The Green Book of Poetry

to Xanthe

THE GREEN BOOK OF POETRY

compiled and edited

Ivo Mosley

Frontier Publishing
Kirstead
Norfolk NR15 1BR

This paperback edition 1994

9 8 7 6 5 4 3 2

First Published in Great Britain by
Frontier Publishing 1993

ISBN 1 872914 06 3

Printed in Great Britain
by Crowes of Norwich

– printed on recycled paper –

Contents

Introduction

End of twentieth century, the world; rivers stinking of effluent, poison waste diffuse in the air, the rain itself become poison;

Trees dying, the soil a sterile holding bank for chemicals; cities, like giant cankers thriving, their millions mostly poor and hungry, their tendrils stretching to the far corners of the earth, draining the land of life;

The earth's riches are plundered for greed then turned to garbage. Man's domination of the earth is all but complete, and some would say almost over.

Amidst all this it's hard to feel good about being human. The bright visions of our ancestors have turned to dust or worse in our hands. The question is not "Is Nature worth preserving?" but "Is humanity worth preserving?".

This book is an argument for "yes". It's a record of the human spirit seeking out what is good, railing at what is bad, wanting to find harmony; trying to create something in that image which we are all born with, and which goes under much-abused names like God, Love and Truth. The poetry here finds beauty in that image, and ugliness in its destruction. That's why it's a 'green' book of poetry. It argues that our exploitation of the planet and our spiritual sickness are the one and the same phenomenon.

The poets represented are from most literatures available in translation as well as from our own. They all speak from that common human voice which is all but lost in what Nadezhda Mandelstam called 'the din of life, the furious drumfire of the demands and aspirations of the moment; the noise such that it drowns out everything else in the world, and amidst which one by one the poets fall silent, because they cannot hear the sound of their own voices.'

As we exploit the world and destroy its beauty we are doing the same to our human spirit. If so, poetry like this will be something of the past, a historical creation best left buried so it does not kindle fierce longing in us for something we may never regain. But if we achieve what seems the impossible – if we cease our poisoning of the earth and our destruction of its other species – we may yet live to feel proud again of our humanity, and of our place in Creation.

There's no point in pretending we can flourish on earth without effort; we have to struggle, like all species, for our well-being. But our dominance must be restrained. The concerted destruction of our planet, involving governments, corporations and all the interlocked economies of the world, is something we as individuals feel powerless to prevent. But the growth of democracy means that, more than ever before, individuals are a powerful part of the whole. We live in an age of mass decision. Whatever their vanity may lead them to believe, leaders in the democratic world are no longer leaders but followers; the voters are in charge. If the great majority of people put the long-term welfare of our species before the immediate gratification of their appetites, the wave of destruction will be halted.

A change of mood is needed among the human population of the planet. The successes of science have led us to believe we can expect everything. When devices for saving labour put many out of work, the response was the creation of employment by waste. Goods are made to deteriorate quickly so more goods will be needed to replace them. More people with more greed and more ability to exploit the Earth have made it a dying place. The limited autonomy within Nature which our technology wins for us is as substantial as a mirage. We have replaced the beautiful cruelty of nature with drab and spirit-murdering wastelands of concrete, asphalt, plastic and plate-glass.

It's said that Chief Seattle looked at our Western materialism and declared, 'This is the beginning not of living but of survival'. Now, even our survival is at risk. This book looks not just to survival but also to the recovery of some of what we've lost. Day by day, species of the earth are disappearing, and what will remain after our orgy is finished no one can tell. We can never recover those species, but we can recover what we have lost inside of us, which is respect for the world and for the joy of being part of it.

Much of the poetry chosen is not widely known to contemporary readers. That's no coincidence; as our civilisation hurls itself towards the cliff-edge the songs it chooses to sing are not those of life. Our materialist civilisation was not born in a day, and poets too have celebrated its values of novelty and conquest. Confused by the orthodox version of poetry, many people no longer know that a poem can express the hopes, anxieties, and above all loves of all of us, for all of us, for as long as there are some of us left. As our destruction of the planet becomes more and more obvious, so does the value of poems like Charlotte Mew's 'The Trees are Down', Farrokhzhad's 'I Pity the Garden' and Judith Wright's 'Australia 1970'.

Most people in industrialised countries now live in cities, and it's hard for them to be aware of the effect their lifestyle is having on the earth. For those who want to know, information is available in nature programmes on the T.V., in the newspapers and in books. If lemmings had newspapers, maybe they wouldn't jump. The aims of this book are not so much to celebrate Nature and warn of impending catastrophe as to understand how we got here and salvage something from the wreckage of our self-esteem. The book argues against the unrestrained pursuit of affluence, and it is worth asking what affluence has done for us. Happiness is subjective, so the question can only be asked; has the single-minded pursuit of material goods made us more happy?

C.D. Darlington, plant geneticist and historian of human society, wrote 'The twentieth century has been devoted to submerging impartially nature and civilisation, art and individuality, under the festering sores of economic growth'. In the attempt to avoid this conclusion, intellectuals have busied themselves trying to re-define nature, civilisation, art and individuality. But a rose by any other name is still a rose, and our knowledge of what these things once meant haunts us. As words, like so many other things, are hacked about and sold to the highest bidder or to the most vociferous lobby-group, poetry is the last stronghold of the sacred word. Poetry depends on the living word for life; it is the guardian of our integrity, our spirituality and our language. In Simone Weil's words, it's the 'light of eternity' as manifest in living words.

Translations: a note

There is a saying, 'poetry is what gets lost in translation'. I would say rather, 'verse is what gets lost in translation'; or, more accurately, translators choose which element – poetry or verse – they favour retaining. I have chosen translations which favour poetry. Successful translations which rhyme are like survivors of a massacre – astonishing mostly for their survival.

Every literate person is familiar with the greatest translation in the English language, the Bible, in its revisions from Tyndale through the King James Version to the New Revised Standard Version. The principle followed in that translation is fidelity to structure, meaning and beauty of language, and that's the principle most translators have adopted here.

Pushkin wrote, 'Translators are the post-horses of enlightenment'. This statement is no less true today, when the post is delivered in vans.

1. Nature

Yes to the Earth

So radiant in certain mornings' light
With its roses and its cypress trees
Is Earth, or with its grain and olives;

So suddenly it is radiant on the soul,
Which stands then alone and forgetful
Though just a moment earlier the soul
Wept bloody tears or dwelt in bitterness;

So radiant in certain mornings' light
Is Earth, and in its silence so expressive,
This wondrous lump rolling in its skies;
Beautiful, tragic in solitude, yet smiling,

That the soul, unasked, replies
"Yes" replies, "Yes" to the Earth,
To the indifferent Earth, "Yes!",

Even though next instant skies
Should darken, roses too, and cypresses,
Or the effort of life grow heavier still,
The act of breathing even more heroic,

"Yes" replies the battered soul to Earth,
So radiant in the light of certain mornings
Beautiful above all things, and human hope.

(Sibilla Aleramo, Italian, 1876–1960, tr. I.M.)

[Nature is our name for everything minus ourselves and our contrivances. As the look of the world is more and more shaped by human interference, the word nature is being replaced by the word environment. But the impoverishment of nature is not to our long-term advantage. The deserts of the world were created by human over-use of nature. The Sahara itself was once green and fertile, its wooded hills and valleys sustaining a large human population. Now, its depleted environment is a permanent home only to creatures tougher and less ambitious than homo sapiens.

While nature was still healthy, human beings both wondered and cursed at its beautiful tyranny. We lived within its framework, and sooner or later it punished our mistakes. Its uncounted species competed with us for resources with which to prosper. It provided us with wonders, as it still does. It also causes us to suffer, and watches with indifference while we die.]

> When I die I don't care how God
> Treats the earth; let it parch, let it flood.
>
> The earth doesn't know what it consumes:
> Skeletons of sheep, carcases of lion.

(Al-Ma'arri, Syrian, 973–1057, tr. Wightman and al-Udhari.)

[As nature sickens under the weight of our demands, we lose the ability to find joy in things around us. This kind of joy is evident in the next five poems, where nature and poet are one in the simple fellowship of co-existence.]

Winter

> Here's my story; the stag cries,
> Winter snarls as summer dies.
>
> The wind bullies the low sun
> In poor light; the seas moan.

Shapeless bracken is turning red,
The wildgoose raises its desperate head.

Bird's wings freeze where fields are hoary.
The world is ice. That's my story.

(Anon., Irish, 9th C., tr. Brendan Kennelly.)

The Moon (1)

At dead of night,
The darkness seems to have deepened.
To the call of geese
The sky is listening; across it
Appears the passing moon.

(Hitomaro, Japanese, 7th c., tr. I.M.)

The Moon (2)

In the sea of heaven,
Waves of cloud arise.
The moon's boat
In a forest of stars
Rows hidden; this I see.

(Hitomaro, Japanese, 7th C., tr. I. M.)

The Blackbird's Song

The little bird is whistling now
From the tip of its yellow beak;
The blackbird on the yellow bough
Is calling over the lake.

(Anon., Irish, 8–9th C., tr. Brendan Kennelly.)

Song of Caribou, Musk Oxen, Women and Men who Would be Manly

Glorious it is to see
The caribou flocking down from the forests
And beginning
Their wandering to the north.
Timidly they watch
For the pitfalls of man.
Glorious it is to see
The great herds from the forests
Spreading out over plains of white,
Glorious to see.
            Yayai, ya, yiya.

Glorious it is to see
Early summer's short-haired caribou
Beginning to wander.
Glorious to see them trot
To and fro
Across the promontories,
Seeking a crossing place.
            Yayai, ya, yiya.

Glorious it is
To see the great musk oxen
Gathering in herds.
The little dogs they watch for
When they gather in herds.
Glorious to see.
            Yayai, ya, yiya.

Glorious it is
To see young women
Gathering in little groups
And paying visits in the houses -
Then all at once the men

Do so want to be manly,
While the girls simply
Think of some little lie.
      Yayai, ya, yiya.

Glorious it is
To see long-haired winter caribou
Returning to the forests.
Fearfully they watch for the little people.
While the herd follows the ebb-mark of the sea
With a storm of clattering hooves.
Glorious it is
When wandering time is come.
      Yayai, ya, yiya.

(Anon., Eskimo, tr. (1921–4) Radmussen and Calvert.)

[Writing is young compared to spoken language; five thousand years compared to perhaps five hundred thousand. A poem written down two thousand years ago is a spring chicken in terms of the spoken tradition, and we have no way of knowing what the earliest poems were like. But historians of language speculate that poetry is as old as language itself, which may have originated as chants cajoling nature into providing for human wants.]

The Rain Man Praises Himself

No house is ever too thick-built
To keep me, the rain, from getting in.
I am well-known to huts and roofs,
A grandson of Never-Been-There,
I am mother of the finest grasses,
Father of green fields everywhere.
My arrows do not miss their aim,
They strike the owners of huts.
I am a terror to clay walls and the architecture of termites,
Fear-inspiring above and below.

When I pour in in the morning, people say:
"He has cut off our lips and stopped our mouths,*
He is giving us juicy fruits.
He has rained and brought us mushrooms,
White as ivory."

* ie made us fall silent

(Oral tradition, Aandonga, southern Africa; written down 1920's; tr. Pettinen, Trask.)

[The word 'poet' comes from the Greek for 'maker' or 'creator'. In the poem that follows, the presence of the poet is as important as the imagery of nature.]

You know the place: then

Leave Crete and come to us
waiting where the grove is
pleasantest, by precincts

sacred to you; incense
smokes on the altar, cold
streams murmur through the

apple branches, a young
rose thicket shades the ground
and quivering leaves pour

down deep sleep; in meadows
where horses have grown sleek
among spring flowers, dill

scents the air. Queen! Cyprian!
Fill our gold cups with love
stirred into clear nectar

(Sappho, Greek, 6th C. B.C., tr. Mary Barnard.)

[Natural imagery can mirror the mood of the poet or it can provide the most extreme contrast, as in the next poem. Sweeney, a pagan prince of ancient Ireland, was driven mad by the curses of priests and the horrors of war.]

The Cliff of Alteran

As Sweeney ranged over Connaught
   He came to a lonely glen
Where a stream poured over a cliff
   And many holy men

Were gathered. Trees, heavy with fruit,
   Grew there by the score.
There were sheltering ivy bowers
   And apple trees galore.

Deer, hares and swine were there.
   On the warm cliff fat seals slept.
Sweeney watched while through his heart
   The raving madness swept.

(Anon., Irish, 12th C., tr. Brendan Kennelly.)

[In the three-line 'haiku' poems of Basho, natural imagery and the poet's observation create a mood so short it's like a flash, a moment seized for contemplation.]

By the road,
In the hedgerow, a rose –
My horse ate it.

(written while looking at the ruins of a great castle)

Summer grasses –
All that remain
Of warriors' dreams.

Withered branch
A crow settles on it –
Autumn dusk.

Red, red,
The sun is unrelenting –
Autumn wind.

(written on a journey)

Fleas, lice;
My horse pisses, right
By my pillow.

(the most famous of all haiku)

Old pond –
Frog jumps in,
Sound of the water.

(Basho, Japanese, 1644–94, tr. I.M.)

[It's frequently observed, by scientists as well as poets, that we humans seem to combine the characteristics of many other animals. We can be fierce like tigers, sadistic like cats, gentle and playful like lambs; or stolid and peaceful like sheep. We can be co-operative like the social insects, rapacious like great black-back gulls, or busy inhabitants of filth like the dung-beetle. We see our characteristics mirrored in nature all around us, some literally, others metaphorically, and this is the source of poetic imagery.

A single natural image – the washing of waves back and forth on the sea shore – pervades the next poem, giving it a sense of the relentless and desolate indifference of time.]

The Old Woman of Beare

The sea crawls from the shore
Leaving there
The despicable weed,
A corpse's hair.
In me,
The desolate withdrawing sea.

The Old Woman of Beare am I
Who once was beautiful.
Now all I know is how to die.
I'll do it well.

Look at my skin
Stretched tight on the bone.
Where kings have pressed their lips,
The pain, the pain.

I don't hate the men
Who swore truth was in their lies.
One thing alone I hate –
Women's eyes.

The young sun
Gives its youth to everyone,
Touching green with gold.
In me, the cold.

The cold. Yet still a seed
Burns there.
Women love only money now.
But when
I loved, I loved
Young men.

Young men whose horses galloped
On many an open plain
Beating lightning from the ground.
I loved such men.

And still the sea
Rears and plunges into me,
Shoving, rolling through my head
Images of the drifting dead.

A soldier cries
Pitifully about his plight;
A king fades
Into the shivering night.

Does not every season prove
That the acorn hits the ground?
Have I not known enough of love
To know it's lost as soon as found?

I drank my fill of wine with kings,
Their eyes fixed on my hair.
Now among the stinking hags
I chew the cud of prayer.

Time was the sea
Brought kings as slaves to me.
Now I near the face of God
And the crab crawls through my blood.

I loved the wine
That thrilled me to my fingertips;
Now the spinster wind
Stitches salt into my lips.

The coward sea
Slouches away from me.
Fear brings back the tide
That made me stretch at the side
Of him who'd take me briefly for his bride.

The sea grows smaller, smaller now.
Farther, farther it goes
Leaving me here where the foam dries
On the deserted land,
Dry as my shrunken thighs,
As the tongue that presses my lips,
As the veins that break through my hands.

(Anon., Irish, 9th C., tr. Brendan Kennelly.)

[Another poem follows where natural imagery, events and feelings are interdependent. It was customary in sixth century Japan to add short poems to the end of a longer one.]

On Seeing a Dead Man lying among Rocks on Samine Island, Sanuki Province

Jewel sea-plants grow
in the province of Sanuki;
is it the nature of the land
that I can gaze on it tirelessly,
is it being the land of the gods
that makes it so beautiful?
With heaven and earth,
sun and moon, together
may it prosper.
The face of a god,
so we are told,
lies on the port of Naka, where
we launched our boat.
Rowing out,
a tidal wind
blew out of the clouds;
as I looked out to sea
waves stood threatening,
as I looked towards the shore
white waves were seething.
The great fish-holding

sea was awesome; so
we pulled our oars to breaking-point.
Here and there,
the islands were many; but
on famous
Samine Island's
wild beach-face
we built a hut for shelter. Then I saw,
amidst the sound of waves,
the beach that served
as a rough-cloth pillow
pillowing you
who on this desolate bed
lay stretched alone.
If I knew your house
I would go and tell them;
if your wife knew
she would come and tend you. But,
although straight as a spear
there is a road, she does not know it;
anxious, longing,
she will be waiting for you,
your precious wife...

Two short poems on the above;

1.   If your wife were here
she would pick wild herbs for you to eat;
but on Mount Sami
even the meadow chickweed
has long since disappeared.

2.   Deep sea-waves
approaching, the shore is
a rough-cloth
pillow, pillowing
you who sleep.

(Hitomaro, Japanese, 6th C., tr. I.M.)

[In the next poem, nature is the setting for love, peace, happiness, rest and magic.]

> I know a bank whereon the wild thyme blows
> Where oxslips and the nodding violet grows
> Quite over-canopied with luscious woodbine,
> With sweet musk-roses and with eglantine;
> There sleeps Titania some time of the night,
> Lull'd in these flowers with dances and delight;
> And there the snake throws her enamelled skin,
> Weed wide enough to wrap a fairy in.

(Shakespeare, 1564–1616, A Midsummer Night's Dream, 2.1.249)

[The comforts of civilisation insulate us from the natural world and allow city-dwellers to more or less ignore it. Eighteenth-century Europeans were so infatuated with the achievments of humanity that untamed nature barely featured in their poetry. The Romantic movement reacted against this human-centred-ness. Poets pointed out that humanity is part of Nature, not its master, and that there is pleasure to be had in feeling a small part of a large whole. Goethe wrote:

'The reason I prefer the society of nature is that nature is always right and the error, if any, can only be on my side. But if I hold converse with men, they will err, and I will err, and so on forever, and we will never get to see matters clearly.'

Wordsworth, like many Romantics, was painfully conscious of humanity's failings. He found an ecstasy in being alone in nature, and a sense of relief that humanity was a small part of nature, not its end-product.]

From 'The Prelude'

One evening (surely I was led by her*)   *Nature
I went alone into a shepherd's boat,
A skiff that to a willow tree was tied
Within a rocky cave, its usual home.

No sooner had I sight of this small skiff,
Discovered thus by unexpected chance,
Than I unloosed her tether and embarked.
The moon was up, the lake was shining clear
Among the hoary mountains; from the shore
I pushed, and struck the oars and struck again
In cadence, and my little boat mov'd on
Even like a man who walks with stately step
Though bent on speed. It was an act of stealth
And troubled pleasure; not without the voice
Of mountain-echoes did my boat move on,
Leaving behind her still on either side
Small circles glittering idly in the moon,
Until they melted all into one track
Of sparkling light. A rocky steep uprose
Above the cavern of the willow tree
And now, as suited one who proudly row'd
With his best skill, I fix'd a steady view
Upon the top of that same craggy ridge,
The bound of the horizon, for behind
Was nothing but the stars and the grey sky.
She was an elfin pinnace; lustily
I dipped my oars into the silent lake,
And, as I rose upon the stroke, my boat
Went heaving through the water, like a swan;
When from behind that craggy steep, till then
The bound of the horizon, a huge cliff,
As if with voluntary power instinct
Upreared its head. I struck and struck again,
And growing still in stature, the huge cliff
Rose up between me and the stars, and still,
With measured motion, like a living thing,
Strode after me. With trembling hands I turned,
And through the silent water stole my way
Back to the cavern of the willow tree.
There, in her mooring-place, I left my bark,
And through the meadows homeward went, with grave

And serious thoughts; and after I had seen
That spectacle, for many days, my brain
Worked with a dim and undetermined sense
Of unknown modes of being; in my thoughts
There was a darkness, call it solitude,
Or blank desertion, no familiar shapes
Of hourly objects, images of trees,
Of sea or sky, no colours of green fields;
But huge and mighty forms that do not live
Like living men moved slowly through the mind
By day and were the trouble of my dreams.

Wisdom and Spirit of the universe!
Thou Soul that art the eternity of thought!
That giv'st to forms and images a breath
And everlasting motion! not in vain,
By day or star-light thus from my first dawn
Of childhood didst thou intertwine for me
The passions that build up our human soul,
Not with the mean and vulgar works of man,
But with high objects, with enduring things,
With life and nature, purifying thus
The elements of feeling and of thought,
And sanctifying, by such discipline,
Both pain and fear, until we recognise
A grandeur in the beatings of the heart.

(William Wordsworth, English, 1770–1850.)

[Holderlin, a German Romantic, set himself the heroic poetic task
of fusing German 'rationality' with the 'holy fire' of ancient
Greece, and went mad trying to fulfil it. The poem which follows
was written during his years of madness, which explains the
signature and date appended. In it, he seems to have thrown off
the trappings of intellectual and civilised life.]

Summer

Still the time of year is here to see, and fields
Of summer stand in lovely glow and mildness.
The green of fields is gloriously laid out,
To where the brook glides down with little waves.

So strolls the day outside through hills and valleys
Unstoppable, and with its fiery beams,
And clouds stroll peacefully in high-up spaces;
The year seems self-restraining in its glory.

9 March 1940   Your humble servant,
                                      Scardanelli.

(Holderlin, 1770–1843, German, tr. I.M.)

[In his madness Holderlin wrote simple poems. His sense of
himself hopped from one living thing to another.]

And little knowledge but much pleasure
Is given to mortal men.

Why dost thou not suffice me O lovely sun
On this May day?
Thou flower of my flowers, what have I more than thee?

Would that I were as children are!
I should be like the nightingale were I to sing
All my delight in one enraptured song!

(Holderlin, German, 1770–1843, tr. David Gascoyne.)

[Leopardi was an Italian Romantic poet. He was born into a
stiflingly claustrophobic family, minor aristocracy fallen on hard
times. He was deformed; not for him Keats' declaration 'Beauty is
truth, truth beauty'. Tormented by his deformity, often stretched

on the rack of unrequited love, longing for the company of like minds but finding himself easily hurt, his poems are triumphs of love over despair.

'The Broom', title of the next poem, refers to yellow-flowering broom that grows in dry, infertile soil. It becomes an image of many parts; beauty in desolation; the fragility of life; the struggle to flourish in the face of assured destruction. Leopardi uses natural imagery to build up and express his vision of the world, of the significance of life, and of human arrogance which seemed dangerous to him then (and how much more to us now!).

Here is no idealised picture of nature. Leopardi calls nature the enemy, in that like all creatures we must struggle against the rest for space and sustenance. But he finds in nature a salutory lesson for humankind, an acceptance of our common fate, and not the arrogance which 'would raise the state of mortal man above the stars'. His love of nature survives contemplation of its most awful face. The poem is a plea for human beings to cooperate, and to forsake the arrogant stupidity which leads to ruin.]

The Broom

Upon the arid shoulder
Of this most terrible mountain,
Vesuvius the destroyer,
Graced by no other tree or flowering plant,
You scatter here your solitary shrubs,
O fragrant-blossoming broom,
Contented with the deserts. So have I seen
Your shoots make beautiful that lonely land
Which girds about the city
Who, once mistress of the world,
Now speaks to travellers of empires lost
With grave and ever-silent face.
I meet you here once more, O you the lover
Of all sad places and deserted worlds,
The constant comrade of afflicted fortune.
Among these fields (now sown

With barren cinders only, covered up
By lava turned to stone
That rings beneath the passing traveller's feet;
Where the snake nestles, coiled in the hot sun,
Or under the south wind
The rabbit seeks again his hollow den)
Were farmsteads and tilled glebe,
And whitening crops of grain, and here the sound
Of lowing herds of cattle,
Gardens and palaces,
Grateful retreats for leisure
Of mighty lords, and here were famous cities
Which the great mountain, from its fiery mouth
Pouring forth streams of flame, did overwhelm
With those that dwelt in them. Now all around,
One single ruin spreads,
Wherein you take your root, O courteous flower,
As if in pity of the doom of others,
And cast a pleasant fragrance to the skies,
Making the desert glad. Now let him come
And view these slopes, whose want it is to flatter
Our mortal state; here he may gaze and see
How loving Nature cares
For our poor human race, and learn to value
At a just estimate the strength of Man,
Whom the harsh Nurse, even when he fears it least
With a slight motion does in part destroy,
And may, with one no less
Slight than the last, even now, and with no warning
Wholly annihilate.
Graven upon these cliffs
Is that '*magnificent,*
Progressive destiny of Humankind'.
Here gaze, and see your image,
O proud and foolish Century,
You who have gone astray
And left the path by reawakening thought
Marked out for you till now, and turning back,
Even of your regress boast,

Proclaiming it advance.
All those fine wits their evil fate has made
You father forth, with flattery receive
Your childish words, although
Deep in their hearts at times
They scorn at you. But I
Would not go to the grave bearing such shame,
Though easily I might
Vie with the rest to imitate their ravings
And make my song acceptable to you;
Rather would I reveal the deep contempt
That lies locked in my breast,
And show it openly, while still I may;
Although I know oblivion
Lies heavy on whom displeases his own age.
But I have learned to laugh
At that bad fate we both will share together.
You dream of liberty, the while you forge
New bonds for thought – through which
Alone Man rose, in part,
From barbarism, whence only civil life
Has grown, and we may guide the common-wealth
To better things. And thus
The truth displeased you, telling
Of that low station and harsh destiny
Nature has given us. So, like a coward,
You turned your back upon the light, which showed
This truth to you, and fleeing it, called base
Those who still followed it; and he
Alone was great of soul who, knave or madman,
Could fool himself or others, and would raise
The state of mortal man above the stars.

A man of poor estate, and weak in body,
Being of a high nobility of soul,
Supposes not, nor claims
That he is rich or handsome,
Nor makes himself a laughing-stock for men
By show of splendid living,

Or valour in his person;
But without shame allows it to appear
In strength and wealth he is a beggar still,
Speaks openly of this, rates his condition
According to the truth.
Nor do I think that creature
Of a high mind, but foolish,
Who, born to perish, and reared up in pain,
Says "I was made for joy,"
And with his festering pride
Covers whole pages, promising on earth
High destinies and new felicity
Which Heaven knows nothing of, much less this earth,
To a people whom one wave
From a troubled sea, one breath
Of poisoned air, one tremor underground
Might utterly destroy
That scarce the memory remained of them.

But noble in soul is he
Who burns to lift his eyes
Against the common doom,
And with free tongue, not docking any truth,
Admits the weak, low state,
The evil lot assigned to us by fate;
He who in suffering,
Shows himself great and strong
And will not add fraternal wrath and hatred –
The worst of all ills – to all
His other miseries
By blaming Man for his unhappiness,
But lays the fault on her who is indeed
The guilty one, the Power who is our mother
In that she brought us forth, step-mother in will.
He calls her enemy, and thus, believing –
As is indeed the truth –
The human race was from the first conjoined
And ranked against the foe,
He takes all men as his confederates,

Embraces all men with a general love
Which is sincere; he offers,
And looks for prompt and valiant aid from them
Amid the anguish and recurring dangers
Of this their common war. But against man
To take up arms, or seek to lay a snare
To cause his neighbour stumble,
Seems mad to him, as if one in the camp
Hemmed in by enemies, beneath the threat
Of their most keen assault,
Forgot the foe, and stirred up bitter strife
Among the allied ranks,
And scattered flight and tumult with his sword
Through his own warriors.
When thoughts like these again
Shall be revealed, as once, unto the crowd,
That horror, which at first
Bound men in fellowship,
Together linked against a cruel Nature,
Shall be in part restored
By knowledge of the truth; honour, right-dealing
In civil intercourse,
Justice and piety shall find a different soil
Than those proud follies, founded upon which
The honour of the mob
Stands firm as all things else rooted in error.

By these deserted banks,
On which the hardened flood
Casts a dark cloak, and still seems moving waves,
Often I sit by night and mark on high
In heaven's purest blue,
The stars burning above this mournful plain,
And where the far-off sea
Becomes their mirror, and the whole world ablaze
With glittering sparks circling the empty sky.
And when I fix my eyes upon those lights,
Which seem to me mere points
Yet are so vast that all

The earth and sea compared to them are truly
Only a point; to which
Not only Man, but this
Globe, wherein Man is nothing,
Is utterly unknown; and when I see –
Beyond even them, infinitely more remote –
Those clustering knots of stars
Which look to us like clouds, and where
Not only Man and Earth, but all our stars,
So infinite in number and in mass,
The golden sun among the rest,
Are unknown (or seem even as they appear
To us on earth – a point
Of nebulous light); then, to my questing thought,
What is it you appear,
O son of man? Remembering
Your state below, of which the soil I tread
Bears testimony still, and yet that you
Think lordship and a purpose
Assigned you by the Whole; how many times
You have been pleased to say, on this obscure
Grainlet of sand, which bears the name of Earth,
The authors of the universal cause
Came down, on your account, often conversing
At pleasure with your race; and how this age,
Which seems in knowledge and in civil arts
The most advanced, heaps insult on the wise,
Renewing once again
These long-derided dreams; what feeling then,
Unhappy children of mortality,
What thought of you at last my heart assails?
I cannot say if pity or scorn prevails.

As a small apple falling from the tree,
Which late in autumn-time
Its ripeness and no other force casts down,
Crushes the loved homes of a tribe of ants,
Tunnelled in the soft loam
With infinite toil, their works,

And all their wealth, which, jealously collecting,
That busy race had garnered with long care
And patient forethought through the summer season –
Burying and laying waste,
All in a moment; so, falling from on high,
Hurled through the utmost heaven,
A cloud of cinders, pumice-stone, and rocks,
Darkness and ruin, mingled
With boiling streams of lava;
Or down the mountain side,
Raging across the fields,
All in a molten mass
Of red-hot sand and metals mixed together,
A mighty flood swept down,
And overwhelmed, destroyed, and covered up
Those cities which the sea
Washed on the further shore,
In a few moments; where above them now
Browses the goat, new towns
Rise in their stead, whose seat is still upon
The sepulcres of those, while the steep mountain
Seems spurning with its foot their prostrate walls.
Nature has no more care
Or value for Man's seed
Than for the ant's; and if disaster falls
More rarely on the former
No other cause can be
Than when he breeds, Man's less fertility.

Full eighteen hundred years
Have passed away, since vanished, overwhelmed
By the force of fire, these peopled seats of men:
And the poor husbandman
Tending his vines, whom scarce the scorched, dead soil
Upon these plains affords a livelihood,
Lifts yet suspicious glances
Towards the fatal summit,
Which, now become no milder than before,
Still full of terror stands, still threatening

Disaster for himself, his sons, and their
Impoverished fields. And often
The wretch, upon the roof
Of his poor cottage, lying
Sleepless all night beneath the wandering air,
Time upon time starts up, to mark the flow
Of that dread simmering, which still pours out
From the unexhausted womb
Over the sandy ridge, and shines upon
The shores about Capri,
And Mergellina, and the Bay of Naples.
And if he sees it coming near, or deep
In his domestic well he hears the water
Gurgling and boiling, he awakes his children,
In haste awakes his wife, and snatching up
Whatever they can seize, they go, and fleeing,
See, far behind, their home,
Their little field, which was
The sole protection they possessed from famine,
Prey to the burning flood,
Which hissing, overtakes it, then unappeased,
Spreads ever-during over all they had.
Returns now to light of day,
Which old oblivion had quenched for her,
Pompeii, a skeleton,
Out of the grave by greed or piety
Dragged forth into the open;
From her deserted forum
Upright among the ranks
Of broken colonnades, the traveller
May gaze long on the forked peak of the mountain,
And on its smoking crest,
Which threatens still the ruins scattered round,
And in the horror of the secret night,
Among the empty theatres,
Temples defaced, and shattered dwelling-houses,
Where now the bat conceals its progeny,
Like an ill-omened torch
Which darkly flickers through deserted halls,

Still runs the glimmer of the deadly lava,
Which far-off through the shadows
Glows red, and tinges everything around.
Even so, knowing naught of Man, or of the ages
Which he calls ancient, or the long succession
Of various generations,
Nature stays ever fresh, or rather she
Travels so long a course,
That still she seems to stay. While empires fall,
While tongues and peoples pass; nothing she sees;
And Man presumes to boast eternity.

And you, O gentle broom,
Who with your fragrant thickets
Make beautiful this spoiled and wasted land,
You too must shortly fall beneath the cruel
Force of the subterranean fire, returning
To this, its wonted place,
Which soon shall stretch its greedy fringe above
Your tender shrubs. You then
Will bend your harmless head, not obstinate
Beneath the rod of fate;
Nor yet till then in vain and cowardly fashion
Bow down to the oppressor yet to come;
Nor upright in mad pride against the stars;
Amid the desert, where
You find your home and birthplace,
Allotted you by fortune, not your will;
But wiser still, and less
Infirm in this than Man, you do not think
Your feeble stock immortal,
Made so by destiny or by yourself.

(Giacomo Leopardi, Italian, 1798–1837, tr. J. Heath-Stubbs.)

[Since the last poem was written, humanity has given up on its presumption to eternal life. In its place it has enshrined the ambition to satisfy every appetite. To satisfy this ambition we force nature to be more and more productive. The world sickens under this exploitation. In hope of future prosperity, we put blind faith in science to come up with new tricks. Machines and technology will, we trust, take the place of care and respect for the earth. Nature's relegation to the status of 'the environment' indicates the depth of joyless self-preoccupation to which we have fallen.

In the following poem a white Australian poet describes her meeting with a black Australian poet (also represented in this anthology) and their joint mourning of the devastated land of Australia.]

Two Dreamtimes

(for Kath Walker, now Oodgeroo Noonuccal)

Kath my sister with the torn heart,
I don't know how to thank you
for your dreamtime stories of joy and grief
written on paperbark.

You were one of the dark children
I wasn't allowed to play with -
riverbank campers, the wrong colour
(I couldn't turn you white.)

So it was late I met you,
late I began to know
they hadn't told me the land I loved
was taken out of your hands.

Sitting all night at my kitchen table
with a cry and a song in your voice,
your eyes were full of the dying children,
the blank-eyed taken women,

the sullen looks of the men who sold them
for rum to forget the selling;
the hard rational white faces
with eyes that forget the past.

With a knifeblade flash in your black eyes
that always long to be blacker,
your Spanish-Koori face
of a fighter and singer,

arms over your breast folding
your sorrow in to hold it,
you brought me to you some of the way
and came the rest to meet me;

over the desert of red sand
came from your lost country
to where I stand with all my fathers,
their guilt and righteousness.

Over the rum your voice sang
the tales of an old people,
their dreaming buried, the place forgotten...
We too have lost our dreaming.

We the robbers, robbed in turn,
selling this land on hire-purchase;
what's stolen once is stolen again
even before we know it.

If we are sisters, it's in this -
our grief for a lost country,
the place we dreamed in long ago,
poisoned now and crumbling.

Let us go back to that far time,
I riding the cleared hills,
plucking blue leaves for their eucalypt scent,
hearing the call of the plover,

in a land I thought was mine for life.
I mourn it as you mourn
the ripped length of the island beaches,
the drained paperbark swamps.

The easy Eden-dreamtime then
in a country of birds and trees
made me your shadow-sister, child,
dark girl I couldn't play with.

But we are grown to a changed world;
over the drinks at night
we can exchange our separate griefs,
but yours and mine are different.

A knife's between us. My righteous kin
still have cruel faces.
Neither you nor I can win them,
though we meet in secret kindness.

I am born of conquerors,
you of the persecuted.
Raped by rum and an alien law,
progress and economics,

are you and I and a once-loved land
peopled by tribes and trees;
doomed by traders and stock-exchanges,
bought by faceless strangers.

And you and I are bought and sold,
our songs and stories too,
though quoted low in a falling market
(publishers shake their heads at poets).

Time that we shared for a little while,
telling sad tales of women
(black or white at a different price)
meant much and little to us.

My shadow-sister, I sing to you
from my place with my righteous kin,
to where you stand with the Koori dead,
"Trust none – not even poets".

The knife's between us. I turn it round,
the handle to your side,
the weapon made from your country's bones.
I have no right to take it.

But both of us die as our dreamtime dies.
I don't know what to give you
for your gay stories, your sad eyes,
but that, and a poem, sister.

(Judith Wright, Australian, b. 1915.)

[The next poem laments the dying of the English countryside. As
the landscape and its wild animals are destroyed, a human way of
life is also being lost. Bats – referred to late in the poem – are now
protected; does this signify a general reversal, or is it a mere token
to pacify an almost silent minority?

The Green Man is accompanied by various local mythical
characters as he renounces his life.]

The Green Man's Last Will and Testament

In a ragged spinney (scheduled
For prompt development as a bijou housing estate)
I saw the green daemon of England's wood
As he wrote his testament. The grey goose
Had given him one of her quills for a pen;
The robin's breast was a crimson seal;
The long yellow centipede held a candle.

He seemed like a hollow oak-trunk, smothered with ivy:
At his feet or roots clustered the witnesses,
Like hectic toadstools, or pallid as broom-rape:
Wood-elves – goodfellows, hobs and lobs,
Black Anis, the child-devouring hag,

From her cave in the Dane Hills, saucer-eyed
Phantom dogs, Black Shuck and Barghest, with the cruel nymphs
Of the northern streams, Peg Powler of the Tees
And Jenny Greenteeth of the Ribble,
Sisters of Bellisama, the very fair one.

"I am sick, I must die," he said. "Poisoned like Lord Randal
From hedges and ditches. My ditches run with pollution,
My hedgerows are gone, and the hedgerow singers.
The rooks, disconsolate, have lost their rookery:
The elms are all dead of the Dutch pox.
No longer the nightjar churns in the twilit glade,
Nor the owl, like a white phantom, silent-feathered
Glides to the barn. The red-beaked chough,
Enclosing Arthur's soul, is seen no more
Wheeling and calling over the Cornish cliffs.
Old Tod has vacated his deep-dug earth;
He has gone to rummage in the city dustbins.
Tiggy is squashed flat on the M1.

"My delicate deer are culled, and on offshore islands
My sleek silkies, where puffin and guillemot
Smother and drown in oil and tar.
The mechanical reaper has guillotined
Ortygometra, though she was no traitor,
Crouching over her cradle – no longer resounds
Crek-crek, crek-crek, among the wheatfields,
Where the scarlet cockle is missing and the blue cornflower.
My orchids and wild hyacinths are raped and torn,
My lenten lilies and my fritillaries.
Less frequent now the debate
Of cuckoo and nightingale – and where is the cuckoo's maid,
The snake-necked bird sacred to Venus,
Her mysteries and the amber twirling wheel?
In no brightness of air dance now the butterflies –
Their hairy mallyshags are slaughtered among the nettles.
The innocent bats are evicted from the belfries,
The death-watch remains, and masticates history.

"I leave to the people of England
All that remains:
Rags and patches – a few old tales
And bawdy jokes, snatches of song and galumphing dance-steps.
Above all my obstinacy – obstinacy of flintstones
That breed in the soil, and pertinacity
Of unlovely weeds – chickweed and groundsel,
Plantain, shepherd's purse and Jack-by-the-hedge.
Let them keep it as they wander in the inhuman towns.

"And the little children, imprisoned in ogrish towers, enchanted
By a one-eyed troll in front of a joyless fire –
I would have them remember the old games and the old dances:
Sir Roger is dead, Sir Roger is dead,
She raised him up under the apple-tree;
Poor Mary is a-weeping, weeping like Ariadne,
Weeping for her husband on a bright summer's day."

(John Heath-Stubbs, English, b. 1918.)

[Can we really live without loving the land, the sky, the trees? It
seems so, but for how long? We have nature in our power now,
just as a peasant has his donkey, but a wise peasant loves his
donkey and looks after it. Dead donkeys do no more work. It's an
old story, that those with power must learn restraint in using it.
    In the next poem, a busy Roman official looks with envy on
an old man who, he imagines, has had a life of carefree toil.]

The Old Man of Verona

This man has lived his life in his own fields.
The house that saw him as a little lad
Sees him an old man: leaning on his staff,
On the same earth he crawled on, he will tell you
The centuries that one low roof has seen.
Fate has not dragged him through the brawling crowds,

Nor ever, as a restless traveller
Has he drunk at unknown springs; no greed of gain
Kept him a-quaking on the perilous seas.
No trumpet sounded for him the attack,
No lawsuit brought him to the raucous courts.
In politics unskilled, knowing naught of the neighbouring town,
His eye takes pleasure in a wider sky.
The years he'll reckon by alternate crops
And not by Parliaments: spring has her flowers,
Autumn her apples: so the year goes by.
The same wide field that hides the setting sun
Sees him return again;
His light the measure of this plain man's day.
That massive oak he remembers a sapling once,
Yon grove of trees grew old along with him.
Verona further seems than India,
Lake Garda is remote as the Red Sea.
Yet, strength indomitable and sinews firm,
The old man stands, a rock among his grandsons.
Let you go gadding, gape at furthest Spain:
You'll have seen life; but this old man has lived.

(Claudian, Roman, c. 370–405, tr. Helen Waddell.)

[Nature's laws do not favour humanity over other species. We make our own laws to do that, and we need new man-made laws to protect us from destroying nature.

In Chinese poetry, nature is a place of retreat from the disappointments of living with one's fellow human beings. Han Shan took to the mountains as a recluse when his efforts to conform with family expectations failed. His poems were said to have been collected from scribbles on rocks and trees by an admiring local bureaucrat. Han Shan means cold mountain; he called himself after the place where he chose to live.]

Life on Cold Mountain

My house is at the foot of the green cliff,
My garden, a jumble of weeds I no longer bother to mow.
New vines dangle in twisted strands
Over old rocks rising steep and high.
Monkeys make off with the mountain fruits,
The white heron crams his bill with fish from the pond,
While I, with a book or two of the immortals,
Read under the trees – mumble, mumble.

(Han Shan, Chinese, 8th–9th C., tr. Burton Watson.)

[Li Po was so venerated during his life that the emperor would personally season his soup. But he too needed the company of nature, and he spent most of his life wandering. If poetry is wine, his poems are distilled spirit.]

Summer in the mountains

Too lazy to shift my white feather fan
I lie naked in the green woods.
Hanging my hat on a rock,
I bare my head to the breeze in the pines.

Silent Night

Moonlight floods the end of my bed.
I wonder, has frost fallen?
Sitting up, I look at the moon.
Lying back, I think of home.

Talk in the Mountains

You ask me, 'Why dwell among green mountains?'
I laugh in silence; my soul is quiet.
Peach blossom follows the moving water;
Here is a heaven and earth, beyond the world of men.

(Li Po, Chinese, 701–762, versions I.M.)

2. Love

The Reign of Love

The world, with steady trust,
Changes in regular seasons.
Seeds that struggle out of earth
Keep to pre-determined bounds.
Daily the golden sun
Leads with his chariot the rosy dawn,
And nightly the evening star
Leads out the moon to rule the sky.
The greedy surging sea
Is kept to certain limits
Lest our uncertain world
Be swamped within its flood.

The sequence of these things is tied –
Seas ruled, lands overseen –
By Love which rules in heaven.

Should love let go the reins,
All things which now are linked
Would move straightway to war;
Things which are beautiful and live in trust
Would fight, and tear apart the scheme of things.

Love, in sacred treaty,
Holds peoples fast in friendship;
Love, in sacred marriage,
Binds lovers fast in innocence;
Love makes laws also for those
Who wish to stay faithful in friendship.

O happy humankind,
If love, by which heaven is ruled,
Could rule your minds too!

(Boethius, Roman, c. 475–524, tr. I.M..)

[Love is the force which binds us together and the motive for making good of our lives. When love goes wrong or is denied, hatred, greed and envy take over, bringing with them a welter of destruction.

Love between the sexes is the most obvious kind of love that we need for our survival. But no less indispensable are the kinds of love between parents and children, between friends, between companions, between us and the world around us; and the greater love that — it sometimes seems — inspires material substance into life.

Poetry is born of love. It plunders the universe for its imagery, not harming but praising as it goes. Love of the world around us is perhaps most important of all right now, when the world lies at our mercy.

As we destroy the loveliness of the world, are we killing love itself?]

The man
who does not love his children
cannot enjoy spring flowers.

(Basho, Japanese, 1644–1694, tr. I.M.)

[In the next poem, love is seen as the one thing left to hang on to in a world where all else of value is being lost.]

Dover Beach

The sea is calm to-night.
The tide is full, the moon lies fair
Upon the straits; — on the French coast the light
Gleams and is gone; the cliffs of England stand,

Glimmering and vast, out in the tranquil bay.
Come to the window, sweet is the night-air!
Only, from the long line of spray
Where the sea meets the moon-blanch'd land,
Listen! You hear the grating roar
Of pebbles which the waves draw back, and fling,
At their return, up the high strand,
Begin, and cease, and then again begin,
With tremulous cadence slow, and bring
The eternal note of sadness in.

Sophocles long ago
Heard it on the Aegean, and it brought
Into his mind the turbid ebb and flow
Of human misery; we
Find also in the sound a thought,
Hearing it by this distant northern sea.

The Sea of Faith
Was once, too, at the full, and round earth's shore
Lay like the folds of a bright girdle furl'd.
But now I only hear
Its melancholy, long, withdrawing roar,
Retreating, to the breath
Of the night-wind, down the vast edges drear
And naked shingles of the world.

Ah, love, let us be true
To one another! for the world, which seems
To lie before us like a land of dreams,
So various, so beautiful, so new,
Hath really neither joy, nor love, nor light,
Nor certitude, nor peace, nor help for pain;
And we are here as on a darkling plain
Swept with confused alarms of struggle and flight,
Where ignorant armies clash by night.

(Matthew Arnold, English, 1822–88)

[Love has to contend with all the violence within and without us, and it gets little help from the culture of our times. Friendship especially suffers when the satisfaction of wants is everyone's goal, and when the economic effectiveness of competition is praised above loyalty and trust. Also, a cultural emphasis on sex (which is marketable) casts a shadow over friendship and other forms of non-sexual love.]

To a Friend

When the moon's splendour shines in a clear sky,
Stand outside and gaze at heaven's brightness,
Marvelling how the pure lamp of the moon
Embraces in its beauty two dear friends
In body separate, but bound in mind by love.
Though face to loving face we may not look,
Yet let this light assure us of our love.
Your faithful friend sends you these small verses,
And if on your part friendship's bond stays firm
May strength and joy be with you all your days!

(Walahfrid Strabo, German, tr. from Latin by I.M.)

Dreaming of Li Po

When death's the cause of parting, tears are finite;
When life's the cause, then grief goes on and on.
The land you're travelling to is full of plague;
As yet, I've heard no news from you in exile.
And now, old friend, you come to me in a dream,
Making me realise how much you're on my mind.
Caught like a bird in a net of trouble,
Have you found feather wings to visit me?
I fear you may no longer be alive –
No living soul could travel a road so far;
You must have left when maple woods were green,
Returning through mountain passes in the dark.

The moon, low over the earth, fills the roof-beams,
And I half expect to see it light your face;
The waters are deep, the waves wide and rolling;
Take care, don't let the river dragons get you!

(Tu Fu, Chinese, 713–70, version I.M. from Hawkes.)

To Tu Fu

On the Mountain of Boiled Rice I met Tu Fu,
Wearing a bamboo hat in the hot midday;
Pray, how is it that you have grown so thin?
Is it because you suffer from poetry?

(Li Po, Chinese, 701–762, tr. Payne.)

Heraclitus

They told me, Heraclitus, they told me you were dead,
They brought me bitter news to hear and bitter tears to shed.
I wept as I remembered how often you and I
Had tired the sun with talking and sent him down the sky.

And now that you are lying, my dear old Carian guest,
A handful of grey ashes, cold and long ago at rest,
Your pleasant voices are not dead, your nightingales[1] yet wake;
For Death, though he takes all away, yet these he cannot take.

(Callimachus, Greek, 305–240 BC, after tr. by William Cory.)

[Sappho's poetry is preserved only in fragments, mostly as short examples of grammar or metre in the work of later ancient writers. But even these fragments have a quality no other poet can match. The following fragments describe a love which – like the love in Shakespeare's sonnets – seems to straddle the boundary between friendship and erotic love.]

[1] Assumed to be the title of a collection of poems.
Only one of Heraclitus' poems is still 'awake'.

Without warning

As a whirlwind
swoops on an oak
Love shakes my heart

(Sappho, Greek, 6th C. B.C., tr. Mary Barnard.)

I have had not one word from her

Frankly I wish I were dead.
When she left, she wept

a great deal; she said to
me, "This parting must be
endured, Sappho. I go unwillingly."

I said, "Go, and be happy
but remember (you know
well) whom you leave shackled by love

"If you forget me, think
of our gifts to Aphrodite
and all the loveliness that we shared

"all the violet tiaras,
braided rosebuds, dill and
crocus twined around your young neck

"myrrh poured on your head
and on soft mats girls with
all that they most wished for beside them

"while no voices chanted
choruses without ours,
no woodlot bloomed in spring without song..."

(Sappho, Greek, 6th C. B.C., tr. Mary Barnard.)

I confess

I love that
which caresses
me. I believe

Love has his
share in the
Sun's brilliance
and virtue

(Sappho, Greek, 6th C. B.C., tr. Mary Barnard.)

[Friendship gone wrong is the subject of the next poem, by a soldier-poet of ancient Greece. Love let down is the origin of bitterness and hatred.]

Shipwreck

Slammed by the surf on the beach
naked at Salmydessos, where the screw-haired men
of Thrace, taking him in
will entertain him (he will have much to undergo,
chewing on slavery's bread)
stiffened with cold, and loops of seaweed from the slime
tangling his body about,
teeth chattering as he lies in abject helplessness
flat on his face like a dog
beside the beach-break where the waves come shattering in.
And let me be there to watch;
for he did me wrong and set his heel on our good faith,
he who had once been my friend.

(Archilochus, Greek, 7th C. B.C., tr. R. Lattimore.)

[Moving on to poetry of sexual love, it's not surprising poets look to Nature for their imagery. In spring, Nature seethes with sexual love; trees and flowers dangle out their organs for airborne copulation on a massive scale, birds meet mid-air in a tangle of feathers, and dogs have to be kept inside not to stop the flow of traffic. It seems only humankind, lustful all the year round, finds these things complicated, as sex is torn different ways between inclination, procreation, conjugation and dissipation.

The next poem is unusual, in that there's no hint of trouble.]

Song

It was a lover and his lass,
　With a hey, and a ho, and a hey nonino,
That o'er the green cornfield did pass
　In the springtime, the only pretty ring time,
When birds do sing, hey ding a ding, ding.
Sweet lovers love the spring.

Between the acres of the rye,
　With a hey, and a ho, and a hey nonino,
These pretty country folk would lie,
　In the springtime, the only pretty ring time,
When birds do sing, hey ding a ding, ding.
Sweet lovers love the spring.

This carol they began that hour,
　With a hey, and a ho, and a hey nonino,
How that a life was but a flower
　In the springtime, the only pretty ring time,
When birds do sing, hey ding a ding, ding.
Sweet lovers love the spring.

And therefore take the present time,
　With a hey, and a ho, and a hey nonino;
For love is crowned with the prime
　In the springtime, the only pretty ring time,
When birds do sing, hey ding a ding, ding.
Sweet lovers love the spring.

(Shakespeare, 1564–1616, 'As You Like It' 4.3.14–31.)

[Mutual erotic attraction is the subject of the next poem.]

Moving fast, a girl came to me one night,
  Hurrying to abscond from innocence.

When she walked, her body said to the wind,
  If you're serious, this is the way you should stir

The branches.

(Mu'tazz, Arabic, 861–908, tr. G. Wightam and A. al-Udhari.)

[A strong sexual urge is favoured in an obvious way by evolution; the stronger it is, the more likely it'll result in an act which passes it on. But to avoid continual promiscuous copulation (which wouldn't favour the successful rearing of children), evolution has made us choosy as to time, place and partner, and given us a strong desire to be faithful, to make a union which will be life-long.

While both sexes share these urges, they seem unequally distributed between the sexes and a lot of poetry by men has been devoted to getting women to say 'yes' when they've said 'no'.]

To His Coy Mistress.

Had we but world enough, and time
This coyness, Lady, were no crime.
We would sit down and think which way
To walk, and pass our long love's day.
Thou by the Indian Ganges' side
Should'st rubies find: I by the tide
Of Humber would complain. I would
Love you ten years before the Flood,
And you should, if you please, refuse
Till the Conversion of the Jews.
My vegetable love should grow

Vaster than empires, and more slow;
An hundred years should go to praise
Thine eyes and on thy forehead gaze;
Two hundred to adore each breast;
But thirty thousand to the rest.
An age at least to every part,
And the last age should show your heart:
For, Lady, you deserve this state;
Nor would I love at lesser rate.
But at my back I always hear
Time's winged chariot hurrying near:
And yonder all before us lie
Deserts of vast eternity.
Thy beauty shall no more be found;
Nor, in thy marble vault, shall sound
My echoing song: then worms shall try
That long-preserved virginity,
And your quaint honour turn to dust;
And into ashes all my lust.
The grave's a fine and private place,
But none, I think, do there embrace.
Now, therefore, while the youthful glue
Sits on thy skin like morning dew,
And while thy willing soul transpires
At every pore with instant fires,
Now let us sport us while we may;
And now, like amorous birds of prey,
Rather at once our time devour,
Than languish in his slow-chapped power.
Let us roll our strength, and all
Our sweetness up into one ball:
And tear our pleasures with rough strife,
Through the iron gates of life.
Thus though we cannot make our sun
Stand still, yet we will make him run.

(Andrew Marvell, English, 1621–1678.)

[Professional poets sometimes string out love affairs into a life-
long occupation. Their work then consists of declarations of love
alternating with expressions of despair, as they either are rejected
by or tire of their beloveds. The next two poems are before-and-
after poems by the same poet.]

Two Requests

O you who are beautiful, you who were born
To hurt me, to be loved, to be beautiful,
O you alone born to be all these things, please
Let me come and see you more often.

My poetry shall make your beauty famous
More than any other woman's in the whole world.
Please, Calvus and Catullus, have mercy and let me
Write better poems than you did!

(Propertius, Roman, c.50 B.C.– c.16 A.D., tr. Jack Lindsay.)

Gone

The girl I loved has left me. She has left me.

Do you tell me, friend, I have no cause for distress?
There are no enemies save those we love...
Kill me, and my anger would be less!
O can I see her leaning on another,
Who was mine, who was mine so lately?
Then, I could say 'You are mine' to her aloud...
But love's king of yesterday becomes by fate
Tomorrow's Fool. That is the way of love.
Great kings have lain in the dust, very great Lords;
There was an old city called Thebes,
And Troy had towers once.
Think of the gifts I gave and the songs I made!
Yet all the time I had her, she would never say the words
'I love you'.

(Propertius, Roman, c.50 B.C.– c.16 A.D., tr. Jack Lindsay.)

[Another poet laments that he's no longer in fashion between the sheets.]

Vixi Puellis Nuper Idoneus...

'I have had times when girls enough...'

They flee from me that sometime did me seek,
    With naked foot stalking in my chamber:
I have seen them gentle, tame, and meek,
    That now are wild, and do not once remember
    That sometime they have put themselves in danger
To take bread at my hand; and now they range,
Busily seeking with a continual change.

Thanked be fortune, it hath been otherwise
    Twenty times better; but once, in special,
In thin array, after a pleasant guise,
    When her loose gown from her shoulders did fall,
    And she caught me in her arms long and small,
Therewith all sweetly did me kiss,
And softly said, *'Dear heart, how like you this?'*

It was no dream; I lay broad waking:
    But all is turned, through my gentleness,
Into a strange fashion of forsaking;
    And I have leave to go, of her goodness;
    And she also to use new-fangleness.
But since that I unkindly so am served,
'How like you this?' – what hath she now deserved?

(Sir Thomas Wyatt, English, 1503–1542.)

[Dante and Petrarch fell in love with unobtainable beloveds. Dante never even met the love of his life; just one glimpse of her in the distance was enough to inspire a lifetime's devotion. Purity of love is perhaps easier to maintain in the absence of mundane stresses like arguments about disgusting personal habits or paying bills. But their poetry served a deeper and higher purpose by

stating that love need not have possession as its object. In an age
when women were more or less the property of men this was a
civilising idea.]

> The stars, the heavens, the elements all applied
> Their various arts and every extreme care
> To make of her a living light, in which
> Nature's reflected, and the peerless sun.
>
> So high is their creation, graceful and fresh,
> That mortals may not gaze on her for long;
> It seems that from her eyes, beyond all measure
> Love allows sweet gracefulness to flow.
>
> The air, beaten by her soft rays,
> Ignites in virtuous fire and soon is such
> That speech and thought are utterly overwhelmed.
>
> No base desire arises, but desire
> Of honour, virtue. Tell me now, when
> Was ever lust assuaged by highest beauty?

(Petrarch, Italian, 1304–74, tr. I.M.)

[The Persian poet Hafiz observes that what the lover wants of the
beloved can never finally be given. The ecstasy and the pain of
love arise from this unobtainability. We are enthralled to natural
law, the 'wheel of heaven' which grants no favours and which
therefore seems flawed.]

I went into the garden at dawn to gather roses,
When suddenly I heard the voice of the nightingale.

Poor thing, he was stricken in anguish for the love of the rose,
And sprinkled the meadows round with his sobs, as he looked for help.

Lost then in thought, slowly I paced in the garden,
Considering this affair of the rose and the nightingale.

The rose is become the image of Beauty, and the nightingale of Love:
The one will grant no favours, yet the other still remains constant.

When the voice of the nightingale prevailed upon my heart,
It seemed I had no power of endurance left.

For many roses have blossomed here in this garden,
But no-one has plucked the rose without the stab of a thorn.

Hafiz, expect no relief from the turning heavens –
That wheel has a thousand flaws, and grants no favours.

(Hafiz, Persian, c.1320–89, tr. P. Avery and J. Heath-Stubbs.)

[In the next two poems, the pain of unrequited love comes close
to overwhelming love's ecstasy.]

He Hears the Cry of the Sedge

I wander by the edge
Of this desolate lake
Where wind cries in the sedge:
Until the axle break
That keeps the stars in their round,
And hands hurl in the deep
The banners of East and West,
And the girdle of light is unbound,
Your breast will not lie by the breast
Of your beloved in sleep.

(W.B.Yeats, Irish, 1865–1939)

Give Me Your Eyes

Give me your eyes.
I do not ask to touch
The hands of you, the mouth of you,
Soft and sweet and fragrant though they be.

No, lift your eyes to mine;
Give me but one last look
Before I step forth forever;
Even though within that moment's crashing space,
I shall know all of life and death heaven and hell.

(Angelina Weld Grimke, American, 1880–1958.)

[Many, if not most, poems of romantic love are about its
difficulties. Good poetry is often born of pain. The subject of the
next two poems is separation; in the first by distance, in the
second by death.]

In Kumano Bay
The crinums grow,
Their leaves piled up in hundreds;
My thoughts of you are the same,
And yet we never meet...

(Hitomaro, Japanese, 7th C., tr. I.M.)

Nocturnal

The sky, the earth, the wind subdued and quiet.
The waves that ripple shoreward from the deep.
The fishes in the sea becalmed in sleep.
The soft reposeful silence of the night.

The fisherman of Helicon who, sprawled
Where in the wind the water ebbs and bobs
Calls the beloved name in vain, and sobs
For it can not be any more than called;

'O waves,' he says, 'before I'm killed by love
Restore to me my nymph, whom you have taken
So early from me and enslaved to death.'

Nobody speaks to him. The sea far off
Slaps. In the wind the grove is gently shaken.
His voice is lifted, borne off on its breath.

(Luis de Camoens, Portuguese, 1524–1580, tr. Keith Bosley.)

[Another troubled poem shows how difficult it is for us to live without love. A Victorian poet lies with a prostitute, lamenting his failure to be with his true love. The attempt to drown love in dissipation has failed.]

Non sum qualis eram bonae sub regno Cynarae

'I am not as I was, under the reign of the good Cynara.'

Last night, ah, yesternight, betwixt her lips and mine
There fell thy shadow, Cynara! thy breath was shed
Upon my soul between the kisses and the wine;
And I was desolate and sick of an old passion,
    Yea, I was desolate and bow'd my head:
I have been faithful to thee, Cynara! in my fashion.

All night upon mine heart I felt her warm heart beat,
Night-long within mine arms in love and sleep she lay;
Surely the kisses of her bought red mouth were sweet;
But I was desolate and sick of an old passion,
    When I awoke and found the dawn was grey;
I have been faithful to thee, Cynara! in my fashion.

I have forgot much, Cynara! gone with the wind,
Flung roses, roses, riotously with the throng,
Dancing, to put thy pale lost lilies out of mind:
But I was desolate and sick of an old passion,
    Yea, all the time, because the dance was long:
I have been faithful to thee, Cynara! in my fashion.

I cried for madder music and for stronger wine,
But when the feast is finish'd and the lamps expire,
Then falls thy shadow, Cynara! the night is thine;
And I am desolate and sick of an old passion,
    Yea, hungry for the lips of my desire:
I have been faithful to thee, Cynara! in my fashion.

(Ernest Dowson, English, 1867–1900.)

[Even when the beloved is attained, emotions like jealousy are apt to spoil things.]

This evening when I spake with thee, beloved,
as in thy face and in thy mien I saw
that I could not persuade thee with my words,
the longing came for thee to see my heart,

and love, abettor of my purposes,
accomplished that which seemed impossible,
for issuing with the tears which sorrow shed
my heart dissolved in misery distilled.

Enough of cruelty, beloved, enough:
let my harsh jealousy torment thee not
nor vile suspicion violate thy virtue

with foolish shadows, vain appearances,
since now in aqueous humour thou hast seen
and held between thy hands my broken heart.

(Juana de Asbaje, Mexican, 1651–95, tr. Samuel Beckett.)

[The poet has premonition that a love affair is doomed even before it begins.]

After the wind and the frost,
It was pleasant to toast myself at the fire.
But I didn't look after my heart
And it was stolen from me.

New Year's Day stretches out luxuriantly,
The stems of the New Year's roses are moist,
And in my breast I no longer feel
The trembling of dragonflies.

Ah, it's not hard for me to guess the thief,
I recognized him by his eyes.
But it's frightening that soon, soon,
He himself will return his prize.

(Anna Akhmatova, Russian, 1889–1966, tr. Judith Hemschemeyer.)

[A poem where love, separated from nature by man-made walls, dies.]

Rooms

I remember rooms that have had their part
In the steady slowing down of the heart.
The room in Paris, the room at Geneva,
The little damp room with the seaweed smell,
And that ceaseless maddening sound of the tide -
    Rooms where for good or ill – things died.
But there is the room where we (two) lie dead,
Though every morning we seem to wake and might just as
                    well seem to sleep again
    As we shall somewhere in the other quieter, dustier bed
    Out there in the sun – in the rain.

(Charlotte Mew, English, 1869–1928).

[The celebrations of love that follow were written twenty-four centuries ago. There is disagreement over many aspects of the Song of Songs. Is it one poem or many? Is a story, or several stories, buried there? If so, what? The first extract is a declaration of love from boy to girl.]

    My beloved speaks and says to me:
      "Arise my love, my fair one,
        and come away;
    for lo, the winter is past,
      the rain is over and gone.
    The flowers appear on the earth,
      the time of singing has come,
    and the voice of the turtledove
      is heard in our land.
    The fig tree puts forth its figs,
      and the vines are in blossom;
      they give forth fragrance.

Arise my love, my fair one,
    and come away.
O my dove, in the clefts of the rock,
    in the covert of the cliff,
let me see your face,
    let me hear your voice,
for your voice is sweet,
    and your face is comely.
Catch us the foxes,
    the little foxes
that spoil the vineyards,
    for our vineyards are in blossom."

(Anon., Hebrew, 4th C. B.C.; Song of Songs, 2, 10–15. Translation from Bible, Revised Standard Version.)

[In the next extract from the Song of Songs, love and desire throw a girl into confusion. Torn between accepting and rejecting her lover, she roams the city and is beaten by night watchmen, perhaps because they think she's a whore.]

I slumbered, but my heart was alert.
    Listen! My beloved is entreating:

(he speaks)   'Open to me, my sister, my darling,
    my dove, my perfect one,
for my forehead is drenched with dew,
    my locks with the mist of the night.'

(she answers)   'I have slipped off my robe.
    How can I put it on?
I have bathed my feet.
    How can I get them soiled?'

My beloved stretched his hand in through the hole,
    and my insides moaned for him.
I arose to open to my beloved,
    and my hands dripped myrrh,

my fingers – liquid myrrh,
      on the handles of the lock.
I opened to my beloved,
      but my beloved had turned away and gone.
Because of him my soul went forth:
      I sought him but did not find him,
            I called him but he did not answer me.
The nightwatchmen who roam the city found me –
      they beat me and bruised me,
took my shawl away from me –
      those who watch the walls.
I ask you to promise, girls of Jerusalem:
      if you find my beloved
do not tell him
      that I am sick with love.

(Anon., Hebrew, 4th C. B.C.; Song of Songs, 5, 3–8, tr. M.V. Fox.)

[The next poem asks playfully the simple question, 'Why can't we have sex whenever we want?']

Comin' thru the Rye

O gin★ a body meet a body,   ★if
  Comin' thru the rye,
Gin a body fuck a body,
  Need a body cry?
      Comin' throu the rye, my jo,
        An' comin throu the rye;
      She fand a staun o' staunin' graith★
        Comin' thro' the rye.

                              ★ found a set of erect equipment.

Gin a body meet a body,
  Comin' throu the glen;
Gin a body fuck a body,
  Need the warld ken★?   ★know

Comin' throu the rye, my jo,
  An' comin throu the rye;
She fand a staun o' staunin' graith
  Comin' thru the rye.

Gin a body meet a body
  Comin' throu the grain;
Gin a body fuck a body
  Cunt's a body's ain*.   *own
    Comin' thro' the rye, my jo,
      An' comin throu the rye;
    She fand a staun o' staunin' graith
      Comin' thro' the rye.

Gin a body meet a body,
  By a body's sel*,   *self
What na* body fucks a body,   *what if a
  Wad a body tell?
    Comin' thro' the rye, my jo,
      An' comin throu the rye;
    She fand a staun o' staunin' graith
      Comin' thro' the rye.

Mony a body meets a body
  They darena weel avow*;   *daren't admit
Mony a body fucks a body,
  Ye wadna think it true.
    Comin' throu the rye, my jo,
      An comin; thro' the rye,
    She fand a staun o' staunin' graith
      Comin' thro' the rye.

(R. Burns, Scottish, 1759–1796.)

[Lots of great literature has been devoted to answering the
question posed in the last song. Burns himself supplied his own
answer, which is an expert one, as he had a great deal of
experience in both 'well-placed' and 'illicit' love.]

The sacred lowe* o' well-placed love,   *flame
Luxuriantly indulge it;
But never tempt the illicit rove,
Though nothing should divulge it;
I waive the quantum of the sin,
The hazard of concealing;
But och! it hardens a' within,
And petrifies the feeling!

(R. Burns, Scottish, 1759–1796; stanza 6 of 'Epistle to a Young Friend'.)

[Pushkin seems to have suffered a 'petrification of feeling' – or at least a jaded appetite – after a dozen or so years of passionate physical affairs with different girls. In the next poem he describes how he needed the coldness of the girl he married to stimulate him. Later he found his wife's flirtations with other men unbearable. He challenged one of them to a duel and was killed.]

No, I don't miss the dissipated nights,
The moans and cries of a young bacchante
Writhing like a serpent in my arms
When, with fierce caresses and love-bites,
She hastens the moment of final spasm.

Dearer to me are you, my quiet friend,
How tormentingly happier I am with you,
When at long last you condescend
To yield to my pleas, tenderly, without rapture,
Cold, ashamed, scarcely responding to
My transports, avoiding them with your lips, your eyes,
More and more coming to life, until
At last you share my pleasure against your will.

(Pushkin, Russian, 1799–1837, tr. D.M. Thomas.)

[Ono no Komachi had many lovers, one of whom is said to have died of exposure under her window while he waited a hundred nights for her to admit him. She wrote the following two poems of disillusion, both using the image of a fading flower; one about men's hearts, the other about her own life.]

1.   A flower which fades
             With no outward sign
                 Is the heart
                 Of man
             In this world.

2.   The colour of the flowers
             Has faded;
             Fruitlessly
             I have spent my life,
             As the long rains fall...

(Ono no Komachi, Japanese, 9th c., tr. I.M.)

[If sexual love without fidelity may prove unsatisfactory in the end, sex without love is unattractive from the very start. It's unattractive because our aesthetic judgements are moulded by our instincts as to what benefits us, as individuals and as a species.]

     The window-frame shakes. What is below?
     A bevy of damp-crotched young pricks
     in the street, on the hunt for sex,
     none of your old-style love. They go

     in their powerful cars anywhere.
     Duty? Down the drain. It is not
     their concern. Nobody has taught
     them anything. And they prefer

     noise to music. Amplified bleats,
     wails and howls, after their disco-
     theques shut, they blare among the streets.

     They have houses, women, snappy
     cars, and that is all they have; no
     wonder they are so unhappy.

(George Faludy, Hungarian, born 1910, tr. George Johnston.)

[When love is absent, what we like to call humanity dies. The next poem sees this death lurking even where new life is being born. The new life in question doesn't seem to have much of a chance of flourishing.]

The Distinct Impression

'I was delivering a child
In this kip of a bedroom in Keogh Square.
The woman jerked and groaned in the bed
Sweat wetting her hair.

Six children lumped and stared at me
As I worked on her.
In the bed with the woman was her man,
Face to the wall, an occasional snore.

"Is it out yet?" he asked of a sudden.
If I'd a bucket o' boilin' water then
I'd have emptied it over his skin.

I had the distinct impression
That the moment the child was out of the woman
The bastard would be back in.'

(B. Kennelly, Irish, b. 1936, from 'The Book of Judas'.)

[Two sonnets of Shakespeare differentiate between lust and love.]

Th' expense of spirit in a waste of shame
Is lust in action; and till action, lust
Is perjured, murd'rous, bloody, full of blame,
Savage, extreme, rude, cruel, not to trust;
Enjoy'd no sooner but despised straight;
Past reason hunted, and, no sooner had,
Past reason hated, as a swallowed bait

On purpose laid to make the taker mad;
Mad in pursuit, and in possession so;
Had, having, and in quest to have, extreme;
A bliss in proof, and proved, a very woe;
Before, a joy proposed; behind, a dream.
   And this the world well knows; yet none knows well
   To shun the heaven that leads men to this hell.

Let me not to the marriage of true minds
Admit impediments; love is not love
Which alters when it alteration finds,
Or bends with the remover to remove.
O, no! it is an ever-fixed mark
That looks on tempests and is never shaken;
It is the star to every wand'ring bark,
Whose worth's unknown, although his height be taken.
Love's nòt Time's fool, though rosy lips and cheeks
Within his bending sickle's compass come;
Love alters not with his brief hours and weeks,
But bears it out even to the edge of doom:-
   If this be error and upon me proved,
   I never writ, nor no man ever loved.

(William Shakespeare, English, 1546–1616; sonnets 129 and 116.)

[The impulse to make a union which is sacred and protected – that is, a marriage – is behind the next poem.]

Two flowers on one stem,
   My heart is in balance with yours.
For you I'll go where love leads me;
   I am in your embrace.
Prayer paints my eyes,
   Seeing you brightens my eyes.
I've drawn near to see your love
   Oh prince of my heart!
How lovely is this hour!
   It flows forth from me for ever!
     It began when I lay with you -

> For sorrow or joy,
>   You have exalted my heart;
>   Do not leave me!

(Anon, Egyptian, c. 13th C. B.C., tr. adapted from M.V. Fox.)

[Married love is not as well documented as the joys and disappointments of courtship. Most trying and testing of all of love's manifestations, it can also have the greatest rewards of trust, intimacy and sexual pleasure.

The next poem, like the poem by Hafiz some pages back, notes that love is born of separate identities in need of each other.]

In Praise of Marriages

Not till life halved, and parted
one from the other,
did time begin, and knowledge;
sorrow, delight.
Terror of being apart, being lost,
made real the night.
Seeking and finding made
yesterday, now and tomorrow.
And love was realized first
when those two came together.

So, perilously joined,
lighted in one small room,
we have made all things true.
Out of the I and the you
spreads this field of power,
that all that waits may come,
all possibles be known -
all futures step from their stone
and pasts come into flower.

(Judith Wright, Australian, born 1915.)

[A world remote from our modern 'post-industrial' society is conjured up by Kalidasa, the most celebrated of poets from India, who wrote plays and poetry about two thousand years ago. This is an extract from 'The Gathering of the Seasons', a poem in praise of married love in which sensuality is celebrated. Erotic description of the female body does not seem, as it sometimes does in Western poetry, to be a spur to possession or violation.]

from '*The Season of Frosts*'

Women now prepare for love's festival,
perfuming their hair with black aloe-smoke,
tracing leafy lines on their lotus-faces,
and rubbing their bodies with white aloe-salve.

With faces pale and drawn from love's weariness,
young women whose lips smart from love-bites
are afraid to laugh out loud,
even when a happy occasion arises.

Seeming sensible of the sensuous beauty
of women's breasts, sad to see them pressed so hard,
the frosty season cries out at dawn, letting fall
dew-drops that cling to the tips of blades of grass.

Fields richly covered with ripening rice
where charming does roam in herds
are sonorous with the calls of damsel cranes.
Ah! What restlessness they arouse!

Where the chill waters of lakes shimmer
blue lotuses open wide in beauty;
mallards court in wild excitement:
all hearts are transported with boundless delight...

Mouths redolent of the fragrance of flower-wine,
Limbs perfumed from mingled breaths -
men and women sleep, twined in one another's arms,
blended in the sweet poetry of love.

Sharp imprint of love-bites on bruised lips,
the lover's fine nail-inscriptions on breasts -
these clearly reveal the passionate enjoyment,
relentless, of women in the first flush of youth.

A certain young woman, mirror in hand,
decorates her radiant lotus-face, basking
in the gentle warmth of the mild morning sun
and gazes with interest, pouting, at the love-bites
her beloved left when he drank his fill
of the nectar of her lower lip.

Yet another, her body limp
from toiling at passion's intense play,
her lotus-eyes painfully red
from the long night's vigil,
– richly-flowing mane of hair waving
wildly over weary, drooping shoulders –
falls asleep,
warmed by a tender sun's gentle rays...

Toiling long hours at love's passionate sport,
other lovely young women, o'ercome with fatigue,
have their slender, languid bodies massaged with oils;
– the chilly air makes their breasts and thighs tingle.

May this season of glittering frosts, delightful
by virtue of its many excellences,
that enthralls the hearts of women;
when the village bournes are brimful
of bountiful harvests of golden grain;
when the dew falls thick
and the air is sweet with the curlew's notes,
fully grant you all happiness.

(Kalidasa, Indian, ? between 100 B.C. and 500 A.D., tr. Chandra Rajan.)

[This short glimpse of a marriage was written by a religious man]

If she believes or wears a cross,
Always be kind to your tired wife

Though she knocks religion and says:
'Friends, don't give a fig for old creeds,

People commit huge crimes having learnt
Only petty acts earn hell fire.'

(Ma'arri, Arabic, 937–1057, tr. G. Wightam and A. al-Udhari.)

[The glorious flowering of a tree after many years is an image of magnificence and sadness in the next poem.]

The Flame-Tree Blooms

It was you planted it;
and it grew high and put on crops of leaves,
extravagant fans; sheltered in it the spider weaves
and birds move through it.

For all it grew so well
it never bloomed, though we watched patiently,
having chosen its place where we could see
it from our window-sill.

Now, in its eighteenth spring,
suddenly, wholly, ceremoniously
it puts off every leaf and stands up nakedly,
calling and gathering

every capacity in it, every power,
drawing up from the very roots of being
this pulse of total red that shocks my seeing
into an agony of flower.

It was you planted it;
and I lean on the sill to see it stand
in its dry shuffle of leaves, just as we planned,
these past years feeding it.

(Judith Wright, Australian, born 1915.)

[The next poem also has an image of the profuse abundance of trees.]

On the Death of His Wife

When in this world
You were still alive
Hand in hand
We two would watch
In front of the house
Where, on a bank, stood
The elm trees,
Their branches spreading here and there.
Though like the spring leaves
Thick and numerous
I loved you
You who were my wife;
Though I leaned on you,
You who were my love,
The laws of this world
You could not disobey.
Like shimmer rising
From burning desolate fields
In a white cloth
Heavenly robe, hidden from my sight
As a bird does
You made a morning journey;
Like the sun going in
You were lost to my sight.
A keep sake for my eyes you left me -
A small child;
When he cries and asks for something,
To give him I have nothing, but,
As a man does, clumsily
I hold him to my side.
Where with my love
I used to sleep,
Our pillows side by side,

In our wedding room,
Through the day now
I'm sad till dark;
Through the night
I sigh until dawn.
Though I weep and moan
I don't know what to do;
Though I love her
I don't know how to meet her.
Then, 'On Bird-like
Hagai Mountain
Your wife is living'
Someone told me; so,
Forcing my way across mountain peaks
I went there with great hardship.
But no good came of it:
For my love
As someone living in this world
Even as a jewel-glow,
Faintly,
I realise now is nowhere to be seen.

Just as last year we saw it
The autumn moonlit night
Once more is bright; but
My love who watched it with me
Grows ever distant on departing time.

Near the road to Fusuma
Among the hills of Hikide
I left my love;
As I came down the mountain road
I felt as one not living.

(Hitomaro, Japanese, 7th. C., tr. I.M.)

[Not all poets are so committed to their marriages. This comment on his marriage comes from Li Po, the most celebrated poet of ancient China.]

To His Wife

Three hundred and sixty-five days
And every day I'm drunk as mud
What difference in being Li Bo's wife
Or married to old Commissioner Flask?

(Li Po, Chinese, 701–762, tr. John Scott.)

[This next song, though written down two and a half thousand years ago, could well be entitled 'Song of the Divorce Courts'.]

Zip, zip the valley wind!
Nothing but wind and rain.
In days of peril, in days of dread
It was always 'I and you'.
Now in time of peace, of happiness,
You have cast me aside.

Zip, zip the valley wind!
Nothing but wind and duststorms!
In days of peril, in days of dread
You put me in your bosom.
Now in time of peace, of happiness
You throw me away like slop-water.

Zip, zip the valley wind
Across the rocky hills.
No grass but is dying,
No tree but is wilting.
You forget my great merits,
Remembering only my small faults.

(Anon, Chinese, 7th C. B.C., Book of Songs 109, tr. A. Waley.)

[The ideal upbringing in most people's mind involves having both a mother and a father around, though one good parent is

preferable to two bad ones. A simple poem connects the themes
of marriage and children.]

> The oddest event in life;
> (God is neither forgetful,
> Nor does he break his promises),
> Two in bed become three.

(Ma'arri, Arabic, 937–1057, tr. G. Wightam and A. al-Udhari.)

[In the next poem a father, a civil servant, is miserable at having to
leave his family to meet the demands of his job.]

Children

> Children don't know what worry means!
> I stand up to go and they hang on my clothes.
> I'm about to scold them
> But my wife eggs them on in their silliness:
> "The children are silly but you're much worse!
> What good does all this worrying do?"
> Stung by her words, I go back to my seat.
> She rinses a wine cup to put before me.
> How much better than Liu Ling's* wife,
> Grumbling at the cost of her husband's drinking!

> *an earlier Chinese poet

(Su T'ung Po, Chinese, 1037–1101, tr. Burton Watson.)

[A poem by a daughter remembering her father]

Father

> They say, his strange, large eyes,
> Opal-like, odd, Nordic eyes,
> Always looked far-off. He could
> Fuss half a day with a flower's root.
> He'd lean over it – and its fragile
> Refined petal's belligerent fragrance.

In women too, he sought the soul.
He collected pictures, books, old embroidery
He also grappled with men.
The table glittered at his opulent feasts.
Servants moved silently, and the wines'
Crystal fire shimmered deep, flaming.
He savoured it, as long as the tablecloth
And flowers were unsplotched. But later
When the word became more and more shrill,
Heated, the smoke more stifling,
The country elite railed at the government.
Ten spoke at once – and roared bent over
Gross, crude jokes – and slumping,
They stammered in brotherly kisses, while
Some started snoring, thick-lipped.
Then he became upset, pensive,
He stared at them with clouded, sad eyes,
And felt that just he was the lonely one there.
Then he whistled for his dog.
The viszla came padding, nuzzled up against him,
And put his smart, pedigreed head in his lap.
In the greying wine-vapour morning
Petting him, they looked at each other.

They say: later I became the light of his eye.
For me, he forgot his celebrated flowers,
He leaned over my lacy, ribboned cradle,
And guarded me like a costly porcelain,
How often he kept watch at my small sickbed!
And when one day, untutored,
I could draw my first two letters, he drew me close,
And whispered, 'That's the way, little one!
When you grow up, the world will be different!'
And then came the disease, and he lingered,
For a long time, knowing his end.
And he wasn't much older than I am today!...
They say, he suffered nights because of me,
If he looked at me he clenched his hands in his lap.
'You'll be a beggar!' he said, and his words choked.

'Why couldn't I have been stingy, for your sake!'
Oh my father, if you could know, that's nothing!
If only I never had a greater worry!
But you see, the world hasn't changed since then;
You were so wrong, father.
Now I hear the news – your grave is so grassy.
The marble bows and the gold letters
Are all washed away, I was there so long ago,
And every year there are downpours.
How many storms! How many have I survived,
And life, father, what chaos!

...If you could see, now you have a grandchild,
Bright-eyed, loud, lively small thing,
But his eyes are different from yours or mine!
Good! Because storms will come! – But maybe
The world will be different when he grows up?
It's been so long that you've slept below!
You weren't much older than I am today,
And time has washed away your golden letters,
And I hear the news, your grave is grassy.
Can I bring my flowers once more?
Who knows? Life is such chaos,
And I am so tired, – father.

(Margit Kaffka, Hungarian, 1880–1918, tr. Laura Schiff.)

[The love between parents and children is crucial for survival, but children must also change with the times. What growing son with a father has not felt the following?]

> father and son
> minds apart
> face to face
> in awkward silence
> why – ?

(Takuboku, Japanese, 1885–1912, tr. Carl Sesar.)

[By the same poet, about his mother:]

> kidding around
> carried my mother
> piggy-back
> I stopped dead, and cried.
> she's so light...

(Takuboku, Japanese, 1885–1912, tr. Carl Sesar.)

[Separation forced on a poet by war sets him thinking of his old home.]

Thinking of My Brothers on a Moonlit Night

> Drums on the watch-tower have emptied the roads -
> At the frontier it's autumn; a wild-goose cries.
> This is a night in which dew becomes frost;
> The moon is bright like it used to be at home.
>
> I have brothers, but they're all scattered.
> My home's broken up; are they dead or alive?
> If letters are sent, they don't arrive;
> The war that separates us seems unending.

(Tu Fu, Chinese, 712–770. Version I.M. after Hawkes.)

[A poem of a mother's love for her child.]

Sleep Close to Me

> Fold of my flesh
> I carried in my womb,
> tender trembling flesh
> sleep close to me!

The partridge sleeps in the wheat
listening to its heartbeat.
Let not my breath disturb you
sleep close to me!

Little tender grass
afraid to live,
don't move from my arms;
sleep close to me!

I have lost everything,
and tremble until I sleep.
Don't move from my breast;
sleep close to me!

(Gabriella Mistral, 1889–1957, Chilean, tr. D.M. Pettinella.)

[Mandelstam, who had no children, reminds us that in the realm
of duties, none stands higher than to do our best for children. The
next poem – written when Mandelstam was facing certain extermination by Stalin – celebrates pleasure, unity with nature, the
integrity of poetry, the defence of freedom, and the continuation
of our human species.]

I sing when my throat is wet, my soul is dry,
and when my eye is moist enough and thinking does not lie.
Is it good, the wine? The furs, are they not fine?
And the swaying dance of Colchis in the blood?
But my breast grows taut, quiet without a tongue:
it is not I who sing, it is my breathing sings,
the mountains' scabbards hold my hearing, and my head is deaf.

The song that has no profit is it's own praise,
delight for friends and burning coals for enemies.

The one-eyed song, growing out of moss,
the one-voiced gift of hunters' lives

sung on horseback and in the heights,
the breath held free and open,
caring only in honour and anger
to get the young ones to their wedding without a fall...

(Osip Mandelstam, Russian, 1891–1938, tr. D. McDuff.)

[Love survives until death in the heart that values it. The next
poem was written not long before the writer committed suicide.
We can even love the earth, that claims us as our grave.]

Moorland Night

My face is against the grass – the moorland grass is wet –
    My eyes are shut against the grass, against my lips there are
                                                 the little blades,
        Over my head the curlews call,
    And now there is the wind in my hair;
My heart is against the grass and the sweet earth; – it has
                                                 gone still, at last.
            It does not want to beat any more,
                And why should it beat?
            This is the end of the journey;
                The Thing is found.

            This is the end of all the roads –
    Over the grass there is the night-dew
And the wind that drives up from the sea along the moorland road;
        I hear a curlew start out from the heath
        And fly off, calling through the dusk,
            The wild, long, rippling call.
    The Thing is found and I am quiet with the earth.
Perhaps the earth will hold it, or the wind, or that bird's cry,
But it is not for long in any life I know. This cannot stay,
Not now, not yet, not in a dying world, with me, for very long.
        I leave it here:

And one day the wet grass may give it back -
One day the quiet earth may give it back
The calling birds may give it as they go by -
To someone walking on the moor who starves for love and will not know
Who gave it to all these to give away;
Or, if I come and ask for it again,
Oh, then to me!

(Charlotte Mew, English, 1869–1928.)

[Rumi argues that our physical mortality – the same for us all, as individuals and as species – makes it imperative that we seek out love.]

One handful of dust shouts 'I was hair!'
One handful of dust shouts 'I am a bone!'
Confusion reigns, until Love appears,
And says, 'Draw close to me – I am life eternal!'

(Rumi, Persian, 1207–73; adapted from a translation by Anne-Marie Schimmel.)

3. Religion

Man, living in the dust,
Is like a bug trapped in a bowl.
All day he scrabbles round and round,
But never escapes from the bowl that holds him.
The immortals are beyond his reach,
His cravings have no end,
While months and years flow by like a river
Until, in an instant, he has grown old.

(Han Shan, Chinese, fl. c. 800 A.D., tr. Burton Watson.)

Hard work was created for everyone,
    and a heavy yoke is laid on the children of Adam,
from the day they come forth from their mother's womb
    until the day they return to the mother of all the living.
Perplexities and fear of heart are theirs,
    and anxious thought of the day of their death.
From the one who sits on a splendid throne
    to the one who grovels in dust and ashes,
from the one who wears purple and a crown
    to the one who is clothed in burlap,
there is anger and envy and trouble and unrest,
    and fear of death, and fury and strife.
And when one rests upon his bed,
    his sleep at night confuses his mind.
He gets little or no rest;
    he struggles in his sleep as he did by day.
He is troubled by the visions of his mind
    like one who has escaped from the battlefield.
At the moment he reaches safety he wakes up,
    astonished that his fears were groundless.

To all creatures, human and animal,
  but to sinners seven times more,
come death and bloodshed and strife and sword,
  calamities and famine and ruin and plague.

(Jesus Ben Sira, Jewish Egyptian, fl. c. 180 BC. Bible, Sirach 40 1–9, New
Revised Standard Version.)

[The grimness of life leads humanity to look for a higher design
behind the apparent arbitrary cruelty of nature. Contemplation of
a divine purpose leads to humility and joy, and in train of these
comes the realisation that God, love, truth, purpose, goodness,
and justice are alive for us in so far as we believe in them, and
disappear from us when we no longer believe in them. By giving
them our loyalty we discover their fruits. By making certain
sacrifices in their favour, we can create our own limited justice
and well-being within the limits set down on us.

    We are also able to join in the delight which all our fellow-
creatures seem to feel, in being part of a continually changing
creation.]

Glory be to God for dappled things –
  For skies of couple-colour as a brinded cow;
    For rose-moles all in stipple upon trout that swim;

Fresh fire-coal chestnut-falls; finches' wings;
  Landscape plotted and pieced – fold, fallow, and plough;
    And all trades, their gear and tackle and trim.

All things counter, original, spare, strange;
  Whatever is fickle, freckled (who knows how?)
    With swift, slow; sweet, sour; adazzle, dim;
He fathers-forth whose beauty is past change:
              Praise him.

(Gerard Manley Hopkins, English, 1844–89.)

[Religions assume that behind nature is a deity whose purpose we are unable fully to comprehend. This assumption seems not unreasonable, since we are limited in understanding by the terms of our existence.]

I see mankind under two lights,
Past and future; and in two states,
Time and place. If we want to know
How God accounts for this oddness
We'll get an evasive answer.

(Ma'arri, Arabic, 973–1057, tr. G. Wightman and A. al-Udhari.)

[Communities all over the world were, and to a great extent still are, bound together internally by religious belief. But religions can be divisive between communities, especially when they claim to have a monopoly on the truth. People complain that religion – or rather, religions, – have caused wars, persecution and civil strife. But who knows how history would have gone without the influence of religions? From the examples of recent societies that rejected religion – those led by Hitler, Stalin and Pol Pot for instance – history would have been an extremely short and bloody affair.

As science gives us more and more knowledge of how the world works, many people think it's inappropriate to believe the old stories of how we came to be. This attitude misunderstands the nature and intention of story-telling, in which literal truth is set aside to arrive at a more profound metaphorical truth. Societies make sacred those stories which seem to them most profoundly true and most helpful for survival. Those in charge of preserving and transmitting the stories, the priests, find they have a power which they often then abuse – but more of that later.

Two contrasting expressions of the ancient and original approach to religion;

'Unspeakable mysteries in the Scriptures are often delivered in a vulgar and illustrative way; and, being written unto man, are delivered, not as they truely are, but as they may be understood.' (Sir Thomas Browne, around 1635.)

'Play consecrated to the Deity, the highest goal of man's endeavour – such was Plato's conception of religion. In following him, we in no way abandon the holy mystery, or cease to rate it as the highest attainable expression of that which escapes logical understanding.' (J. Huizinga, 1938.)

A recent version[1] of civilisation in Europe has it that our remote ancestors, wandering hunter-gatherers, worshipped a Mother Goddess (c 20,000–10,000 B.C.). Later, the same people settled down. They began sowing seeds and keeping animals in captivity. Worship of the Mother Goddess continued and there was a golden age of peace and prosperity (c 10,000–4,500 B.C.). This was interrupted when warlike tribes, worshipping male gods, ransacked these communities.

Whatever poems were chanted to this Mother Goddess of life and death are lost. Poems to goddesses that survive are from thousands of years later, by which time the Father God is supreme. The original character of the Mother Goddess was by then split into various attributes, some re-assigned to the Supreme Father and others to lesser female goddesses, of Earth, Love, War, the Moon and so on. The poem that follows addresses Gaia, Greek goddess of the earth.]

Hymn to Earth, Mother of All

Gaia, mother of all, hard, splendid as rock,
Eldest of all beings; I sing the greatness of Earth!
She feeds the world's creatures; those on the sacred land,
Those in the paths of the sea, and those that fly in air;
All are hers; she feeds them, from her sacred store.
Fair children and fair harvests depend on her blessing;
She provides for us to live, and when she witholds we die.
Happy the man she delights to honour! Abundance is his,
His trees grow heavy with fruit, his land heavy with corn.
His pastures teem with cattle, his house is full of good things.
Such men rule with just laws in cities of fair women;
Beauty, wealth and fortune follow them in plenty.

[1] Marija Gimbutas, 'The Civilisation of the Goddess', 1991.

Their sons exult in ever fresh delight; and, garlanded,
Their daughters skip merrily on the soft flowers of the field.
Such are those you honour, holy goddess, generous spirit.
    Mother of gods, bride of the starry sky, farewell!
To cheer my heart, please give me things for making you this song;
In this, and in my other songs, I will remember you.

(Anon., Greek, 6th C. B.C. Version I.M. from existing translations by
Shelley, Evelyn-White, Boer and Cashford.)

[The next poem tells of the goddess Aphrodite, called 'the
Cyprian' because she was born in Cyprus, goddess of love in all
its manifestations.]

Aphrodite

Listen, my children; Love is not only Love,
But many are the names whereby she is called.
She is Death; she is indomitable Force;
She is wild Frenzy, and vehement Desire;
She is Lamentation. All things meet in her,
Virtue, Tranquillity, and Violence.
Into all living hearts she instils herself.
Of this goddess what creature is not the prey?
Into the shoals of fish that swim the sea
She enters, and within the four-foot tribes
On land she harbours; and among the birds
On divine wing she flits. What deity
Who wrestles with her is not overthrown?
If I may tell − and the truth may be told −
She rules the heart of Zeus. Without a spear,
Without sword, all the purposes of mortals
And gods the Cyprian has power to confound.

(Sophocles, Greek, 495–406 B.C., tr. R.C. Trevelyan.)

[The next poem is from a hymn addressed to Inanna, goddess of
the Moon and of War. The poet (a high priestess) curries Inanna's

favour by describing the goddess's ability to lay waste those who don't worship her. It was written during a time of war, and goddesses had to be fierce to maintain their place in the pecking order.]

from 'The Adoration of Inanna in Ur'

My Queen; the Anunna, the great gods,
Fled before you like fluttering bats,
Could not stand before your awesome face,
Could not approach your awesome forehead.
Who can soothe your angry heart!
Your baleful heart is beyond soothing!
Queen, happy of liver, joyful of heart,
But whose anger cannot be soothed; daughter of Nanna,
Queen, first in the land, who has ever paid you enough homage!

The mountain which did not pay you homage –
Vegetation was accursed on it,
You burnt down its great gates,
Its rivers ran with blood because of you,
its people had nothing to drink,
Its troops were led off willingly before you.
Its forces disbanded willingly before you.
The amusement places of its cities were filled with turbulence.
Its adult males were driven off as captives before you.

Against the city that said not 'Yours is the land,'
That said not 'It belongs to the father that begot you,'
You spoke your holy word, turned away from it,
Kept your distance from its womb.
Its woman spoke not of love with her husband,
In the deep night she whispered not tenderly with him,
Revealed not to him the holiness of her heart.

Rampant wild cow, elder daughter of Nanna,
Queen greater than An, who has ever paid you enough homage!

(Enhuedanna, Sumerian, b. c. 2300 B.C., tr. S.N. Kramer.)

[For most of recorded history, male gods have been predominant. Even the supreme deity – God, Jehovah, Zeus, Allah, or Buddha – has been sexed as a male. The Hindu supreme deity Brahman, however, is officially beyond gender.

Though it would seem that female deities are more protective of the earth and vengeful of transgressions against nature, religions overseen by male gods haven't neglected values of conservation. Mankind is seen as God's steward, and it's his duty to look after nature. When Jehovah gave Israel the Laws he said 'Land will not be sold absolutely, for it belongs to me, and you are only strangers and guests of mine' (Leviticus 25, 23). The trouble is, prosperity brings with it a belief that we can do without God's laws. The consequences of this are described in the next two extracts, the first of which could hardly be more like a description of the present day.]

> Hear the word of the Lord,
>   O people of Israel;
> for the Lord has an indictment
>   against the inhabitants of the land.
> There is no faithfulness or loyalty,
>   and no knowledge of God in the land.
> Swearing, lying and murder,
>   and stealing and adultery break out;
>   bloodshed follows bloodshed.
> Therefore the land mourns,
>   and all who live in it languish;
> together with the wild animals
>   and the birds of the air
>   even the fish of the sea are perishing.

(Hosea, Hebrew, 8th C. B.C. Bible, Hosea, 4, 1–3. New Revised Standard Version.)

[A later stage in the desecration of law and the land is described in the Book of Isaiah:]

The earth mourns and withers,
    the world languishes and withers
    the heavens languish together with the earth.
The earth lies polluted under its inhabitants;
for they have transgressed the laws,
    violated the statutes,
    broken the everlasting covenant.
Therefore a curse devours the earth,
    and its inhabitants suffer for their guilt;
therefore the inhabitants of the earth are scorched,
    and few men are left.
The wine mourns,
    the vine languishes,
    all the merry-hearted sigh.
The mirth of the timbrels is stilled,
    the noise of the jubilant has ceased,
    the mirth of the lyre is stilled.
No more do they drink wine with singing;
    strong drink is bitter to those who drink it.
The city of chaos is broken down,
    every house is shut up so that none can enter.
There is an outcry in the streets for lack of wine;
    all joy has reached its eventide;
    the gladness of the earth is banished.
Desolation is left in the city,
    the gates are battered into ruins.

(Isaiah, Hebrew, c. 700 B.C. Bible, Isaiah, 24, 4–12, Revised
Standard Version.)

[Religions differ greatly, but they have in common the notion
that in order to flourish we must live in accordance with rules not
of our making.

    In the following poem, the poet rants against his servitude to
God, entertaining all sorts of ideas of indulging himself, until he is
interrupted by a voice to which he cannot help but respond.]

The Collar

I struck the board and cried, 'No more.
　　　I will abroad.
　　What? shall I ever sigh and pine?
My lines and life are free; free as the rode★, ★wildfowl
　　Loose as the wind, as large as store.
　　　Shall I still be in suit?
　　Have I no harvest but a thorn
　　To let me blood, and not restore
What I have lost with cordial fruit?
　　　Sure there was wine
Before my sighs did dry it: there was corn
　　Before my tears did drown it.
　　Is the year only lost to me?
　　Have I no bays to crown it?
No flowers, no garlands gay? All blasted?
　　　All wasted?
　　Not so, my heart; but there is fruit,
　　　And thou hast hands.
　　Recover all thy sigh-blown age
On double pleasures: leave thy cold dispute
Of what is fit, and not. Forsake thy cage,
　　　Thy rope of sands,
Which petty thoughts have made, and made to thee
Good cable, to enforce and draw,
　　　And be thy law,
While thou didst wink and wouldst not see.
　　　Away, take heed:
　　　I will abroad.
Call in thy deaths head there: tie up thy fears.
　　He that forbears
　　To suit and serve his need,
　　　Deserves his load.'
But as I raved and grew more fierce and wild
　　At every word,
Methought I heard one calling, 'Child!'
　　And I replied, 'My Lord!'

(George Herbert, English, 1593–1633.)

[In Taoism, the idea of God is replaced by the idea of 'the way'. This represents the laws and the order behind the physical universe. If we live in conformity with the way, we flourish; if we go against it, we don't.]

There is a thing confusedly formed,
Born before heaven and earth.
Silent and void
It stands alone and does not change,
Goes round and does not weary.
It is capable of being the mother of the world.
I know not its name
So I style it 'the way'.
I give it the makeshift name of 'the great'.
Being great, it is further described as receding,
Receding, it is described as far away,
Being far away, it is described as turning back.

Hence the way is great; heaven is great; earth is great; and man is also great. Within the realm there are four things that are great, and man counts as one.

Man follows earth,
Earth follows heaven,
Heaven follows the way,
The way follows itself.

(Lao Tzu, Chinese, 4th–3rd C. B.C.; from the Tao Te Ching. Compiled from tr.'s by D.C.Lau and R.Payne.)

[The theme that God is everywhere is common to most religions. The next poem is by a Muslim; the one after, by a Hindu.]

O God,
Whenever I listen to the voice of anything you have made –
The rustling of the trees
The trickling of water
The cries of birds

The flickering of shadow
The roar of the wind
The song of the thunder
I hear it saying:
God is One!
Nothing can be compared with God!

(Rabi'a, b. 717, Iraq. Tr. Charles Upton.)

I laugh when I hear the fish in the water is thirsty.
Don't you know, God's in your own house,
That you wander the forests so listlessly?
In your home is the truth; go where you will,
To Benares or Mathura; [2]
If your soul is a stranger to you, the whole world is unhomely.

(Kabir, Hindi, 1440–1518, tr. Tagore and Bridges, modernised.)

[In the next poem, Kabir describes in simple terms the love that exists
between God and himself.]

How could the love between You and me sever?
As the leaf of the lotus lies on the water,
    so You are my Lord and I am your servant.
As the moon-bird 'chakor' gazes all night at the moon,
    so You are my Lord and I am your servant.
From the beginning until the end of time there is
            love between You and me;
    and how shall such love be extinguished?

Kabir says; As a river arriving at the ocean,
    so my heart touches You.

(Kabir, Hindi, 1440–1518, tr. Tagore and Bridges, modernised.)

[2] Places holy to the Hindus.

[The next poem goes deeper into the same subject. It is a mystical poem; that is, the language of metaphor overwhelms the sense of reason which we need for everyday life.]

Gaze on the cheeks of love, that you may gain the attributes of true men; sit not with the cold ones so you will not be chilled by their breath.

From the cheeks of love seek something other than the form; your business is to be a fellow sufferer with love.

If you have the attributes of a clod, you will never fly in the air; you will fly in the air if you break to pieces and become dust.

If you do not break to pieces, he who composed you will break you; when death breaks you, how will you become a unique pearl?

When a leaf becomes yellow, the fresh root makes it green; why are you content with a love from which you turn yellow?

(Rumi, Persian, 12071273, tr. Arberry.)

[Most religions see humility as appropriate to our station, and pride as coming before a fall.]

He is walking in the road
As proud as any king.
He looks down on everyone,
For his house is full of riches.
  If you don't bow down to someone,
  God himself will humble you.

(Anonymous song, Gond (India), written down and translated c. 1930 by V. Elwin and S. Hivale).

[The intoxication of religious ecstasy is compared to drunkenness in the next poem. Hafiz was by profession a lecturer on the Koran, in which wine is forbidden. Poets have often got into trouble for not being earnest enough concerning religion, but

Shiraz, where Hafiz lived, was governed with relative
tolerance.]

The dawn is breaking, cup-bearer; fill up with wine:
The revolving heavens will not delay, so hurry!

Let us get drunk with a cup of the rose-red wine -
Before this transient world has itself passed out.

The sun of wine has risen upon the east of the bowl:
If pleasure is what you aim at, waste no time in sleep.

Since one day we'll be clay for Fate to make pitchers of,
Let my skull be a cup kept sweet, being filled with wine.

We are not bigots or puritans; we need no penance:
Preach to us only with a cup of unmixed wine.

This worship of wine, Hafiz, is a virtuous business,
So be resolute in pursuit of righteous works!

(Hafiz, Persian, c.13201389, tr. J. Heath-Stubbs and Peter Avery.)

[In the next poem, the beauty of nature inspires the poet to praise
God. Marbod writes of spring with one eye on the fruits of
harvest; he was a medieval monk, and not forgetful of his belly.
The edible is evidence of the credible.]

A Description of the Beauty of Spring

Now I must mend my manners
    And lay my gruffness by.
The earth is making merry,
    And so, I think, must I.
The flowers are out in thousands,
    Each in a different dress.
The woods are green and like to fruit,
    The earth has donned her grassy fleece,

And blackbirds, jackdaws, magpies, nightingales
Are shouting each other down in equal praise.

There's a nest in the tree with young ones in it
    And lurking in the branches are the unfledged birds.
The bearded grain is whitening to harvest,
    Lovely are the gardens with the half-blown rose;
Add to these the vines, and the grapes, and the hazel nuts,
The young girls dancing, and their mothers dancing too,
And the young men at play, and the good feast toward,
    And the quiet shining day.

So many lovely things, and if a man looks on them,
And his mood is not softened, nor a smile on his face,
An intractable clod is he, at odds with his heart is he,
For who can behold earth's beauty without praising it
Has a grudge against earth's Maker, whose honour all these serve,
    Cold winter, summer, autumn, comely spring.

(Marbod of Rennes, French, c.1035–1123; tr. from Latin by Helen
Waddell.)

[When war wreaks havoc and society is in turmoil, people
withdraw from the world and try to find peace within
themselves, some in religious communities, some as hermits. Han
Shan was a Chinese Buddhist hermit whose poems were collected
by an admirer (a local civil servant) from the rocks and trees on
which Han Shan wrote them.]

    The clear water sparkles like crystal,
    You can see through it easily, right to the bottom.
    My mind is free from every thought,
    Nothing in the myriad realms can move it.
    Since it cannot be wantonly roused,
    For ever and for ever it will stay unchanged.
    When you have learned to know in this way,
    You will know there is no inside or out!

(Han Shan, Chinese, fl. c. 800 A.D., tr. Burton Watson.)

[The next poem concerns the search for wisdom, as different from
knowledge as life is from matter.]

Silver has its mines,
   and gold a place for refining.
Iron is extracted from the earth,
   the smelted rocks yield copper.
Man makes an end of darkness,
   to the utmost limit he digs
   the black rock in shadow dark as death.
Foreigners bore into ravines
   in unfrequented places,
   swinging suspended far from human beings.
That earth from which bread comes
   is ravaged underground by fire.
There, the rocks have veins of sapphire
   and their dust contains gold.
That is a path unknown to birds of prey,
   unseen by the eye of any vulture;
a path not trodden by the lordly beasts,
   where no lion ever walked.
Man attacks the flint,
   upturning mountains by their roots.
He cuts canals through the rock,
   on the watch for anything precious.
He explores the sources of rivers,
   bringing hidden things to light.
But where does Wisdom come from?
   Where is Intelligence to be found?

No human being knows the way to her,
   she is not to be found on earth where they live.
'She is not in me,' says the Abyss;
   'Nor here,' replies the Sea.
She cannot be bought with solid gold,
   nor paid for with any weight of silver,
nor valued against gold of Ophir,,
   precious agate or sapphire.
Neither gold nor glass compares with her,

for her, a vase of fine gold would be no exchange,
let alone coral or crystal:
    better go fishing for Wisdom than for pearls!
Topaz from Cush is worthless in comparison,
    and gold, even refined, is valueless.
But where does Wisdom come from?
    Where is Intelligence to be found?

She cannot be seen by any living creature,
    she is hidden from the birds of the sky.
Perdition and Death both say,
    'We have heard only rumours of her.'
God alone understands her path
    and knows where she is to be found.
(For he sees to the remotest parts of the earth,
    and observes all that lies under heaven.)
When he willed to give weight to the wind
    and measured out the waters with a gauge,
when he imposed a law on the rain
    and mapped a route for thunderclaps to follow,
then he saw and evaluated her,
    looked her through and through, assessing her.
Then he said to human beings,
    'Wisdom? – that is fear of the Lord;
Intelligence? – avoidance of evil.'

(Anon, Hebrew; Book of Job, ch. 28. 5th c. B.C. Translation from 'The New Jerusalem Bible'.)

[Religious teaching both helps and limits our understanding of God. Human societies conceive of God in an image that suits them, in their particular time and place. In order to justify cannibalism, Aztec priests conceived of God as thirsty for human blood.[3] The corpses that remained after sacrifice were eaten by a populace starved of protein. This view of God is obviously limited. Limited too, though in a different way, is the view of

---

[3] Marvin Harris argues this in 'Cannibals and Kings'.

God as a nice chap, a view conceived to assure prosperous people that they deserve their prosperity. God is not some of what we can conceive of, or all we can conceive of, but more than we can conceive of.

Sacrifice is an ancient and important part of religion. The idea is to give up one thing in order to gain something better. Even without religion we make sacrifices, like suppressing the desire to be rude to someone in the interests of peace and harmony. If the gain is more long-term – the welfare of the planet, for example – voices of short term self-interest grow very loud. How much do we have to sacrifice, to allow the planet to regain its health? First of all we have to sacrifice the dream of ever-increasing prosperity. It's doubtful whether law can replace religion in enforcing such large-scale sacrifice.

Anyone making a sacrifice does so with a benefit in mind. In the next poem George Eliot wants to make a sacrifice of her life, not by destroying it but by living for a higher ideal. By being 'to other souls the cup of strength in some great agony' she will experience the heaven of joining the 'choir invisible whose music is the gladness of the world'.]

'O May I Join the Choir Invisible'

Longum illud tempus, quum non ero, magis me movet, quam hoc exiguum. – Cicero, ad Atticum, xii, 18. [4]

O may I join the choir invisible
Of those immortal dead who live again
In minds made better by their presence: live
In pulses stirred to generosity,
In deeds of daring rectitude, in scorn
For miserable aims that end with self,
In thoughts sublime that pierce the night like stars,
And with their mild persistence urge man's search
To vaster issues.

[4] 'The great extent of time when I shall no longer be alive moves me more than this paltry span...'

So to live is heaven:
To make undying music in the world,
Breathing as beauteous order that controls
With growing sway the growing life of man.
So we inherit that sweet purity
For which we struggled, failed, and agonised
With widening retrospect that bred despair.
Rebellious flesh that would not be subdued,
A vicious parent shaming still its child
Poor anxious penitence, is quick dissolved;
Its discords, quenched by meeting harmonies,
Die in the large and charitable air.
And all our rarer, better, truer self,
That sobbed religiously in yearning song,
That watched to ease the burthen of the world,
Laboriously tracing what must be
And what might yet be better – saw within
A worthier image for the sanctuary,
And shaped it forth before the multitude
Divinely human, raising worship so
To higher reverence more mixed with love –
That better self shall live till human Time
Shall fold its eyelids, and the human sky
Be gathered like a scroll within the tomb
Unread for ever.

This is life to come,
Which martyred men have made more glorious
For us who strive to follow. May I reach
That purest heaven, be to other souls
The cup of strength in some great agony,
Enkindle generous ardour, feed pure love,
Beget the smiles that have no cruelty –
Be the sweet presence of a good diffused,
And in diffusion ever more intense.
So shall I join the choir invisible
Whose music is the gladness of the world.

(George Eliot, English, 1819–80.)

[The why and how of leading a good life have pre-occupied Judaeo-Christian religious thinking. The simple answer to why − in order to feel good − is offset in many people's minds by the prosperity of many who lead bad lives, and also by the short-term pleasures that can be had from behaving badly. But life would be a very simple affair if good behaviour was rewarded by prosperity.

The subject of good and bad behaviour is tackled at length in the Book of Wisdom, chapters 2 and 3, from which the following is extracted.]

                                                     * the unrighteous

For they* reasoned unsoundly, saying to themselves,
"Short and sorrowful is our life, unrighteous
and there is no remedy when a life comes to its end,
and no one has been known to return from Hades.
For we were born by mere chance,
and hereafter we shall be as though we had never been,
for the breath in our nostrils is smoke,
and reason is a spark kindled by the beating of our hearts;
when it is extinguished, the body will turn to ashes,
and the spirit will dissolve like empty air.
Our name will be forgotten in time,
and no one will remember our works;
our life will pass away like the traces of a cloud,
and be scattered like mist
that is chased by the rays of the sun
and overcome by its heat...

"Come, therefore, let us enjoy the good things that exist,
and make use of the creation to the full as in youth.
Let us take our fill of costly wine and perfumes,
and let no flower of spring pass us by.
Let us crown ourselves with rosebuds before they wither.
Let none of us fail to share in our revelry;
everywhere let us leave signs of our enjoyment,
because this is our portion, and this our lot.
Let us oppress the righteous poor man;
let us not spare the widow
or regard the grey hairs of the aged.

But let our might be our law of right,
for what is weak proves itself to be useless.

"Let us lie in wait for the righteous man,
Because he is inconvenient to us and opposes our actions;
he reproaches us for sins against the law,
and accuses us of sins against our training...
Let us test him with insult and torture,
so that we may find out how gentle he is,
and make trial of his forbearance.
Let us condemn him to a shameful death,
for, according to what he says, he will be protected."

But the souls of the righteous are in the hand of God,
and no torment will ever touch them.
In the eyes of the foolish they seemed to have died,
and their departure was thought to be a disaster,
and their going from us to be their destruction;
but they are at peace.
For though in the sight of others they were punished,
their hope is full of immortality...

But the ungodly will be punished as their reasoning deserves,
those who disregarded the righteous
and rebelled against the Lord;
for those who despise wisdom and instruction are miserable.
Their hope is vain, their labours are unprofitable,
and their works are useless.
Their wives are foolish, and their children evil;
their offspring are accursed.

(Anon., Jewish Greek, c 50 B.C. Bible, from 'The Wisdom of Solomon',
chapters 2,3, New Revised Standard Version.)

[Why is there so much suffering in the world? In the Book of Job,
Job asks this question, adding 'In particular, why me?'. None of
the replies he gets satisfy him, and eventually he calls on God
himself to answer. God breaks his usual silence and tells Job that

the mysteries of creation are not Job's to comprehend. Here is
how God begins.]

> Then the Lord answered Job out of the whirlwind:
> "Who is this that darkens counsel
>   by words without knowledge?
> Gird up your loins like a man,
>   I will question you, and you shall declare to me.
> Where were you when I laid the foundations of the earth?
>   Tell me, if you have understanding.
> Who determines its measurements – surely you know!
>   Or who stretched the line upon it?
> On what were its bases sunk,
>   or who laid its cornerstone
> when all the morning stars sang together
>   and all the heavenly beings shouted for joy?'

(Anon., Hebrew, 5th C. B.C. Bible, Book of Job 38, 1–7, New Revised
Standard Version.)

[In the Book of Job, God allows Job to suffer at Satan's hand. Job
'persists in his integrity' and demonstrates that his loyalty to God
is not dependent on good fortune. Though he wins through to
further good fortune, it may be that his true reward is his dialogue
with God.

In a more recent poem, Edwin Muir notices that the finer
qualities of hope, faith, charity, love and pity are inconceivable
without 'shapes of terror and grief'. Suffering and nobility of
spirit are inextricably interlinked. On this linkage materialism –
with its fierce avoidance of any sort of pain – breaks down.]

One Foot in Eden

> One foot in Eden still, I stand
> And look across the other land.
> The world's great day is growing late,
> Yet strange these fields that we have planted
> So long with crops of love and hate.
> Time's handiworks by time are haunted,
> And nothing now can separate

The corn and tares compactly grown.
The armorial weed in stillness bound
About the stalk; these are our own.
Evil and good stand thick around
In the fields of charity and sin
Where we shall lead our harvest in.

Yet still from Eden springs the root
As clean as on the starting day.
Time takes the foliage and the fruit
And burns the archetypal leaf
To shapes of terror and of grief
Scattered along the winter way.
But famished field and blackened tree
Bear flowers in Eden never known.
Blossoms of grief and charity
Bloom in these darkened fields alone.
What had Eden ever to say
Of hope and faith and pity and love
Until was buried all its day
And memory found its treasure trove?
Strange blessings never in Paradise
Fall from these beclouded skies.

(Edwin Muir, Scottish, 1887–1959.)

[Under the protection of organised religions, ways of life grow up that are comfortable and fruitful. Four poems follow which express the comforts and consolations of a religious way of life in a difficult or hostile world.

In the first, Mahadevi explains that her love for the god Krishna fulfils her desire for perfection.]

Other men are thorn
under the smooth leaf.
I cannot touch them,
go near them, nor trust them,
nor speak to them confidences.

Mother,
because they all have thorns
in their chests,
    I cannot take
any man in my arms but my lord

    white as jasmine.

(Mahadevi, 12th C., Kannada (India), tr. A.K. Ramanujan.)

[Milton, incapacitated by blindness, reassures himself that there is a place for him in God's creation even though he is unable to work. God's mercy does not demand of us more than we can give.]

When I consider how my light is spent,
  Ere half my days in this dark world and wide,
  And that one talent which is death to hide,
  Lodg'd with me useless, though my soul more bent
To serve therewith my Maker, and present
  My true account, lest he returning chide;
  Doth God exact day-labour, light deny'd,
  I fondly ask; But patience to prevent
That murmur, soon replies, God doth not need
  Either man's work or his own gifts; who best
  Bear his mild yoke, they serve him best, his state
Is kingly. Thousands at his bidding speed
  And post o'er land and ocean without rest:
  They also serve who only stand and wait.

(Milton, English, 1608–1674.)

[The poet of the next piece lives in a ghetto. Outside are people who hate him because they are anti-Semites brought up on hatred of Jews, and who value nothing but 'the swill and guzzle' of democratic materialism.]

Goodnight, Wide World

Good night, wide world
Big stinking world!
Not you but I slam shut the door.
With my long gabardine,
My fiery, yellow patch,
With head erect,
And at my sole command,
I go back into the ghetto.
Wipe off all markings of apostasy!
I roll my body in your grime;
Glory, glory, glory to you,
Crippled Jewish life!
I cast out all your unclean cultures, world!
Though all has been laid waste,
I burrow in your dust,
Sorrowing Jewish life.

Swinish German, hostile Polack,
Thievish Amalekite – land of swill and guzzle,
Slobbering democracy,
With your cold compress of sympathy,
Good night, brash world with your electric glare.

Back to my kerosene, my shadowed tallow candles,
Endless October and faint stars,
To my twisting streets and crooked lantern,
To my sacred scrolls and holy books,
To tough Talmudic riddles and lucid Yiddish speech,
To law, to duty, and to justice,
To what is deeply mine.
World, joyously I stride
Toward the quiet ghetto lights.

Good night, I give you in good measure
All my redeemers;
Take your Jesus Marxes; choke on their daring
Burst with each drop of our baptized blood.

And still I trust that though He tarry,
My waiting will spring newly day by day.
Green leaves again will rustle
On our withered tree.
I need no comforting.
I walk again my straight and narrow way;
From Wagner's heathen blare to Hebrew chant
And the hummed melody.
I kiss you, cankered Jewish life,
The joy of homecoming weeps in me.

(Jacob Glatstein, Yiddish, 1896–1971, tr. Marie Syrkin.)

[In the next poem, the poet speaks of the healing power of trees on his master Jesus, who, knowing he will soon be betrayed and put to death, goes into the woods for consolation.]

Ballad of Trees and the Master

Into the woods my Master went,
Clean forspent, forspent.
Into the woods my Master came,
Forspent with love and shame.
But the olives were not blind to him:
The little grey leaves were kind to him:
The thorn-tree had a mind to him
When into the trees He came.

Out of the woods my Master went,
And He was well content.
Out of the woods my Master came,
Content with death and shame.
When Death and Shame would woo Him last:
'Twas on a tree they slew Him – last
When out of the woods He came.

(Sidney Lanier, American, 1842–1881.)

[Religion is often rejected because its representatives behave badly. However, since they're only human it'd be odd if they didn't; likewise with religious institutions, whatever their claims of divine authority.

The subject of the next poem is a man who hijacks religion to the cause of hatred and lust for power. Calvin described in his journals his inappropriate sexual arousals, which he ascribed to the devil's influence.]

John Calvin

His forehead was unlined but moist, and shone
above his long French nose. He didn't care
to touch his wife, so he caressed his beard
into smooth waves as he proclaimed the Lord
thrust sin into men's souls so he could hurl
them latterly to Hell. It was so vile,
so horrible, it had to be believed.
In dreams he loved to hone castrating knives
and in Geneva did away with lust,
jailed loving couples, poets, all who smiled
with happiness, or laughed, or studied books,
and well-dressed men that danced, especially if
their pants were bulging with distended pricks.
He himself had rarely such ill luck,
though thirty years or so ago, in Paris,
when a student, he once watched a colleague
being soundly caned in the College yard
and saw the victim shaking on his bunk,
blood welling from his wealed and naked arse,
and did get an erection. Poor Servetus,
whom he had first denounced to the inquisition,
like a fool sought sanctuary in Geneva,
and Calvin had him burnt on a slow fire,
his followers herding all the people there
to watch the blaze as, at his window, sniffing
that rank smoke, he licked his swollen lips,
himself remote from lechery – yet how come
his prick swelled stiff and jutted its bald head?
The ways of God are mysteries indeed!

(George Faludy, Hungarian, b. 1910, tr. Robin Skelton.)

[The history of religion is sprinkled with such revolting creatures, but the history of atheism is spread with even worse. The first society to institute compulsory atheism was Marxist Russia. Then Fascist Germany substituted worship of a man — a very inadequate man — for worship of God. What happened next makes up the nastiest chapter in human history.

Dogma originally meant opinion, but it becomes a weapon when used by those who would hijack religion in the interests of power and wealth. Religion relies on intuition, contemplation, instinct, tradition, faith and inspiration as guides to what will do us good. Dogma, when it becomes tyrannical, is an enemy, and so is an absolute belief in reason, for both refuse to know their limitations.

In the next poem Ma'arri warns us not to believe all we're told. In the first couplet of this poem he's referring to the doctrine of re-incarnation.]

> They say the soul's ferried corpse to infant
> Till, cleaned by each crossing, it's fit for God.
>
> Don't believe what you're told unless your mind
> Confirms its truth: palm trunks, lofty as clouds,
>
> Stay wood. Be calm, take care and bear in mind
> The Indian sword is worn thin as it's honed.

(Ma'arri, Arabic, 973–1057, tr. G. Wightman and A. al-Udhari.)

[Hafiz, an Islamic theologian as well as a great poet, wrote in one of his poems,
> Hypocrisy and zeal are burning religion's harvest;
> Throw off your woollen cassock, Hafiz, and go!

Religious organisations and individuals have vested interests like the rest of us. Religions in the West tend to require exclusive allegiance from their followers. In many lands, however, individuals follow several religions simultaneously, in recognition that no one religion holds a monopoly on truth.

When religions foment hatred and rivalry, they do us no service.]

When will mankind realise it is one?
Will it ever bridge the gulfs that divide it?
The white tramples the black,
The Jew is proud that he is chosen of the Lord,
Another thinks he's best because he came from Brahma's mouth.

When shall we give up rotting in fancied poses by the grace of the
    Lord?

Like a bunch of puppies, some with eyes just open,
Some with just one eye open, others yet to open their eyes,
Engaged in unseemly scrabble for the mother's breast,
Alas! we are all absorbed in wrangling and recrimination.

(Srinivasa, Kannada (India), b. 1891, translator not known.)

[Goethe makes a similar point;]

"Jews and Heathens out!" – that's the tolerance of Christian fanatics;
"Christ and Heathens, curse them!" mutters a Jewish beard.
"Roast Christians on the spit, burn Jews in the fire" –
So sings a Turkish child, despising both Christians and Jews.
Which is the cleverest? Choose! – But if these
Fools are in your Palace, Lord, I'll give it a miss.

(Goethe, 1749–1832, German, tr. I.M.)

[But, 'without God, anything goes.' As Christianity began to lose
its grip on European civilisation under the onslaught of
'enlightened' thinking, Christians found little barring them from
behaving as brutally as they wished. As democracy gained
ground, the will of the people replaced Christian authority – and
the will of the people was not benevolent.
    The next poem expresses the disgust of a Jewish poet
watching Jews everywhere threatened and violated by those who
still called themselves Christians, inheritors of the Jewish God.]

The Last Word

Pluck, O prophet, the firebrand from your altar,
And cast it to the villains -
Let it serve them for roasting, to set their kettles on,
And to warm their palms.
Fling the ember from your heart
And let it light their pipes,
Let it illume the stealthy smirk on their lips
And the evil cunning in their eyes.
Lo, they come, these villains,
Mouthing the prayers you've taught them,
Feeling your pain and sharing your hope,
Their souls straining towards your ruined shrine,
So as to pounce on the wreckage,
Burrow in its rubble heap,
And cart away its scattered stones
To pave their floors and fence their gardens,
To mount as tombstones over graves.
And when they find your scorched heart in the rummage,
They'll throw it to their dogs.

Trample upon your altar, stamp it with contempt
And scatter its fire and smoke.
Sever with one sweep of the hand the spider web
Strung like harp strings in your heart,
Whence you wove a song of life
And a dream of salvation -
Vain oracles beguiling the ear.
Disperse them to the winds,
Frayed and shimmering let them drift
On a sunny day at summer's end,
So that no soul will find its mate,
No filament match its comrade,
But all melt away in a first downpour of rain.
Smash your hammer, your iron hammer,
Fractured by many vain poundings against stony hearts,

And mould it into a spade
To dig a grave for us.

Speak the curse God's wrath sets on your tongue,
Let not your lips falter;
Though your word be bitter as death,
Yea, death itself,
We'll hear and know it.

Lo, the bloated night has hemmed us in,
Darkness has overwhelmed us,
And we reel like the blind.
Something has happened,
We know not what,
There is none to see and none to tell
Whether the sun rose for us or set –
Set forever.
Boundless, frightful is the encompassing void,
And there is no refuge;
If we pray or wail in the dark,
Who will give ear?
If we voice God's harrowing malediction,
On whose head will it fall?
And if we gnash our teeth and clench our fist,
On whose skull will it descend?
Chaos will swallow them all,
The wind carry them off,
Doom lies in wait for them,
No stay, no strength, no road.
And the heavens are silent,
They know their iniquity against us,
They have sinned to hell,
And bear their guilt in silence.

Open now your lips, O prophet of the end.
If you have a word, speak out!
Though it be bitter as death,
Yea, death itself,

Speak out!
Wherefore shall we fear death,
His angel already astride upon our shoulders
And his bridle in our mouth?
With shouts of resurrection on our lips,
And with frolickers' mirth
We gambol to the grave.

(H. N. Bialik, Hebrew, 1873–1934, tr. A.A. Steinbach.)

[Temporarily horrified at crimes against humanity, materialist
man nevertheless proceeds full speed with crimes against the
planet. But as our lifestyle exhausts the world's riches, there will
be a struggle over what is left; who can tell when the human
holocaust will resume? Meanwhile banality invades religion to
numb the pain of thought.]

Open Your Hearts

Open your hearts to the Holy Spirit
For Christ's sake.
We'll be back to you in a moment
After this commercial break.

(Brendan Kennelly, Irish, b. 1936. From 'The Book of Judas'.)

[It's an old story, that when people desert religion they adopt the
criterion of profit to decide whether something is good. In the
next poem Gotama, the first Buddha, argues that wealth is an
unreliable provider of happiness.]

The man whose heart's desires are gratified,
is glad indeed to see success secured.

But, if his heart's desires and aims are foiled,
he smarts as if a dart had wounded him.

Yet, should he shun desires as he would shun
a snake's head underfoot, by vigilance
he overcomes the world's seductive lures.

Whoso with boundless appetite desires
fields, lands, or gold, herds, horses, women, serfs
and kinsfolk – him tumultuous desires

(weak tho' they seem) o'ercome at last; they crush
their victim. Here on, ills come surging in
like waves that flood some wrecked ship's crazy hold.

Therefore by watchfulness discard desires;
expel them: bale your ship: and cross the Flood
to safety's haven on the further shore.

(Gotama, India, 6th C. B.C., tr. from Pali by Lord Chalmers.)

[Han Shan takes up the theme, looking to peace and beauty to
give him happiness and mocking those obsessed with
possessions.]

In a tangle of cliffs I chose a place -
Bird-paths, but no trails for men.
What's beyond the yard?
White clouds clinging to vague rocks.
Now I've lived here – how many years -
Again and again, spring and winter pass.
Go tell families with silverware and cars
"What's the use of all that noise and money?"

(Han Shan, Chinese, lived c. 800, modern tr. by Gary Snyder.)

[Our age of materialism fosters the notion that we have no need
of God or religion. We – humanity – are then the most

important, intelligent and god-like creatures in the known universe. The other side of the coin is that when we have such high opinion of ourselves we are apt to make a terrible mess.

Poetry often insults God; calls God a trickster, a sadist, even evil; but atheists mostly write in prose. An atheist worth quoting for his lucid and scrupulous comments is Sigmund Freud, who wrote on religion as a pure enlightened materialist. His view of our rational human goal is a state where

'...undisturbed by internal discord, men might devote themselves to the acquisition of wealth and its enjoyment. That would be the golden age...' On religion he wrote: 'The origin of the religious attitude can be traced back in clear outline as far as the feeling of infantile helplessness. There may be something further behind that, but for the present it is wrapped in obscurity.' And of the 'religion of the common man': 'The common man cannot imagine Providence otherwise than in the figure of an enormously exalted father... The whole thing is so patently infantile, so foreign to reality, that to anyone with a friendly attitude to humanity it is painful to think that the great majority of mortals will never be able to rise above this view of life.' [7]

Freud devoted his life to uncovering truth at a time when most organised religions were fighting a rearguard action against it in the effort to hold on to influence and power. His life's work contributed enormously to the welfare of his fellow human beings while religions were failing to prevent catastrophe. It's an irony that some atheists lead the kind of morally admirable lives which most religious people can only dream of. Such people seem to behave well naturally, and to view the struggles of others as a bird might view the flight of a plane; noisy, cumbersome, alarming and at best only partially successful.

The next two poems attack the notion that scientific knowledge does away with the existence of God.]

[5] 'The Future of an Illusion', Penguin Freud Library 12, p. 185.

[6] Civilisation and its Discontents, Penguin Freud Library 12, p. 260. Freud's use of the word 'mortal' seems odd in the context.

[7] Idem, Penguin Freud Library 12, p. 261.

To Hafiz of Shiraz

The rose has come into the garden, from
Nothingness into being.

Once I did not know the birds were described,
classified, observed, fixed in their proper localities.
Each bird that sprang from the tree, passed overhead,
    hawked from the bough,
was sole, new, dressed as no other was dressed.
Any leaf might hide the paradise-bird.

Once I believed any poem might follow my pen,
any road might beckon my feet to mapless horizons,
any eyes that I met, any hand that I took, any word that
    I heard,
might pierce to my heart, stay forever in mine, open worlds
    on its hinge.
All then seemed possible; time and world were my own.

Now that I know that each star has its path, each bird
is finally feathered and grown in the unbroken shell,
each tree in the seed, each song in the life laid down -
is the night sky any less strange; should my glance less follow
    the flight;
should the pen shake less in my hand?

No, more and more like a birth looks the scheduled rising of
    Venus:
the turn of a wing in the wind more startles my blood.
Every path and life leads one way only,
out of continual miracle, through creation's fable,
over and over repeated but never yet understood,
as every word leads back to the blinding original Word.

(Judith Wright, Australian, born 1915.)

[Reacting to the inroads of science on wonder, Auden celebrates the god Terminus, who in the ancient world was responsible for boundaries. Here, Terminus is given new life. He is called on to distinguish between the tall stories of science and the world we really live in, to temper our outlandish extravagance, and to provide limits in which we may be intimate and play.]

Ode to Terminus

The High Priests of telescopes and cyclotrons
keep making pronouncements about happenings
    on scales too gigantic or dwarfish
    to be noticed by our native senses,

discoveries which, couched in the elegant
euphemisms of algebra, look innocent,
    harmless enough but, when translated
    into the vulgar anthropomorphic

tongue, will give no cause for hilarity
to gardeners or housewives: if galaxies
    bolt like panicking mobs, if mesons
    riot like fish in a feeding-frenzy,

it sounds too like Political History
to boost civil morale, too symbolic of
    the crimes and strikes and demonstrations
    we are supposed to gloat on at breakfast.

How trite, though, our fears beside the miracle
that we're here to shiver, that a Thingummy
    so addicted to lethal violence
    should somehow have secreted a placid

tump with exactly the right ingredients
to start and cocker Life, that heavenly
    freak for whose manage we shall have to
    give account at the Judgement, our Middle-

Earth, where Sun-Father to all appearances
moves by day from orient to occident,
    and his light is felt as a friendly
      presence not a photonic bombardment,

where all visibles do have a definite
outline they stick to, and are undoubtedly
    at rest or in motion, where lovers
      recognize each other by their surface,

where to all species except the talkative
have been allotted the niche and diet that
    become them. This, whatever micro-
      biology might think, is the world we

really live in and that saves our sanity,
who know all too well how the most erudite
    mind behaves in the dark without a
      surround it is called on to interpret,

how, discarding rhythm, punctuation, metaphor,
it sinks into a drivelling monologue,
    too literal to see a joke or
      distinguish a penis from a pencil.

Venus and Mars are powers too natural
to temper our outlandish extravagance:
    You alone, Terminus the Mentor,
      can teach us to alter our gestures.

God of walls, doors and reticence, nemesis
overtakes the sacrilegious technocrat,
    but blessed is the City that thanks you
      for giving us games and grammars and metres.

By whose grace, also, every gathering
of two or three in confident amity
    repeats the pentecostal marvel,
      as each in each finds his right translator.

In this world our colossal immodesty
has plundered and poisoned, it is possible
>You still might save us, who by now have
>learned this: that scientists, to be truthful,

must remind us to take all they say as a
tall story, that abhorred in the Heav'ns are all
self-proclaimed poets who, to wow an
audience, utter some resonant lie.

(W.H. Auden, English, 1907–73.)

[Restraints of sacred and taboo are used by religions to protect the welfare of their communities. In a 'rational' society these ideas are abandoned, in the theory that decisions can be taken based on knowledge. The trouble is, we never know enough to be sure we are deciding correctly. Furthermore, even the knowledge we have is ignored if it impinges on our comfort. In the words of the poet Ma'arri, 'if you go to bed with Reason, you wake up bruised.'

Most of us want to be accepted and admired by our fellow human beings. As long as the profits which accrue from the rape of the earth are so generally admired, we can expect the rape to continue. Compared to a moral climate created by religion, the law is comparatively ineffectual at restraining undesirable behaviour.

The final poem, written by a Japanese Buddhist monk, asks a question normally asked by children. Later it can get forgotten, not because it's been answered, but because a literal answer is impossible. Ryokan's poem seems to anticipate a view of contemporary science, that life is the playfulness of atoms.]

To Inscribe on a Picture of a Skull I Painted

All things born of causes end when causes run out;
but causes, what are they born of?
That very first cause − where did it come from?
At this point words fail me, workings of my mind go dead.
I took these words to the old woman in the house to the east;

THE GREEN BOOK OF POETRY 121

the old woman in the house to the east was not pleased.
I questioned the old man in the house to the west;
the old man in the house to the west puckered his brow and walked away.
I tried writing the question on a biscuit, fed it to the dogs,
but even the dogs refused to bite.
Concluding that these must be unlucky words, a mere jumble of a query,
I rolled life and death into a pill, kneading them together,
and gave it to the skull in the meadowside.
Suddenly the skull came leaping up,
began to sing and dance for me,
a long song, ballad of the Three Ages,
a wonderful dance, postures of the Three Worlds.
Three worlds, three ages, three times danced over - [8]
"the moon sets on Chang-an and its midnight bells."

(Ryokan, Japanese, 1758–1831, tr. Burton Watson.)

[Religion is in a continual state of change, and we can only wait
to see what new ideas the future brings. Humanity needs both
wise government and the influence of religion to flourish
peacefully. Religious leaders who claim they know all about God
have a lot to answer for. The long-established religions are even
slower than governments in waking up to what is happening to
the earth. Some 'religious' proscriptions – against birth control is
an obvious example – serve only to encourage disaster and
bringing catastrophe nearer.

In Western civilisation, the influence of religion grows ever
weaker. The ideals of our civilisation almost make up a religion in
themselves; tolerance, fairness, a sharing of prosperity, a striving
towards common goals and freedoms for all humanity. But these
ideals haven't restrained the all-out pursuit of wealth and creature
comforts, or the even more Earth-consuming pursuit of employment by waste. The horrors of other atheist cultures may well be
rivalled or even outdone in the twenty-first century, as full scale
degeneration of our world gets under way.]

[8] The three ages are past, present and future. The three worlds are desire, form,
and formlessness. The last line is a quote from a famous poem of farewell,
written when a monk was setting off on the long journey from China back to
India where Buddhism began. Chang-an was the capital of China.

4. War

[The existence of nuclear weapons threatens instantaneous destruction on a massive scale. Even without nuclear weapons, war wreaks environmental havoc, as we saw all too painfully during the Gulf War of 1990. But the habit of war is hard to give up, and more wars were recorded in the 1980's than in any previous decade.

War has played a large role in our human history. The conquest of territory and the migration of peoples contributed to the flourishing of our species, as different cultures mixed and added to each other's vitality. War also helped control population growth. Nowadays, more peaceful methods are available to both these ends, and war is seen as a sickness and a scourge, the most obvious of 'those facts of filth and violence/that we're too dumb to prevent.' [1]

The first poem is an insight into war as waged by early human peoples in competition with one another for living space and glory. It is particularly eloquent on war's devastation of the natural world.]

Where the Lilies Were in Flower

Fish leaping
in fields of cattle;

easy unplowed sowing
where the wild boar has rooted;

big-eyed buffalo herds
stopped by fields of lilies
flowering in sugarcane beds;

[1] W.H. Auden, from 'Thank You, Fog'.

ancient cows bending their heads
over water flowers
scattered by the busy dancers
swaying with lifted hands;

queen's-flower trees full of bird cries,
the rustle of coconut trees,
canals from flowering pools
in countries
with cities sung in song;

but your anger
touched them, brought them terror,
left their beauty in ruins,
bodies consumed by Death.

The districts are empty, parched;
the waves of sugarcane blossom,
stalks of dry grass.
The thorny babul of the twisted fruit
neck to neck with the giant black babul.

The she-devil with the branching crest
roams
astraddle on her demon,
and the small persistent thorn
is spread in the moving dust
of ashen battlefields.

Not a sound, nothing animal,
not even dung,
in the ruins of public places
that kill the hearts of eager men,
chill all courage,
and shake those who remember.

But here,
the sages have sought your woods.

In your open spaces, the fighters play
with bright-jewelled women.
The traveller is safe on the highway.
Sellers of grain shelter their kin
who shelter, in turn, their kin.

The silver star will not go near
the place of the red planet: so it rains
on the thirsty fields.
Hunger has fled
and taken disease with her.

Great one,
your land blossoms
everywhere.

(Kumattur Kannanar, Tamil, 1st C. A.D.?, tr. A.K. Ramanujan.)

[Kings courted poets and sages, who brought civilised values to
bear on them, as we see in the next poem.]

A Poet's Counsel

*to a cruel king when he was about to have his enemy's children
trampled to death by elephants in a public place*

You come from the line of a Cola[2] king
who gave his flesh
for a pigeon in danger,
      and for others besides,

and these children also come
from a line of kings
who in their cool shade
share all they have

[2] Translator's note: 'The Cola ancestor was famous in legend for an act of
extreme generosity. When a pigeon, hunted by a hawk, sought his protection,
he satisfied the hawk's hunger by offering the predator his own flesh in place of
the pigeon's.

lest poets,
those tillers of nothing
but wisdom,
should suffer hardships.

    Look at these children,
    the crowns of their heads are still soft.

    As they watch the elephants,
    they even forget to cry,

    stare dumbstruck at the crowd
    in some new terror
    of things unknown.

Now that you've heard me out,
do what you will.

(Kovur Kilar, Tamil, 1st C. A.D.?, tr. A.K. Ramanujan.)

[As we become more civilised, we accept as 'kin' a wider circle of
people, and religious or tribal wars seem not glorious but obscene.
We recognise that humanity is one species, and that its different
races are of value to one another. Our governments are asked to
direct their efforts more at avoiding war than planning the next
one.

   Li Po and Tu Fu, China's greatest poets, both wrote many
poems against war.]

The Chariots Go Forth to War

Chariots rumble and roll; horses whinny and neigh;
Men are marching with bows and arrows at their hips.
Their parents and wives hurry to bid farewell,
Raising clouds of dust over Hsien-Yang Bridge.
They pull at the soldiers' clothes, stamp their feet and cry out.
The sound of their crying soars to the clouds.

A passer-by questions the soldiers;
They shake their heads dumbly and say:
'Since the age of fifteen we have defended the northern rivers.
Till we are forty we shall serve on the western front.
We leave our homes as youths and return as gray-haired men.
Along the frontier there flows the sea of our blood.
The King hungers for territory – therefore we fight.

'Have you not heard, sir,
How through the two hundred countries east of the Tai-Yeng
    Mountains,
Through thousands of villages and tens of thousands of hamlets
Thorns and nettles run wild?
Sturdy peasant women swing the hoe and drive the plow,
But neither in the east nor west is anything raised or sown.
The soldiers of Sh'ang will fight to the end,
But they cannot be slain like dogs or like hens.

'It's kind of you to ask, sir,
But how dare we express our resentment?
Winter has come and the year is passing away;
The war on the western passes is still going on.
The magistrates are pressing us to pay taxes,
But where shall we get the money?
If only I had known the fate in store for boys,
I would have had my children all girls,
For girls may be married to the neighbours,
But boys are born only to be cut down and buried beneath the
    grass.

'Do you not see, sir,
The long dead ancient bones near the Blue Sea bleached by the
    sun?
And now the lament of those who have just died
Mingles with the voices of those who died long ago,
And darkness falls, and the rain, and the ghostly whimpering of
    voices.'

(Tu Fu, Chinese, 713–770, tr. Nee Wen-yei.)

Fighting South of the Ramparts

Last year we were fighting at the source of the Sang-kan;
This year we are fighting on the Onion River road.
We have washed our swords in the surf of Parthian seas;
We have pastured our horses among the snows of the T'ien Shan.
The King's armies have grown grey and old
Fighting ten thousand leagues away from home.
The Huns have no trade but battle and carnage;
They have no fields or ploughlands,
But only wastes where white bones lie among yellow sands.
Where the House of Chi'n built the great Wall that was to keep
    away the Tartars,
There, in its turn, the House of Han lit beacons of war.
The beacons are always alight, fighting and marching never stop.
Men die in the field, slashing sword to sword;
The horses of the conquered neigh piteously to Heaven.
Crows and hawks peck for human guts,
Carry them in their beaks and hang them on the branches of
    withered trees.
Captains and soldiers are smeared on the bushes and grass;
The General schemed in vain.
Know therefore that the sword is a cursed thing,
Which the wise man uses only if he must.

(Li Po, Chinese, 701–762, tr. Arthur Waley.)

[The next poem, by a contemporary of Li Po and Tu Fu, follows on
from the last line of the last one, describing the kind of man society can
make use of when it's under attack. The old commander's poverty and
loneliness are a legacy of the isolating responsibilities of his command
and of his memories of slaughter.]

The Old Commander

A lad in his teens, he seized
a horse from the enemy and
rode it; he went into the wild
mountains, hunted a great tiger

and killed it; over our long
frontiers he stood, like the Yellow-
Bearded Hero, his one sword
holding back many.

At times our armies of Han
would sweep over the plains
like peals of thunder,
encircling the tribesmen, as
in a snare; yet the fact
that one general was
not defeated was sheer good
luck; while that another
gained no glory was just
the opposite;

so it came that this commander,
grey with the worries of human
affairs, was retired; though when
on service he could pick the eye
of a bird with an arrow, now
his left arm hangs listlessly, like
a cut sapling; he gains his living
selling melons by the roadside, or
learning how to do farmwork around
his hut, stuck away up on a lonely
path, looking out over cold mountains;
a pitiful end for him who was able,
they say, to find water anywhere
when his men needed it; who never
wasted his strength on wine.

Now again from behind the frontiers
tribesmen gather like clouds; despatches
from the front tell of urgency; from
out of the heart of our country, youth
is called up to meet the threat; hurriedly
the old commander is summoned back to arms;
he polishes his armour; his sword with

its jade hilt dances in delight; his
great bow is anxious to strike down
the invaders' chief, so this insult to
his land may be wiped out;
one thinks back on that old leader
in history, who despite his age,
gained victory with one bold stroke.

(Wang Wei, Chinese, 699–761, tr. Rewi Alley.)

[European civilisation has been the most expansionist of all human civilisations. Its culture and its peoples have taken over most of the earth, depleting and sometimes exterminating other peoples. Not surprisingly, it has held war in high esteem, and many of its poets have praised war. Our male ancestors regarded war as a glorious duty.

Ironically, the greatest long poem of Western civilisation, the Iliad, is anti-war. It was performed regularly and with the utmost veneration during the war-filled years of Ancient Greece, and has been held in the highest regard ever since.

In this extract, the Danaans (Achaeans, Greeks) are losing the day's fighting against the Trojans. Achilles is sulking and won't fight. His friend Patroclus is begging Achilles' permission to lead his Myrmidons and fight, and to put on Achilles' armour to frighten the Trojans. We see in this extract the allure of war as well as its folly.]

from 'The Iliad'

'... send me forth now at the head of the Myrmidon host,
That I may be a light of hope to the Danaans.
And let me strap on my shoulders that armour of yours,
That the zealous Trojans may take me for you and quickly
Withdraw from the fighting. Then the battling, war-worn sons
Of Achaeans may have a chance to catch their breath –
Such chances in battle are few – and we who are fresh
May easily drive, with little more than our war-screams,
The exhausted Trojans away from the ships and the shelters
And back toward the city'
Such was his plea, poor childish

Fool that he was, for it was his own hard death
And doom for which he pleaded.

(Homer, Greek, ? 9th–6th C. B.C.; from book 16, tr. Ennis Rees.)

[For European civilisation, the First World War was a watershed. The idea of war as a good thing grew dim in the slaughter of the males of a generation. From then on, the poetry of war would be represented not so much by this:]

> The naked earth is warm with spring,
> And with green grass and bursting trees
> Leans to the sun's gaze glorying,
> And quivers in the sunny breeze;
> And life is colour and warmth and light,
> And a striving evermore for these;
> And he is dead who will not fight;
> And who dies fighting has increase.

(Julian Grenfell, English, 1888–1915; 1st stanza of 'Into Battle'.)

[as by this]

Dulce et Decorum Est⋆

⋆sweet it is, and fitting

Bent double, like old beggars under sacks,
Knock-kneed, coughing like hags, we cursed through sludge,
Till on the haunting flares we turned our backs
And towards our distant rest began to trudge.
Men marched asleep. Many had lost their boots
But limped on, blood-shod. All went lame; all blind;
Drunk with fatigue; deaf even to the hoots
Of tired, outstripped Five-Nines that dropped behind.

Gas! Gas! Quick, boys! – An ecstasy of fumbling,
Fitting the helmets just in time;
But someone still was yelling out and stumbling,

And flound'ring like a man in fire or lime...
Dim, through the misty panes and thick green light,
As under a green sea, I saw him drowning.

In all my dreams, before my helpless sight,
He plunges at me, guttering, choking, drowning.

If in some smothering dreams you too could pace
Behind the wagon that we flung him in,
And watch the white eyes writhing in his face,
His hanging face, like a devil's sick of sin;
If you could hear, at every jolt, the blood
Come gargling from the froth-corrupted lungs,
Obscene as cancer, bitter as the cud
Of vile, incurable sores on innocent tongues, -
My friend, you would not tell with such high zest
To children ardent for some desperate glory,
The old Lie: Dulce et decorum est
Pro patria mori.★

★sweet it is, and fitting, to die for one's country

(Wilfrid Owen, English, 1893–1918.)

[In the next poem – of the Second World War – the poet feels for a
dead enemy's beloved.]

Vergissmeinnicht★

★forget-me-not

Three weeks gone and the combatants gone
returning over the nightmare ground
we found the place again, and found
the soldier sprawling in the sun.

The frowning barrel of his gun
overshadowing. As we came on
that day, he hit my tank with one
like the entry of a demon.

Look. Here in the gunpit spoil
the dishonoured picture of his girl
who has put: *Steffi. Vergissmeinnicht**   * 'Steffi.
in a copybook gothic script.   Forget-me-not'

We see him almost with content,
abased, and seeming to have paid,
and mocked at by his own equipment
that's hard and good when he's decayed.

But she would weep to see today
how on his skin the swart flies move;
the dust upon the paper eye
and the burst stomach like a cave.

For here the lover and killer are mingled
who had one body and one heart.
And death who had the soldier singled
has done the lover mortal hurt.

(Keith Douglas, English, 1920 – 1944.)

[The act of killing a fellow human being is described by the same poet.
Empathy for the enemy and a horror of horror make war more
difficult to wage.]

How to Kill

Under the parabola of a ball,
a child turning into a man,
I looked into the air too long.
The ball fell into my hand, it sang
in the closed fist: *Open Open
Behold a gift designed to kill.*

Now in my dial of glass appears
the soldier who is going to die.

He smiles, and moves about in ways
his mother knows, habits of his.
The wires touch his face; I cry
NOW. Death, like a familiar, hears

and look, has made a man of dust
of a man of flesh. This sorcery
I do. Being damned, I am amused
to see the centre of love diffused
and the waves of love travel into vacancy.
How easy it is to make a ghost.

The weightless mosquito touches
her tiny shadow on the stone,
and with how like, how infinite
a lightness, man and shadow meet.
They fuse. A shadow is a man
When the mosquito death approaches.

(Keith Douglas, English, 1920 – 1944.)

[The poems of Owen and Douglas were youthful and conventional
before they experienced war. There is a terrible sense of war forging
their versifying metal into hardened poetic steel, then with its final
blow destroying it.

The strange exhilaration of war and the enlivening proximity of
death are described in the next poem.]

A whole night,
Thrown down near a friend
Already butchered
With his mouth
Baring its teeth
Towards the full moon:
With the congestion
Of his hands
Penetrating my silence,

I've written letters
Full of love.

Never have I been
So
Attached to life.

(Giuseppe Ungaretti, Italian, 1888–1970, tr. I.M.)

[War, though it involves women's cooperation, is waged largely by men. There are questions around this point. The more society is dominated by men, is it the more likely to wage aggressive war? Are cultures overseen by male deities more warlike than those overseen by female deities? These questions are explored in the chapters 'Religion' and 'Men and Women', and the answers would seem to be 'yes'. But there's no doubt that women are capable of being warlike, as women political leaders of our time have demonstrated. The next poem describes such a woman, and is by a woman poet.]

The old woman's shoulders
were dry, unfleshed,
with outstanding veins;
her low belly
was like a lotus pad.

When people said
her son had taken fright,
had turned his back on battle
and died,

she raged
and shouted,

"If he really broke down
in the thick of battle,
I'll slash these breasts
that gave him suck,"

and went there,
sword in hand.

Turning over body after fallen body,
she rummaged through the blood-red field
till she found her son,
quartered, in pieces,

and she rejoiced
more than on the day
she gave him birth.

(Kakkaipatiniyar Naccellaiyar, Tamil, ? 1st. C. A.D., tr. A.K. Ramanujan.)

[The next two poems express more familiar sentiments of those
left behind when fighting men go to war.]

I climb that wooded hill
And look towards where my father is.
My father is saying, 'Alas, my son is on service;
Day and night he knows no rest.
Grant that he is being careful of himself,
So that he may come back and not be left behind!'

I climb that bare hill
And look to where my mother is.
My mother is saying, 'Alas, my young one is on service;
Day and night he gets no sleep.
Grant that he is being careful of himself,
So that he may come back, and not be cast away.'

I climb that ridge
And look towards where my elder brother is.
My brother is saying, 'Alas, my younger brother is on service;
Day and night he toils.
Grant that he is being careful of himself,
So that he may come back and not die.'

(Anon, Chinese, 7th C. B.C., Book of Songs 124, tr. A. Waley.)

May, 1915

Let us remember, Spring will come again
To the scorched, blackened woods, where the wounded trees
Wait, with their old wise patience for the heavenly rain,
Sure of the sky: sure of the sea to send its healing breeze,
    Sure of the sun. And even as to these
        Surely the Spring, when God shall please,
        Will come again like a divine surprise
To those who sit today with their great Dead, hands in their hands,
            eyes in their eyes,
At one with love, at one with Grief: blind to the scattered things
            and changing skies.

(Charlotte Mew, English, 1869–1928.)

[War ravages the landscape and destroys the careful work of generations. The aftermath for country people who have survived is described with a touch of wry humour in the next poem.]

After the Wars

The soldiers have gone, the villagers return
The snows have ceased, the flowers are opening up
Last year's yellowed grass still stands
Smoke puffs again from the little hamlets
Tired rats squeak among the empty walls
Starving crows peck in the barren fields
I seem to hear people muttering:
'The taxman's coming round again'.

(Xin Yuan, Chinese, 13th c., tr. John Scott.)

[The millions of lives thrown into ruin by war are represented here by a poem written 1800 years ago by a Chinese noble-woman. She was captured by nomadic tribesmen during one of their periodic rampages in China. She was forced to marry a chief, by whom she had two children. When he died, tribal custom forced her to marry his son. After twelve years she was ransomed. She had to return to China and leave her children behind. Back in China, she was scorned for her two marriages to barbarians, the second of which was to their minds incestuous. She remarried a Chinese, but the translator speculates that her new husband was ordered to marry her by the emperor who had ransomed her.]

Poem of Sorrow

...Cho's company came down upon the east,
Their metal armour glinting in the sun.
The men of the plains were weak and cowardly,
The invading soldiers were all Hu and Chi'ang.
Trampling across the fields, they invested the cities;
In the towns they attacked, everything was destroyed.
Heads were lopped off till no one was left to kill,
Just bones and corpses propping each other up.
On their horses' flanks they hung the heads of men,
On their horses' backs they carried off women and girls.
We galloped for days westwards into the passes,
The endless road was dangerous and steep.
When I looked back, into the mist-hung distance,
I felt as though my very heart was breaking.
In all they captured over ten thousand women,
Our captors would not let us keep together.
Sometimes when sisters found themselves side by side,
Longing to speak, they dared not utter a word.
If by some trivial fault we angered the soldiers,
At once they'd bawl out 'Kill these prisoners!
We'd better take knives and finish them off,
Why waste our time on keeping them alive?'
I had no desire to go on living longer,
I could not bear their cursing and reviling.
Sometimes they flogged us with rods as well,
And the pain we felt was mingled with our hatred.
During the day we trudged on weeping and crying,
At night we sat there, groaning to ourselves.

We longed to die, but could not get the chance,
We longed to live, with nothing left to live for.
How could the Blue Above be so unjust
To pour on us such anger and misfortune?
The border wilds are different from China,
And men know little of Righteousness and Truth.
It is a place where frost and snow abound,
And the northern wind blows spring and summer long.
It sent my clothes flapping about as it blew,
And whistled shrilly all around my ears.
Moved by the seasons, I thought of my father and mother,
My grief and sighing never came to an end.
When a stranger arrived from the world outside,
I was always overjoyed to hear of it,
I would welcome him, ask what news he had,
Only to find his district was not mine.
By luck my constant wish was gratified,
My relatives sent someone to rescue me.
But now when I was able to escape,
I found I had to leave my children there.
Natural bonds tie children to a woman's heart,
I thought of our parting, never to meet again,
In life and death eternally separated –
I could not bring myself to say goodbye.
My children came and clung around my neck,
Asking their mother where she was going to.
'They say that you have got to go away,
How can you ever come back to us again?
Mother, you were always so loving and so kind,
Why have you now become so harsh to us? We have not
    even grown into men,
How can you not look back and think of us?'
The sight of them destroyed me utterly,
I grew confused, behaved like one run mad.
Weeping and wailing, I fondled and caressed them,
When I had to set out, I turned back time and again.
The women who were taken captive with me

Came to bid me farewell and see me off.
They were glad that I could go back, though alone;
The sound of their crying hurt me grievously.
Because of this the horses stood hesitating,
Because of this the carriage did not move.
All the lookers-on were crying and wailing,
Even the passsers-by were crying too.
But I had to go, I had to harden my heart.
Daily our caravan hurried me further away.
On and on we went, three thousand leagues,
When would I ever see those I had left behind?
I brooded on the children of my womb,
The heart in my breast was broken evermore.
I got home to find my family was wiped out,
Nor had I any kin at all alive.
My home town had become a mountain-forest,
In its ruined courts the thorns and mugworts grew,
And all around, white bones of unknown men
Lay scattered with no one to bury them.
Outside the gates I heard no human voices,
Only wolves were howling, barking all around.
I stood alone, facing my lonely shadow,
My cry of anguish battered at my heart.
I climbed a hill and gazed into the distance,
And soul and spirit suddenly fled from me.
A bystander encouraged me to patience,
Kept urging me to try and go on living.
Though I went on living, what had life left for me?
I entrusted my fate to yet another man,
Exhausted my heart to summon strength to go on.
My wanderings have made all men despise me,
I live in fear of being cast aside once more.
How long can a woman's life go dragging on?
I shall know sorrow till the very end of my days.

(Tsai Yen, Chinese, fl. c. 190 A.D., tr. Frodsham and Cheng Hsi.)

[Displaced victims of war are the subjects of the next poem. The poet notes with irony how the victims' presence illuminates the limitations of a more normal way of life.]

Victims

They are ageing now, some dead.
In the third-class suburbs of exile
their foreign accents
continue to condemn them. They should
not have expected more.

They had their time
of blazing across headlines,
welcomes, interviews, placings
in jobs that could not fit,
of being walked round carefully.
One averts the eyes
from horror or miracle equally.

Their faces, common to humankind,
had eyes, lips, noses.
That in itself was grave,
seen through such a flame.

The Czech boy, talking,
posturing, desperate to please,
restless as a spastic trying
to confine his twitches
into the normal straightjacket -
what could we do with him?

The neighbours asked him
to children's parties,
being at sixteen a child;
gave him small jobs
having no niche to hold him
whether as icon, inhabitant
or memento mori.

He could not be a person
having once been forced to carry
other children's corpses
to the place of burning.

But when we saw him walk
beside our own children
darkness rose from that pit.
Quickly but carefully
(he must not notice)
we put our bodies
between our children and the Victim.

Absit omen*, you gods –   *may this omen
avert the doom,   keep its distance
the future's beckoning flame.

Perhaps he did not notice. At last
he went away.

In what back-street of what city
does he keep silence, unreadable
fading graffito of half-
forgotten obscenity?

Think: such are not to be pitied.
They wear already
a coat of ash seared in.
But our children and their children
have put on, over the years,
a delicate cloak of fat.

(Judith Wright, Australian, born 1915.)

[The theme of ash continues in the most famous poem about the
Holocaust. Celan's parents died in an internment camp, his father
of typhus, his mother murdered. He himself survived but with a
legacy of mental torment. He committed suicide in 1970.

Margarete is a German girl, Shulamith a Jewish girl. Shulamith is the name traditionally given to the girl in the Song of Songs. In concentration camps, some inmates were forced to play 'civilised' music while others were burnt. The poem is not so much about war itself as about the madnesses war unleashes.]

Death fugue

Black milk of daybreak we drink it at sundown
we drink it at noon in the morning we drink it at night
we drink and we drink it
we dig a grave in the breezes there one lies unconfined
A man lives in the house he plays with the serpents he writes
he writes when dusk falls to Germany your golden hair Margarete
he writes it and steps out of doors and the stars are flashing
he whistles his pack out
he whistles his Jews out in earth has them dig for a grave
he commands us strike up for the dance

Black milk of daybreak we drink you at night
we drink in the morning at noon we drink you at sundown
we drink and we drink you
A man lives in the house he plays with the serpents he writes
he writes when dusk falls to Germany your golden hair Margarete
your ashen hair Shulamith we dig a grave in the breezes there
one lies unconfined.

He calls out jab deeper into the earth you lot you others sing now and play
he grabs the iron in his belt he waves it his eyes are blue
jab deeper you lot with your spades you others play on for the dance

Black milk of daybreak we drink you at night
we drink you at noon in the morning we drink you at sundown
we drink and we drink you
a man lives in the house your golden hair Margarete
your ashen hair Shulamith he plays with the serpents

He calls out more sweetly play death death is a master from Germany
he calls out more darkly now stroke your strings then as smoke you will

rise into air
then a grave you will have in the clouds there one lies unconfined

Black milk of daybreak we drink you at night
we drink you at noon death is a master from Germany
we drink you at sundown and in the morning we drink and we drink you
death is a master from Germany his eyes are blue
he strikes you with leaden bullets his aim is true
a man lives in the house your golden hair Margarete
he sets his pack on to us he grants us a grave in the air
he plays with the serpents and daydreams death is a master from Germany

your golden hair Margarete
your ashen hair Shulamith

(Paul Celan, German, 1920–70, tr. Michael Hamburger.)

[Long ago there was a saying, 'The god of war is just, killing only those who kill'. That was never wholly accurate, but now those who kill are remote from those they kill. Those who get killed are for the most part poor and uneducated, conscripts or civilians, the least privileged and least influential of the populations involved. Technology allows war to be waged from a distance and vastly increases its potential for destruction.

The politics of war have also changed. Second– and third-world tyrants are befriended and used by the democratic powers, who profitably supply them with arms in return for the right to strip the land of oil, minerals and timber. The tyrants may use their armaments to slaughter and oppress their own populations, but if they upset the Western powers they are slapped down.[3] In this way, armaments and warfare contribute to the asset-stripping of the earth.

The proliferation of armaments is described in the next poem, first published in 1953. Great powers, too frightened of each others' armaments to go to war with each other (especially when the leaders themselves would be incinerated in such a conflict), conduct wars that are sporadic and continuing but far from home, while the threat – or promise – of mass destruction hangs over us all.]

[3] This paragraph follows closely the ideas and some of the wording of C.D. Darlington in 'The Little Universe of Man', pp. 265–6.

Every Day

War will no more be declared,
just continued. The unheard-of
has become the commonplace. The hero
stays far from the fighting. The weakling
is moved to the zone of fire.
The uniform of the day is patience;
the decoration, the shabby star
of hope above the heart.

It will be awarded
when nothing more is happening,
when the barrage falls silent,
when the enemy has become invisible,
and the shadow of eternal armament
fills the sky.

It will be awarded
for flight from banners
for bravery in front of friends
for the treachery of unworthy secrets,
and the non-action
of every briefing.

(Ingeborg Bachmann, Austrian, 1926–73, tr. I.M.)

[As nuclear weapons proliferate, the overcast skies of the last poem threaten to break and engulf us in storm. Looking ahead, a new reason for warfare presents itself. Environmental disasters in one country increasingly affect the welfare of neighbour states. Deforestation in Tibet causes flooding in Bangladesh. Industrial pollution in England and Germany cause acid rain across Northern Europe. Accidents in nuclear power stations affect whole continents. As environmental degradation becomes more acute, and living standards impossible to maintain, war over such issues is an ugly possibility. More than ever, it's in our interests to look to our common interests as a species.

In light of this emphasis we must not forget the sacrifice many people have made in defence of their right to freedom under familiar skies. Slavery, extermination or the yoke of foreign domination are examples of things worth fighting against, and the last poem celebrates sacrifice made in war.]

Behold, O Earth, how wasteful we have been
Spreading our seed in your secret sacred lap;
Not shining barley seed, nor heavy wheat,
Nor gold-streaked grain of rye, nor tasselled corn;
Behold, O Earth, how wasteful we have been!
The fairest of our flowers are in your dust,
Flowers that hardly witnessed the morning sun,
Some half in bud, some full in fragrant bloom,
Before life's noon, their innocence our grief;
Their dew not dry, they met a light that was new.
Accept these best, youth of the purest dream,
Whole in heart, not stained by the guilt of the world,
The weave of their days to be finished in life yet to be.
These are our best: what better have you seen?
Cover them over; the corn will soon be green,
Strong with their strength; the sanctity of earth
Increased by sacrifice; in death's mystery
May they make splendid amends for us that live.
Behold, O Earth, how wasteful we have been!

(Saul Tchernikhovsky, 1875–1943, Hebrew; version I.M. from translation by H. Auerbach.)

5. Civilisation

Reporter: Mr Gandhi, what do you think of modern civilisation?
Mahatma Gandhi: That would be a good idea!

[There are two meanings to the word civilisation. One refers to the accumulation of material and organisational strengths by which people dominate Nature and other people, and win for themselves some respite from the harsh conditions of primitive life. The other meaning refers more to a state of mind in which people behave towards each other with decency and consideration, so that different groups and individuals may live cooperatively and at peace with one another. Gandhi pointed out that the two don't necessarily go together.

Looking back, civilisations (in the first sense of the word) seem to behave like organisms, in that they live their lives then die. Conceivably our own civilisation could last till the sun explodes and the planet boils – or even longer, if by then we are colonisers of space. Alternatively, it may collapse soon, as the effects of our waste products damage the living world of which we are part.

As Europeans explored and conquered territory from the sixteenth century onwards, they came across the remains of many collapsed civilisations. Unable to accept the implication that their own civilisation would one day too collapse, they developed theories of lost races who built the civilisations then mysteriously disappeared. The thought that the peasants tilling the ground among the ruins could be descendants of those who had built and enjoyed the civilisations was unbearable to them.

It is said, 'forests precede civilisations, deserts follow'.]

Ozymandias

I met a traveller from an antique land
Who said: Two vast and trunkless legs of stone
Stand in the desert... Near them, on the sand,
Half sunk, a shattered visage lies, whose frown,
And wrinkled lip, and sneer of cold command,
Tell that its sculptor well those passions read
Which yet survive, stamped on these lifeless things,
The hand that mocked them, and the heart that fed:
And on the pedestal these words appear:
'My name is Ozymandias, king of kings:
Look on my works, ye Mighty, and despair!'
Nothing beside remains. Round the decay
Of that colossal wreck, boundless and bare
The lone and level sands stretch far away.

(P.B. Shelley, English, 1792–1822.)

[Damage to the land is a classic prelude to the collapse of
civilisation. Trees attract rainfall. If too many trees are cut down,
other vegetation also suffers. Over-intensive farming methods in
support of large city populations impoverish the soil. Warfare is
destructive of land, people and resources. Pollution is a relative
newcomer to the list, though today it's the most threatening item
of all. An early short poem about pollution:]

> Saucepan-soot
> Drifts ashamed
> Among the irises

(Kagu no Chiyo, Japanese, 1701–1755, tr. I.M.)

[In the next poem the poet asks, where does responsibility lie for
the system which tyrannises our lives and poisons our world?]

A Voiced Lament

Who's sprinkled salt on our children's milk
Who's muddied our waters
Hey, who goes there?

Are we living a fairy-tale, which century is this
Whence can the poison have seeped
Into our apple, onto our comb?

The light of day comes to our room unbidden
Wakes us and takes us away, forces
A pick-axe, a pen into our hands
The wagonloads go past, go past
Pushed into harness, we climb the slope
We pluck night from the forty thieves
Sing it a lullaby in our arms
Should not its arms enfold our sleep
Who is rocking whom?

They are walking the dead away
Mindful of proper ceremony
Is that the wind, is someone blowing
The living are in their lockers
Then who is it whose breath
Ruffles these well-kept files
Hey, who goes there?

(Gulten Akin, Turkish, b. 1933, tr. Nermin Menemencioglu.)

[This all seems a long way away from the high hopes with which
Western civilisation began.]

Numberless are the world's wonders, but none
More wonderful than man; the stormgray sea

Yields to his prows, the huge crests bear him high;
Earth, holy and inexhaustible, is graven
With shining furrows where his plows have gone
Year after year, the timeless labour of stallions.

The lightboned birds and beasts that cling to cover,
The lithe fish lighting their reaches of dim water,
All are taken, tamed in the net of his mind;
The lion on the hill, the wild horse windy-maned,
Resign to him; and his blunt yoke has broken
The sultry shoulders of the mountain bull.

Words also, and thoughts as rapid as air,
He fashions to his good use; statecraft is his,
And his the skill that deflects the arrows of snow,
The spears of winter rain: from every wind
He has made himself secure – from all but one:
In the late wind of death he cannot stand.

O clear intelligence, force beyond all measure!
O fate of man, working both good and evil!
When the laws are kept, how proudly his city stands!
When the laws are broken, what of his city then?
Never may the anarchic man find rest at my hearth,
Never let it be said that my thoughts are his thoughts!

(Sophocles, Greek, 495–406 B.C.; from 'Antigone', tr. Dudley Fitts.)

[Three centuries later, Greek civilisation was in ruins, destroyed
by its love of war. But out of the ruins of Greek civilisation grew
the Roman; out of the ruins of Roman civilisation grew modern
Europe.

Today, poets are no longer so full of praise for our species,
nor are they themselves held in high esteem. There is mutual
contempt between the destroyers and the impotent guardians of
our human spirit.]

(Monsieur Majora, technocrat)

Our neighbour's forty, an engineer, Swiss,
but could be anything – French, Belgian, German.
The policeman slaps his back. The whore squeals bliss.
He is a treasured guest of King Hassan.
Prospecting for oil in the desert and long gone,
his faucets are still running, his TV on.

On his bedside table are rings of cognac,
as on the year-old book he borrowed from Lily.
He only reads machines, writes only cheques.
We visited, we drank, the boredom deadly.
Cretinous technocrat, our century's pet -
Just seeing him, the Princess ached to vomit.

In his brand-new Rolls he barrelled out
the other morning, glancing up to check
the balconies for admirers, at the gate

ran down a puppy, didn't turn a hair.
Kill him? No point. We can't escape his like;
our very air is thick with murderers'sperm.

(George Faludy, Hungarian, born 1910, tr. Robin Skelton.)

[Today's dream is that everyone will be able to share in the fruits of civilisation. For those who know poverty, the escape from hardship is a powerful dream.]

Shanty Town

She sees a husband in her dream;
a toff with a salary of one hundred liras.
She marries, and moves to the city.
Letters arrive at their address,
The Happy Nest Apartments, basement floor.
They live in a flat neat as a box.

No more laundry, no more washing windows,
if she washes dishes, they are her own.
She has children, like angels, like drops of light.
She buys a second-hand pram,
mornings she goes to the Red Crescent Gardens,
so that little Yilmaz may play in the sand,
like the children of toffs.

The sewage-worker's best dream
is of the Turkish bath.
He stretches out on a marble platform,
a row of masseurs line up at his head.
One pours water,
one soaps him,
another waits his turn with a loofah.
As new customers enter,
the snow-white sewage worker leaves the bath.

(Orhan Veli Kanik, Turkish, 1914–50, tr. N. Menemencioglu.)

[After a while, the magic of material comfort wears off, and once again we are left with the age-old unanswerable puzzle of why we are here. The materialist solution to this puzzle – 'to acquire as much as we can' – leads to endless hard work, guilt at achieving our aims at others' expense, the collapse of family life starved of love and attention, and damage to the planet.]

I work, work
and still
no joy in my life
I stare
at my hands

(Ishikawa Takuboku, Japanese, 1885–1912, tr. Carl Sesar.)

[Civilisation isn't just a way to get more for ourselves. It provides us with ideas of how to behave if we would live in peace and happiness, and with ideas of how to enjoy ourselves without strife. It provides us with the recorded efforts of fellow humans to do these things, and to understand the nature of our human predicament. And, because time never stands still and perfection is always beyond us, it provides us with the opportunity to share in the making of civilisation, with all its possibilities of beauty, and its equally great potential for cruelty and disaster.

The next poem describes the lure of civilisation. A barbarian is attracted by what he has been summoned to destroy.]

Draktulf

Draktulf? Ragwulf? However did they say it
in Vizigoth? We only know him fair,
attractive, a great lout of a lad who lived
with his parents in a tent of bearskins
in the tangled reed-beds of Lake Balaton.
He'd not heard of villages or houses
or faced an abstract notion, and for him
the one and only landscape was the marshes.
One day the Chieftain of the nearby tribe
sent for him and equipped him with sword and shield,
then, with fifty others, marched him through
thick forests, over looming mountains, wild
secret pathways, always by night, in silence,
dawn behind them, touching their left shoulders,
until one day they stood before Ravenna,
a barbarian host below the walls
crowding the meadow in full battle order.
He was put in the front rank straight away.
The leader pointed to the sun-washed bastions,
said, 'Here's the stronghold of our enemy!
We'll capture it and kill off all those Romans.'
The walls were dirty yellow and half ruined,
standing upon the battlements some scattered
listless, helmeted soldiers, and behind
their backs a peristyle, a deep blue fountain,
and, near a temple poised in cypresses,
a marble statue of a naked Venus

saved somehow from the fury of the priests.
Draktulf stared at the goddess's naked breasts
and the little stars that sparkled on them.
His comrades shook their clenched fists at the city
but he immediately knew his home
was here, that he belonged to Her for ever.
His knees were shaking. Almost he fell down.
His mouth seeped crystal sweetness at Her call,
and sharp excitement gripped and throbbed his loins.
That night he joined the defenders on the walls.

(George Faludy, Hungarian, b. 1910, tr. Robin Skelton.)

[The process of 'barbarians' becoming civilised – that is, joining
or forming the ruling class of a civilisation – is part of the story of
civilisation itself. But the attempt to distribute more equally the
fruits of civilisation is relatively recent.[1] In the past, beneficiaries of
civilisation depended on the work of their fellow human beings.
If we are all to benefit, we depend on the work of machines. But
these very machines give us the power to destroy the world, and
ourselves along with it.]

The Secret of the Machines

We were taken from the ore-bed and the mine,
  We were melted in the furnace and the pit -
We were cast and wrought and hammered to design,
  We were cut and filed and tooled and gauged to fit.
Some water, coal, and oil is all we ask,
  And a thousandth of an inch to give us play:
And now, if you will set us to our task,
  We will serve you four and twenty hours a day!

  We can pull and haul and push and lift and drive,
  We can print and plough and weave and heat and light,
  We can run and race and swim and fly and dive,
  We can see and hear and count and read and write!

[1] There is a theory that Mayan civilisation foundered on just such an attempt.

Would you call a friend from half across the world?
  If you'll let us have his name and town and state,
You shall see and hear your crackling question hurled
  Across the arch of heaven while you wait.
Has he answered? Does he need you at his side?
  You can start this very evening if you choose,
And take the Western ocean in the stride
  Of seventy thousand horses and some screws!

    The boat express is waiting your command!
    You will find the *Mauretania* at the quay,
    Till her captain turns the lever 'neath his hand,
    And the monstrous nine-decked city goes to sea.

Do you wish to make the mountains bare their head
  And lay their new-cut forests at your feet?
Do you want to turn a river in its bed,
  Or plant a barren wilderness with wheat?
Shall we pipe aloft and bring you water down
  From the never failing cisterns of the snows,
To work the mills and tramways in your town,
  And irrigate the orchards as it flows?

    It is easy! Give us dynamite and drills!
    Watch the iron-shouldered rocks lie down and quake,
    As the thirsty desert-level floods and fills,
    And the valley we have damned becomes a lake.

But remember please, the Law by which we live,
  We are not built to comprehend a lie,
We can neither love nor pity nor forgive.
  If you make a slip in handling us you die!
We are greater than the Peoples or the Kings -
  Be humble, as you crawl beneath our rods! -
Our touch can alter all created things,
  We are everything on earth except – the Gods!

    Though our smoke may hide the Heavens from your eyes,
    It will vanish and the stars will shine again,

Because, for all our power and weight and size,
We are nothing more than children of your brain!

(Rudyard Kipling, English, 1865–1936.)

[Now that machines do much of the work, human labour has become a sought-after commodity. Goods are made to perish quickly, to keep up the need for human labour – and to keep expensive machinery busy.

To maintain this system, we must want goods more than anything. Our sense of wonder is directed away from the wonders of Nature and towards the wonders of human creation.]

The Motoka★   ★ motor car

You see that Benz sitting at the rich's end?
Ha! That motoka is motoka
It belongs to the Minister for Fairness
Who yesterday was loaded with a doctorate
At Makerere with whisky and I don't know what
Plus I hear the literate thighs of an undergraduate.

You see those market women gaping their mouths?
The glory of its inside has robbed them of words,
I tell you the feather seats the gold steering
The TV the radio station the gear!
He can converse with all the world presidents
While driving in the back seat with his darly
Between his legs without the driver seeing a thing! ha! ha! ha!
Look at the driver chasing the children away
They want to see the pistol in the door pocket
Or the button that lets out bullets from the machine
Through the eyes of the car-sshhhhhhhhhhhhhhhh!
Let's not talk about it.

But I tell you that motoka can run
It sails like a lyato, speeds like a swallow

And doesn't know anyone stupid on its way
The other day I heard -
But look at its behind, that mother of twins!
A-ah! That motoka is motoka
You just wait, I'll tell you more
But let me first sell my tomatoes.

(Theo Luzuka, contemporary, African.)

[Lost in wonder at our own creations we lose our sense of wonder
at the world – at what used to be called God's creation. The voice
of the next poem is Judas, spirit of betrayal through the ages.]

Whenever That Happened

Hell is the familiar all stripped of wonder.
Was there a moment
When wonder at the world died in my eyes?
Had I a friend I could recognise?
When did I take friendship for granted?
When did I get used to the thought of murder?
When did my flesh cease to astonish me?
When did my mind become grey-familiar?
Whenever that happened is when I knew
I could do anything.
When wonder died in me power was born.
I can change the world because I no longer dream of blue,
I can betray a god because I never heard a girl sing
Of steps in the street or sunlight blessing a field of corn.

(Brendan Kennelly, Irish, b. 1936.)

[Being in work has become what divides the affluent from the
poor. Being busy is a status symbol. The affluent are never at rest;
when they are not working they are enjoying a leisure pursuit.
Contemplation has become the preserve of the unemployed, who
are powerless to influence human affairs. In these circumstances, a
change of direction becomes less and less likely.

As democracy gained precedence in England in the nineteenth century, the saying 'we must educate our masters' became popular among the ruling classes. Voters should know about the issues, it was reasoned, so they would not misuse their new power. But this was in conflict with another attitude – that ignorant voters are more easily exploited.

In the next poem, an old poet reflects on the limitations of his education.]

Flycatchers

Sweet pretty fledgelings, perched on the rail arow,
Expectantly happy, where ye can watch below
Your parents a-hunting i' the meadow grasses
All the gay morning to feed you with flies;

Ye recall me a time sixty summers ago,
When, a young chubby chap, I sat just so
With others on a school-form rank'd in a row,
Not less eager and hungry than you, I trow,
With intelligences agape and eyes aglow,
While an authoritative old wise-acre
Stood over us and from a desk fed us with flies.

Dead flies – such as litter the library south-window,
That buzzed at the panes until they fell stiff-baked on the sill,
Or are roll'd up asleep i' the blinds at sunrise,
Or wafer'd flat in a shrunken folio.

A dry biped he was, nurtured likewise
On skins and skeletons, stale from top to toe
With all manner of rubbish and all manner of lies.

(Robert Bridges, English, 1844–1930.)

[Education became a battle ground for rival ideologies. Ideologies are systems of ideas designed to get power for their holders, and are akin to superstition not wisdom. Because truth is not their primary objective, they always lead to more or less grief. One ideology says education should be used to make us more economically effective, another says it should be used to make us all equal. The idea that it should be used for what it was designed for – to make us more understanding – got lost, leaving us in the land of Shakespeare's King Lear:

> 'To wilful men,
> The injuries that they themselves procure
> Must be their schoolmasters.'

More recently, the trend has been to give children freedom to explore their own paths, as if children are innately decent and civilised, and as if we grown-ups might discover civilisation from our children. This freedom has produced a generation even keener on consumer pleasures than their parents.]

To a young man driving his own car

So you're already driving your own car
I'll bet your friends are jealous
As you were learning to drive
I thought how splendid for you
to go speeding everywhere
Getting any kind of licence is good
I often said
Now you speed about in your car
you can't see the roadside trees changing
with the seasons
you can't see the merchants selling fruit
or fish at the roadside
you can't see the woman running along
with a sick child slung on her back
Always on the look-out for traffic-patrols
and red lights
your eyes fixed straight ahead'
you speed about
your eyes have grown sharper
your mind has grown busier

and though the price of fuel
may go up even more
and exhaust fumes block your view
you drive around
and do not intend to walk anywhere I'm sure
and those years of youth that people spend
walking or running
getting about by bus or subway
you are spending at over 40 mph
When I see you speeding along in your car
I feel you have isolated yourself
too lightly
and my heart grows heavy

((Kwang-kyu Kim, Korean, b. 1941, tr. Brother Anthony of Taize.)

[The failure of education to bring up young people with an understanding of human society is squandering the potential of democracy. Education is provided to a basic level with which the victim of the process might be able to get a job. Everything is done on the cheap; teachers are low-paid, buildings are cheap and tatty, and there's a lack of books. The message is not, flourish!, not even, survive!, just – exist!

Today, young people have to face the fact that generations preceeding them have made of the world a place poisoned, sick and dying. Even to exist as a consuming human being in the way they have been brought up is to contribute to the poisoning of the world. To get a job – 'if they are lucky' – is almost certain to add more to this process of destruction.

Meanwhile, the yearning of young people for a decent world is exploited by the entertainment and music industries. These industries, along with fashion, drugs, and the lure of powerful comforts like owning a car, direct the energy and attention of young people towards getting and spending. Stupified, they are incapable of working for or even thinking about a better society. In the next poem, the character speaking is Judas the betrayer.]

Money in Love

My good friend, the Pinstripe Pig, says
There's money in love
Especially in shining teenage eyes.
Pinstripe's mind, all bonny-bladed edge,
Hires me to write songs
That shiver their little fannies
While they pour out tears and screams
And tidal monies.

Pinstripe sits in his office all day
Breaking record after record.
'Thanks be to God' he sighs 'for the fucking young,
The fucking young.'
Child, if you're lucky,
Pinstripe will blow you a kiss, he's music-lord
Thrilling your days with love's old sweet song.

Listen to Pinstripe, child, and you can't go wrong.

(Brendan Kennelly, Irish, b. 1936.)

[Along with affluence comes the illusion that we can do without moral restraint. We forget that we owe our survival as a species to morality, which enables us to trust each other and co-operate. Such co-operation, as Charles Darwin noted, gives us an edge over other species.

The curse Timon uttered on the citizens of Athens describes a state of affairs in many ways similar to how we live today. Timon speaks as he leaves the city, whose citizens loved him while he was rich but deserted him once he was poor. The curse he utters is with a view to their extinction. Much of what he wishes on them, we have embraced voluntarily.]

Let me look back on thee. O thou wall,
That girdles in those wolves, dive in the earth,
And fence not Athens! Matrons, turn incontinent!

Obedience fail in children! Slaves and fools,
Pluck the grave wrinkled Senate from the bench,
And minister in their steads! To general filths
Convert o' th' instant, green virginity!
Do't in your parents' eyes! Bankrupts, hold fast:
Rather than render back, out with your knives,
And cut your trusters' throats! Bound servants, steal!
Large-handed robbers your grave masters are
And pill★ by law. Maid, to thy master's bed!   ★pillage
Thy mistress is o' the brothel. Son of sixteen,
Pluck the lined crutch from thy old limping sire,
With it beat out his brains! Piety and fear,
Religion to the gods, peace, justice, truth,
Domestic awe, night-rest and neighbourhood,
Instruction, manners, mysteries and trades,
Degrees, observances, customs and laws,
Decline to your confounding contraries,
And yet confusion live! Plagues incident to men,
Your potent and infectious fevers heap
On Athens, ripe for stroke! Thou cold sciatica,
Cripple our senators, that their limbs may halt
As lamely as their manners! Lust and liberty
Creep in the minds and marrows of our youth,
That 'gainst the stream of virtue they may strive,
And drown themselves in riot! Itches, blains,
Sow all th'Athenian bosoms, and their crop
Be general leprosy! Breath infect breath,
That their society, as their friendship, may
Be merely poison! Nothing I'll bear from thee
But nakedness, thou detestable town!
Take thou that too, with multiplying bans!
Timon will to the woods, where he shall find
The unkindest beast more kinder than mankind.
The gods confound – hear me, you good gods all! –
Th'Athenians both within and out that wall!
And grant, as Timon grows, his hate may grow
To the whole race of mankind, high and low!
Amen.

(Shakespeare, English, 1564–1616; Timon, Act 4, Scene 1.)

[The green movement comes not from governments, not from those who should know and be responsible, but from individuals who see and hate what our civilisation is doing to the world. Politicians in democracies are no longer leaders; their job is to sniff the direction the herd wants to travel in. So it's up to voters to be wise, and the burden of knowledge and responsibility lies on them.

To make things worse, politicians try to persuade voters to stay with the jamboree – partly because they don't want to derail the gravy-train, partly because the change we need is so alarmingly radical. The next poem is in the semi-literate voice of a well-known Australian politician.]

God Gave Us Trees to Cut Down

My Goodness;
if I was to have a say in the way things should be done in
    Victoria:
like we run them and have them here in Queensland,
then by Crikey;
those forests – rainforests and what have they – in Gippsland
    there;
and let me tell you,
we have been down this road with the conservationists too:
and, by golly, we gave them what for.

And why should they cut down their trees?
What use are they? well I'll tell you:
the Japanese – I know they're a funny mob of people –
but they make paper out of trees, see,
and we all need paper.
You know this – what a stupid question to ask.
What would you do without paper and cardboard and
    – goodness, I ask you.
Of course we must cut down trees;
golly, what did God give them to us for.

And look at the other States, and all of them and what have
    you;
they have taken a leaf out of our Queensland way of doing
    things.
Just look at Mr. Grey in Tasmania; he cuts down many trees,
now; unfortunately they don't seem to have the courage
to stand up to the Federal Government and sit firmly on their
    position
– but let me tell you, they cut down many trees in Tasmania.
And in Western Australia
– just look at them – well –
they cut down their Jarra, and all their other sorts there.
And in New South Wales previous governments,
and even the present government sells their trees to the
    Japanese,

and my goodness, so they should.
Don't worry about South Australia, they don't have any
    trees.
Unfortunately the Northern Territory has been given to the
    Aboriginals,
and we all know they worship trees and sticks and plants and
    things
and what have you
and all sorts of things so we all know where that place is
    going;
and what a pity;
minerals and the Casino and Ayers Rock
– as they now call it: Uluru; and what a shame – don't you
    think it a shame?
And you see? they worship rocks too. All the minerals will
    go down the drain.

But here in Queensland we don't let the Federal
    Government
down there in Canberra tell us what to do
– and why should we?
If they come up here we soon give them short shrift and
    short change.

We send them running back down south with their tails
    between their legs
and their hats behind their backs like little schoolboys.
That's the way to do it – you've got to show them who's
    boss.
And so I would tell Mr. Cain not to worry about those
    conservationists,
just run right over them:
cut right through the lot of them as if they weren't there.
Golly, that's the way we do it in Queensland.

My goodness, you should know
God gave us those rainforests to cut down....

(W. Les Russell, Aboriginal Australian, b. 1949.)

[The great nightmare of civilisation is that control of it will be
given into the wrong hands. It wasn't somewhere wild and un-
civilised that the Holocaust took place, it was in the heart of
civilised and democratic Europe. In the absence of religion and
good education, continually increasing affluence is relied on to
keep voters happy – a foolish reliance if ever there was one. The
next poem is about what happens when power is handed over to
extremists, whose promises of order and plenty lead to
nightmare.]

The Shield of Achilles

She looked over his shoulder
    For vines and olive trees,
Marble well-governed cities,
    And ships upon untamed seas,
But there on the shining metal
    His hands had put instead
An artificial wilderness
    And a sky like lead.

A plain without a feature, bare and brown,
  No blade of grass, no sign of neighbourhood,
Nothing to eat and nowhere to sit down,
  Yet, congregated on its blankness, stood
  An unintelligible multitude,
A million eyes, a million boots in line,
Without expression, waiting for a sign.

Out of the air a voice without a face
  Proved by statistics that some cause was just
In tones as dry and level as the place:
  No one was cheered and nothing was discussed;
  Column by column in a cloud of dust
They marched away enduring a belief
Whose logic brought them, somewhere else, to grief.

  She looked over his shoulder
    For ritual pieties,
  White garlanded heifers,
    Libation and sacrifice,
  But there on the shining metal
    Where the altar should have been,
  She saw by his flickering forge-light
    Quite another scene.

Barbed wire enclosed an arbitrary spot
  Where bored officials lounged (one cracked a joke)
And sentries sweated, for the day was hot:
  A crowd of ordinary decent folk
  Watched from without and neither moved nor spoke
As three pale figures were led forth and bound
To three posts driven upright in the ground.

The mass and majesty of this world, all
  That carries weight and always weighs the same,
Lay in the hands of others; they were small
  And could not hope for help and no help came;
  What their foes liked to do was done, their shame
Was all the worst could wish; they lost their pride
And died as men before their bodies died.

She looked over his shoulder
  For athletes at their games,
Men and women in a dance
  Moving their sweet limbs
Quick, quick, to music,
  But there on the shining shield
His hands had set no dancing-floor
  But a weed-choked field.

A ragged urchin, aimless and alone,
  Loitered about that vacancy; a bird
Flew up to safety from his well-aimed stone:
  That girls are raped, that two boys knife a third,
  Were axioms to him, who'd never heard
Of any world where promises were kept
Or one could weep because another wept.

The thin-lipped armourer,
  Hephaestos,[2] hobbled away;
Thetis[3] of the shining breasts
  Cried out in dismay
At what the god had wrought
  To please her son, the strong
Iron-hearted man-slaying Achilles
  Who would not live long.

(W.H. Auden, English, 1907–73.)

[There are other aspects of modern civilised life which encourage materialism. Comfort and affluence isolate us physically from our fellow humans. Community life breaks down, to be replaced by consumer enjoyments. We begin to treat each other as if we are ourselves no more than objects to be used.]

---

[2] God of fire.

[3] A sea-nymph, Achilles' mother.

Every Decent Family

Every decent family should have a brothel attached
Instead of a half-hearted garage.
How else can they be expected to survive
In this age of hate and rage?
Keep a whore instead of a car
Your man is happy
Driving her to work
Nearly every morning of the year.

The whore keeps the wife alive
The wife hates the whore
The whore screws the man, the man loves the wife,
It is always possible to entertain a guest,
The garage boasts old tyres and plastic bags
Though there are times when the desire to burn
Everything to the ground can scarcely be suppressed.

(Brendan Kennelly, Irish, b. 1936.)

[Civilisation has a long reach. If a buyer of cat litter knew that a sacred aboriginal mountain was being disembowelled to produce it, would the purchase go ahead? Though we don't know the price of our petty comforts, we can (if we want to) form a fair impression of the general price of civilisation.]

Time is Running Out

The miner rapes
The heart of the earth
With his violent spade.
Stealing, bottling her black blood
For the sake of greedy trade.
On his metal throne of destruction,
He labours away with a will,
Piling the mountainous minerals high
With giant tool and iron drill.

In his greedy lust for power,
He destroys old nature's will.
For the sake of the filthy dollar,
He dirties the nest he builds.
Well he knows that violence
Of his destructive kind
Will be violently written
Upon the sands of time.

But time is running out
And time is close at hand,
For the Dreamtime folk are massing
To defend their timeless land.
Come gentle black man
Show your strength;
Time to take a stand.
Make the violent miner feel
Your violent
Love of land.

(Oodgeroo Noonuccal, Aboriginal Australian, b. 1920.)

[Systems of oppression grow when a dream is followed without enough regard to the cost of the dream. In the next poem, a Palestinian woman watches an Israeli boy, mourning that some of his 'human heart and face' will be lost as, chasing the worthy dream of a national homeland, he is brought up to be an oppressor of those who lived there before him.]

To Etan, *An Israeli child from the Kibbuts Ma'oz Hayim*

He falls
under the star that branches
a wild tree in his hands
a web woven with the threads of steel stretching walls of blood
around The Dream.
He is caught.

Opening his eyes
Etan, the child, asks,
"How long do we have to watch over this land?"
And time deformed
dragged in khaki, bypasses him
through flames and smoke
sorrows and death.

If only the star could foretell the truth.

Etan, my child
Like the harbour that is drowning
I can see you drown
through the lie
The bloated dream is a sinking load.
I am afraid for you, my child
to have to grow up in this web of things
to be gradually stripped of your human heart and face
you could fall again, my child
    and fall
        and fall
            fading into a fathomless end.

(Fadwa Tuqun, Palestinian, b. 1917, tr. Kamal Boullata.)

[The ideals of Western civilisation as it expanded across the globe were material prosperity, good government and the Christian religion. It offered these to the peoples who came under its sway, but with many a slip 'twixt cup and lip.

In the theft of land occupied by other people, civilised theory and civilised practise are at their most divergent. Australia was declared ' terra nullius', land of no one, by the explorer Captain James Cook, as if the native population did not exist or were animals. Later, racial contempt enabled colonists to maintain their view of themselves as civilised while they slaughtered those who were there before them.

In the next poem, Christian colonists are taken to task by an Aboriginal poet for hypocrisy.]

Memo to JC

When you were down here JC and walked this earth,
You were a pretty decent sort of bloke,
Although you never owned nothing, but the clothes on your back,
And you were always walking round, broke.
But you could talk to people, and you didn't have to judge,
You didn't mind helping the down and out
But these fellows preaching now in your Holy name,
Just what are they on about?
Didn't you tell these fellows to do other things,
Besides all that preaching and praying?
Well, listen, JC, there's things that ought to be said,
And I might as well get on with the saying.
Didn't you tell them 'don't judge your fellow man'
And 'love ye one another'
And 'not put your faith in worldly goods'.
Well, you should see the goods that they got, brother!
They got great big buildings and works of art,
And millions of dollars in real estate,
They got no time to care about human beings,
They forgot what you told 'em, mate;
Things like, 'Whatever ye do to the least of my brothers,
This ye do also unto me'.
Yeah, well these people who are using your good name,
They're abusing it, JC,
But there's still people living the way you lived,
And still copping the hypocrisy, racism and hate,
Getting crucified by the fat cats, too,
But they don't call us religious, mate.
Tho' we've got the same basic values that you lived by,
Sharin' and carin' about each other,
And the bread and wine that you passed around,
Well, we're still doin' that, brother.
Yeah, we share our food and drink and shelter,
Our grief, our happiness, our hopes and plans,
But they don't call us 'Followers of Jesus',
They call us black fellas, man.
But if you're still offering your hand in forgiveness

To the one who's done wrong, and is sorry,
I reckon we'll meet up later on,
And I got no cause to worry.
Just don't seem right somehow that all the good you did,
That people preach, not practise, what you said,
I wonder, if it all died with you, that day on the cross,
And if it just never got raised from the dead.

(Maureen Watson, Aboriginal Australian, contemporary.)

[The dream of modern civilisation requires widespread exploitation of the earth and its far-flung peoples. Previously, European countries wanted to expand both in search of wealth and in search of land for burgeoniong populations. Medicine, longevity, hygiene and better nutrition all played a part in burgeoning population growth, as did laws against the old-fashioned methods of population control; abortion, infanticide and sexual deviance.

Populations in the most civilised countries are now more stable. The old system of colonialism has been replaced by a new one, which is in many ways worse. Corrupt·third world governments are maintained by Western supplies of arms in return for the right to strip the land of its assets. A global system of interlocked and powerful interests has developed. Liberals are the token conscience of our civilisation. Tolstoy wrote, over a hundred years ago,

'I sit on a man's back, choking him and making him carry me, and yet assure myself and others that I am very sorry for him and wish to ease his lot by all possible means – except by getting off his back.'

Destroying the planet, and robbing many peoples of their land and livelihood – what's it all for? When we consider how much of the world's riches are consumed to produce trash, and how little effort is directed to making things that are fine and will give long enjoyment, we can only feel doubly angry. Many goods are designed to perish in as short a time as the manufacturers can get away with. It is this process – of consuming forests, ripping up the land for minerals, polluting transportation, and the rubbish, much of it poisonous – which is killing the earth.

But our lifestyle doesn't make us happy. What we've done to Nature we've done to ourselves. We live like we make chickens live, cooped up in boxes, only functioning to consume and produce. Who would ask chickens in a battery if they are happy? Who would believe them if they answered?]

The Unhappy Race

White fellow, you are the unhappy race.
You alone have left nature and made civilized laws.
You have enslaved yourselves as you enslaved the horse and
    other wild things.
Why, white man?
Your police lock up your tribe in houses with bars,
We see poor women scrubbing floors of richer women.
Why, white man, why?
You laugh at 'poor blackfellow', you say we must be like
    you.
You say we must leave the old freedom and leisure,
We must be civilised and work for you.
Why, white fellow?
Leave us alone, we don't want your collars and ties,
We don't need your routines and compulsions.
We want the old freeedom and joy that all things have but
    you,
Poor white man of the unhappy race.

(Oodgeroo Noonuccal, Aboriginal Australian, b. 1920.)

[The cry of 'Leave us alone!' is heard wherever our civilisation comes to stay in a foreign land.]

Hope

    Time has triumphed, the wind has scattered all,
    Alexander, Caesar, empires, cities are lost,
    Tara and Troy flourished a while and fell
    And even England itself, maybe, will bite the dust.

(Anon., Irish, 17th–19th c., tr. Brendan Kennelly.)

The ever-touring Englishmen have built their bungalows
All over our sweet forest
They drive their trains with smoke
O look at them, how they talk on wires to one another
With their wires they have bound the whole world together
   for themselves.

(Anonymous song, Gond, 1930's, tr. V. Elwin and S. Hivale.)

[The further people move away from dirt and physical work, the less they are aware of their dependance on Nature. It's this sense of unreality that allows corporations, governments and highly paid dwellers in luxury apartments to make decisions which, for short-term profit, devastate the globe. Insulated from the earth by plate glass and concrete they don't even see what they're doing. The next poem contrasts the builders of high-rise buildings with the people who will inhabit them later.]

Builders

On great Ur-slabs of concrete terraces,
or rust-red bones of girder and cross-member,
they sit, eating their sandwiches
at noon. They look at home there
among the stylized trunks of metal forests,
the unfinished work.
Maybe the half-built is our proper habitat,
manhandling raw material
in basic contact, manipulation, direction
of various substances. Simple...

Later, the place changes.
Dressed in plastic wall boards, fitted
with doors and windows, connected
by cables, wires and pipes to the feed-in world,
it becomes part of a circuit.

Coming in later to consult officials,
sign papers, buy, sell, argue over contracts,
they observe the fake marble, the carpets
covering those bare encounters of concrete and steel,
the corridors scurrying with unfamiliar errands:
wondering. Wondering about building.
How whatever we construct gets complicated,
gets out of order and beyond our control.

(Judith Wright, Australian, b. 1915.)

[In a poem that's a bit unfair on pigs, Brendan Kennelly describes
the kind of man who thrives among the fake marble and
carpets.]

The Pig

You, Heavenly Muse, how will you justify
The pig's ways to men?
How will you sing
Of the pig's origin?
What thighs opened wide
To let out that snout
Rammed on a carcase of timeless slime?
When the old sly juices went to work
What womb
Sheltered our little darling?
What breasts
Gave it suck?

Suck, suck.

And on our treacherous planet
What hearts worry for its welfare?

The pig is everywhere.

He grunts between the lovers in their bed
His hot sperm flooding the girl

His dungeon breath rutting into her skin
Where a man's fingers move in what he thinks
Are patterns of enchantment.
The pig's eyes smile in the dark.

The pig's eyes glow with ambition.
He knows that where his head won't go
His tail will enter,
His little corkscrew tail.

The pig sits on committees,
Hums and haws, grunts yes and no,
Is patient, wise, attentive,
Wary of decision (alternatives are many).
When he hefts his bottom from the chair
The seat is hot.
His head is dull
But, maybe, he's just a little stronger now.

The pig knows how to apologise.
He would hurt nobody.
If he did, he didn't mean it.
His small eyes redden with conviction.
Remorse falls like saliva from his jaws.

The pig is bored
But doesn't know it.
The pig gobbles time
And loves the weekend.
The pig is important
And always says 'It seems to me' and 'Yes, let's face it'.
The pig chews borrowed words,
Munching conscientiously.
Sometimes he thinks he's a prophet, a seer so elegant
That we should bow down before him.
He is more remote from a sense of the unutterable
Than any words could begin to suggest.

The pig knows he has made the world.
Mention the possibility of something beyond it –

He farts in your face.

The pig's deepest sty is under his skin.
His skin is elegantly clad.
The pig knows might is right.
The pig is polite.
The pig is responsible and subtle.
How can this be so?
I don't know, but I have seen the pig at work
And know the truth of what I see.

The pig has lived in me

And gone his way, snouting the muck
In the wide sty of the world.

His appetite for filth is monstrous
And he knows
There is more sustenance in filth
Than in the sweet feast at the white table
Where friends gather for a night
Talk and laugh
In a room with warm light.

The pig might enter that room
And swallow everything in sight.

But the pig's sense of timing
Is flawless.
His own throat is fat, ready to cut,
But no one will do that.
Instead, the pig will slit
Some other throat.
There will be no blood but a death,
The pig will hump into the future

Huge
Hot
Effective

His eyes darting like blackbirds for the worm
Waiting to be stabbed, plucked, gulped,
Forgotten.

And still our darling lives
As though there were no
Oblivion.

(Brendan Kennelly, Irish, b. 1936.)

[There is a story in Greek mythology about a giant named
Antaeus. He was only strong when standing on his mother Earth.
Hercules realised this, and managed to kill the giant by holding
him up in the air; the giant lost his strength and Hercules squeezed
him to death. Hercules himself was an earthy kind of hero.

We have truly come a long way from mother Earth. Even
our farmers traverse their fields in machines, usually with
headphones on, substituting pop music or other people's chatter
for the grinding mechanical noise. The countryside itself has been
transformed into a semi-industrial landscape. Most of the
population now lives in towns, and most voters have no
experience of life in the countryside. In the next poem Pan, god of
wildness and fear, moves from the country to the city.]

Panic

Not in deserted meadows Pan wanders
But in the crowded cities where millions live.
Asphalt and concrete are his stamping ground
At noon, during the long hot summers.

From luxury flats in block apartments
He leaps into the latest cars.
He lives with giant banks for background
Surrounded by his minions.

He singles out the silent, the helpless
Avoiding those who bare their teeth

Near factory walls and muffled fortress gate
He pounces on the meagre joys
Of vanquished men, discouraged women.

Not in the sultry summers alone
But any day, almost, in the big cities
He combs the boulevards with mute malicious laughter.
Seeing him face to face the unemployed
Turn giddy as they pace the hard dank pavements.

Where the poor, the sick, the hungry crawl,
In the city's belly, in remote alleyways,
His sense of mischief unassuaged, he vents
More fury on Man's cruel civilisation
Of atom bombs and guided missiles.

Tomorrow? If there is a trace of him in the news,
The bread, the water with its taste of hemlock,
Or if his shadow falls on the faces of children,
There is little hope in tomorrow for such as us.

(Behcet Necatigil, Turkish, b. 1916, tr. N. Menemencioglu.)

[The great effort of building a civilisation is its own exhilaration;
but what are people to do once it's largely built? Is frustration
inevitable? We are living organisms, and the essence of life is
struggle. If civilisation is so constricting that struggle is done away
with, apathy, boredom, and the desire to knock it all down
result.]

Twentieth Century

I am being consumed by life
Wasting, not doing anything,
Between the four symmetrical
Walls of my house.

Oh, workers! Bring your picks!
Let my walls and roof fall,
Let air move my blood,
Let sun burn my shoulders.

I am a twentieth century woman.
I spend my day lounging,
Watching, from my room,
How a branch moves.

Europe is burning,
And I'm watching its flames
With the same indifference
With which I contemplate that branch.

You, passer-by, don't look me
Up and down; my soul
Shouts its crime aloud, yours
Hides under its words.

(Alfonsina Storni, Argentinian, 1892–1938, tr. M. Freeman.)

[The same feelings of claustrophobia and frustration, voiced by a
young man, lead him to violence.]

The Lament of a Discontented Young Man

(at the beginning of a conscripted century)

Paris, Peking... London, or Rome?
How desolate is this city, the world!
City or village, it all means the same: Nothing.
To change one's surroundings
is utterly senseless now.
If only something different
if only a great riot would begin.

For who can still bear this greyness
which lets liars sparkle and gleam?
O clenched fist, come:
let this so worthless life crash down,
then let the great doctor, Death, arrive,
and after death the opening of eyes,
the horrors,
let something different come,
rebellions, why do you hesitate?

Blood, blood, blood.
Man will be much more beautiful
once he is cleaned with blood,
and better too.
Then come with your angels and trumpets,
O Resurrection,
and come with your armies of millions,
drive the vigour of youth into this desolate
globe, the earth,
and let the redeeming rifle come,
Amen.

(Endre Ady, Hungarian, 1877–1919, tr. F Marnau and M Hamburger.)

[The same poet wrote, a few years later, of the fruits his prayers
had borne.]

Prayer after the War

Lord, I have come from the war,
all is departed and past:
now reconcile me to to yourself, and to myself,
since you are peace.

Look, my heart is a fiery
ulcer, and nothing gives relief.
Then with a kiss overpower my heart
to soften it.

For a long time already
my sad great eyes have been shut
to this world, there's nothing to see, but you:
you they embrace.

These two running legs have been
knee-deep in blood, look, O Lord,
look down, now no feet remain, only knees,
Lord, only knees.

I do not fight now, nor kiss,
My mouth is bloodless, withered,
my devoured arms are crutches, so are
all other parts.

Look at me therefore, O Lord,
all is departed and past,
now reconcile me to yourself, and to myself,
since you are peace.

(Endre Ady, Hungarian, 1877–1919, tr. F Marnau and M Hamburger.)

[Another pair of contrasting pieces gives impressions of what civilisation is trying to uphold, and of the terrible consequences when it breaks down. In Germany, during the Thirty Years War, religious bigots joined secular rulers in the struggle for power. Armed bands looted and robbed; no one was safe. Gryphius describes the results:]

Tears of the Fatherland

So, now we are destroyed; utterly; more than utterly!
The gang of shameless peoples, the maddening music of war,
The sword fat with blood, the thundering of the guns
Have consumed our sweat and toil, exhausted our reserves.
Towers are on fire, churches turned upside down;
The town hall is in ruins, the strong cut down, destroyed.
Young girls are raped; wherever we turn our gaze,

Fire, plague, and death pierce heart and spirit through.
Here, town and ramparts run with ever-fresh streams of blood.
It's three times six years now, since our mighty river's flow
Was blocked almost by corpses, just barely trickling through.
Yet, I pass over in silence something more terrible than death,
More desperate even than plague, fire and famine;
That so many were bereaved of their soul's treasure too.

(Gryphius, German, 1616–64, tr. I.M.)

[A contemporary of Gryphius, the poet Grimmelshausen, described his astonishment at arriving in Switzerland and finding civilised conditions of a kind he had never experienced in his native Germany, so long had the war been going on:

'There I saw people trading and walking about in peace. The stables were full of cattle, the barnyards were full of chickens, geese, and ducks running about, the streets were safely used by travellers. Taverns were full of people, who sat there enjoying themselves. There was no fear of an enemy, no concern of plunder, and no anxiousness about losing property or life. Everyone lived securely beneath his vine or fig tree, and indeed, measured against German countries, they lived in pure voluptiousness and joy. I took the country for an earthly paradise.'

This truly sounds like civilisation. The simplicity of the scene is a reminder that most of the developments necessary for civilisation were made in Neolithic times, between seven and twelve thousand years ago: cultivation of crops, herding of animals, the making of tools, the control of fire, the development of language, the accumulation and handing on of knowledge, and the formation of cities. Add to these the wheel and writing, and all that's needed for the establishment of a permanent civilisation is a reform of human nature!

Civilisation is essentially the attempt to rise out of the dirt and hard constraints of life within nature. Freed somewhat from these constraints, we have time to enjoy ourselves and create things of which we feel proud – whether homes, families, pastimes, objects of art or beauty, or a society well-ordered but free enough so that most of its individuals may flourish. Time to think is a luxurious pleasure, if we are not harried by anxiety or guilt. The next fourteen poems are about the pursuit of civilised pleasures which are not destructive, either to humanity or to the planet.]

It's a pleasure
When, rising in the morning,
I go outside and
Find that a flower has bloomed
That was not there yesterday.

It's a pleasure
When, a most infrequent treat,
We've fish for dinner
And my children cry with joy
'Yum-yum!' and gobble it down.

It's a pleasure
When, without receiving help,
I can understand
The meaning of a volume
Reputed most difficult.

(Tachibana Akemi, Japanese, 1812–68, tr. Donald Keene.)

Sitting in silence
and looking wise
isn't half as good
as drinking wine
and making a riotous shouting!

(Otomo no Tabito, Japanese, 665–731, tr. I.M. after A. Waley.)

Let me go home now;
The feast can go on without me;
My child may be crying,
And my patient wife
Waiting for me to come home!

(Yamanoue Okura, Japanese, c. 660–733, tr. I.M.)

[By delighting in beauty we imitate both Nature and God. In the
next poem, the poet reflects on the beauty of his patron's house,
then compares it humourously with the squalor of his own.]

Your house gleams with calm light,
its ceilings brightly painted in the new fashion,
the many colours gaily reflect at the dome
and several designs gleam in their beauty.
The garden of the Hesperides does not bloom in this way;
it wilts quickly, suddenly losing its flowers,
but the violets and lovely roses that belong to you
are fastened to the dome, their permanent setting;
and so your shades of bramble-purple and hyacinth
have no fear of the south wind's bluster or gusts.
My house is black with unending night,
inside there is no gleam of light or good cheer.
It lacks beautiful and elegant tapestries;
no door-key or bar keeps it in order,
nor does the ceiling gleam, adorned with pictures;
soot sticks to the high dome.
If Neptune ever teems down in black showers
it just increases the thick coating on my home;
when the east wind bellows wildly
it strikes this old hall and makes it tremble.
Like the foul mansion of Cacus
or the dark Labyrinth
which resembled blackest night
is my home – alas what a monstrous injustice! –
as it stands shuddering, dark, and covered with a black pall,
for even in the light of day an appearance of night

lies heavy on these decrepit buildings.
Believe you me, this is not a fitting home for scholars
who love the boon of bright light;
it is a house suitable for bats,
an ideal property for a pack of moles.
O Lantbert, gather all your sightless and blind men,
I pray, and send them here,
and let this dark house thrive forever and ever
under its proper name of Home For The Blind!
But now, exalted father and splendid shepherd,
help me in these troubles, o dear and honoured one,
kindly speak the word so that this gloomy house,
devoid of daylight, may be redecorated.
Let there be a panelled ceiling, finely painted,
a new door-key and a strong lock;
then let there be blue and green windows,
into which Phoebus can shine his welcome rays,
and with his lovely gleam, famous bishop, illumine
your scholars who love the sunshine.
So, too, lord may you be granted
a beautiful, fine and radiant place in the heights of heaven,
decorated by the Almighty's hand,
in the happy city of Jerusalem.

(Sedulius Scotus, Irish, fl. 848–874; tr. from Latin by Peter Godman.)

[There are many poems on the pleasures of gardens, which can represent to perfection the harmony that's possible between human beings and nature.]

Planting Flowers on the Eastern Embankment

I took money and bought flowering trees
And planted them out on the bank to the east of the Keep.
I simply bought whatever had most blooms,
Not caring whether peach, apricot, or plum.
A hundred fruits, all mixed up together;
A thousand branches, flowering in due rotation.

Each has its season coming early or late;
But to all alike the fertile soil is kind.
The red flowers hang like a heavy mist;
The white flowers gleam like a fall of snow.
The wandering bees cannot bear to leave them;
The sweet birds also come there to roost.
In front there flows an ever-running stream;
Beneath, there is built a little flat terrace.
Sometimes, I sweep the flagstones of the terrrace;
Sometimes, in the wind, I raise my cup and drink.
The flower-branches screen my head from the sun;
The flower-buds fall down in my lap.
Alone drinking, alone singing my songs,
I do not notice the moon is level with the steps.
The people of Pa do not care for flowers;
All the spring no one has come to look.
But their Governor-General, alone with his cup of wine,
Sits till evening, and will not move from the place!

(Po Chu-I, Chinese, 772–846, tr. Arthur Waley.)

[The hard work of gardening is not mentioned in the last poem.
The next, written by a mediaeval monk, celebrates the labour as
well as the results; it is the introduction to a much longer poem,
which goes on to celebrate the plants of the medieval garden.]

A quiet life has many rewards: not least of these
Is the joy that comes to him who devotes himself to the art   4
They knew at Paestum, and learns the ancient skill of obscene
Priapus – the joy that comes of devoting himself to a garden.
For whatever the land you possess, whether it be where sand
And gravel lie barren and dead, or where fruits grow heavy
In rich moist ground; whether high on a steep hillside,
Easy ground in the plain or rough among sloping valleys –
Wherever it is, your land cannot fail to produce
Its native plants. If you do not let laziness clog
Your labour, if you do not insult with misguided efforts

---

4 He was cursed with a permanent erection.

The gardener's multifarious wealth, and if you do not
Refuse to harden or dirty your hands in the open air
Or to spread whole baskets of dung on the sun-parched soil -
Then, you may rest assured, your soil will not fail you.
This I have learned not only from common opinion
And searching about in old books, but from experience -
Experience of hard work and sacrifice of many days
When I might have rested, but chose instead to labour.

(Strabo, German, 808–849, tr. from Latin by Raef Payne.)

[On imagination, and the reading of books:]

On First Looking into Chapman's Homer

Much have I travell'd in the realms of gold
And many goodly states and kingdoms seen;
Round many western islands have I been
Which bards in fealty to Apollo hold.
Oft of one wide expanse had I been told
That deep-brow'd Homer ruled as his demesne:
Yet did I never breathe its pure serene
Till I heard Chapman speak out loud and bold:

Then felt I like some watcher of the skies
When a new planet swims into his ken;
Or like stout Cortez when with eagle eyes
He stared at the Pacific – and all his men
Look'd at each other with a wild surmise -
Silent, upon a peak in Darien. [5]

(John Keats, English, 1795–1821.)

[Elsewhere in this book are 'Heraclitus' on the pleasure of talk and
'Pangur Ban' on the pleasure of learning. The next poem

[5] The Isthmus of Panama, between Central and South America.

concerns the enjoyment of music. Salinas was a blind organist, musical theorist and collector of folk-songs, who lived in Spain from 1513 to 1590. Sadly, none of his music survives.]

Ode to Salinas

The air grows calm, is
Bathed in loveliness and unusual light,
Salinas, when your music sounds
Extreme in its refinement
Under your skilled well-governed hand.

At this divine sound,
My soul, from cowering in oblivion,
Arises to regain
A sense and memory of
The glory of its first exalted state.

And, as it greets itself,
In destiny and thoughts it now grows stronger;
Estranged is the gold
Which the blind crowd adores
So fleeting and so fickle in its beauty.

Through and out of air
It soars, arriving at the highest sphere,
And there it hears another
Mode imperishable,
The music that is origin of all.

There it sees the great
Master, industrious on a zither immense,
Produce with adept motion
The sacred harmony
By which the eternal temple is sustained.

And now my soul, composed
Of numbers that agree, sends in reply
Consonant music;
Both, insistently,
Combine to make the softest harmony.

Here my soul navigates
Upon a sea of gentleness until
At last it drowns,
Its senses deaf
To any outside mishap or occurrence.

Oh blessed unawareness!
Oh death that gives us life! Oh sweet oblivion!
Would it but last, that I
Might never be thrust back
To this base and vile way of being!

To this good I call you,
You glory of Apollo's sacred choir -
My friends, whom I love
And treasure above all -
For everything but this is lamentation.

Play on, play on, Salinas!
Your music sound for ever in my ears!
To divine goodness it
Awakens my senses,
Leaving them deaf to all other things.

(Luis de Leon, Spanish, ?1527–1591, tr. I. M.)

[The pleasures of living in the country are celebrated in many poems. In the next two, the poet has been disappointed by his reception in the city and is making the best of things in the country.]

Drinking Wine; Two Poems

1. In the quiet of the morning I heard a knock at my door;
   I threw on my clothes and opened it myself.
   I asked who it was who had come so early to see me;
   He said he was a peasant, coming with good intent.
   He brought with him a full flagon of wine,
   Believing my household had fallen on evil days.
   'You live in rags under a thatched roof
   And seem to have no desire for a better lot.
   The rest of mankind have all the same ambitions;
   You too must learn to wallow in their mire.'
   'Old man, I am impressed by what you say,
   But my soul is not fashioned like other men's.
   To drive in their rut I might perhaps learn;
   To be untrue to myself could only lead to muddle.
   Let us drink and enjoy together the wine you have brought;
   For my course is set now and cannot be altered.'

2. I built my hut in a zone of human habitation,
   Yet near me there sounds no noise of horse or coach.
   Would you know how that is possible?
   A heart that is distant creates a wilderness round it.
   I pluck chrysanthemums under the eastern hedge,
   Then gaze long at the distant hills.
   The mountain air is fresh at dusk of day;
   The flying birds two by two return.
   In these things there lies a deep meaning;
   Yet when we would express it, words suddenly fail us.

(Tao Yuan Ming, Chinese, 372–427, tr. Arthur Waley.)

[A walk was a cure for depression long before shopping sprees were invented.]

Third Day of the Third Month, Rain: Written to Dispel My Depression

1. I go out the door; it's raining, but I can't go back now,
   so I borrow someone's bamboo hat to wear for a while.
   Spring has tinted ten thousand leaves, and I didn't even know;
   the clouds have taken a thousand mountains and swept them away.

2. I look for flowers in the village
   but they hide from me on purpose;
   and even when I find them, they only sadden me.
   It would be better to lie down
   and listen to the rain
   in the spring mountains -
   a quick downpour, then a few scattered drops.

3. As spring dies, the scenes grow more beautiful:
   the poet will remember them for the rest of his life.
   Level fields overflowing with green -
   wheat in every village;
   soft waters reflecting red -
   flowers on every bank.

(Yang Wan-Li, Chinese, 1127–1206, tr. J. Chaves.)

[The next poem concerns the way civilisation affects the way we enjoy the world around us. The story behind the poem is this. A Chinese king, feeling guilty at the enormous gap in wealth between himself and his subjects, reflects aloud that at least the delightful breeze he is enjoying can be enjoyed by his subjects. A courtier, the poet Sung Yu, doesn't let the Emperor get away with such sloppy thinking. Whether we enjoy the wind, he says, depends on where we are when it's blowing.]

"The wind is born from the land
And springs up in the tips of the green duckweed.
It insinuates itself into the valleys
And rages in the canyon mouth,

Skirts the corners of Mount T'ai
And dances beneath the pines and cedars.
Swiftly it flies, whistling and wailing;
Fiercely it splutters its anger.
It crashes with a voice like thunder,
Whirls and tumbles in confusion,
Shaking rocks, striking trees,
Blasting the tangled forest.
Then, when its force is almost spent,
It wavers and disperses,
Thrusting into crevices and rattling door latches.
Clean and clear
It scatters and rolls away.
Thus it is that this cool, fresh hero wind,
Leaping and bounding up and down,
Climbs over the high wall
And enters deep into palace halls.
With a puff of breath it shakes the leaves and flowers,
Wanders among the cassia and pepper trees,
Or soars over the swift waters.
It buffets the mallow flower,
Sweeps the angelica, touches the spikenard,
Glides over the sweet lichens and lights on willow shoots,
Rambling over the hills
And their scattered host of fragrant flowers.
After this, it wanders round the courtyard,
Ascends the jade hall in the north,
Clambers over gauze curtains,
Passes through the inner apartments,
And so becomes Your Majesty's wind.
When this wind blows on a man,
At once he feels a chill run through him,
And he sighs at its cool freshness.
Clear and gentle,
It cures sickness, dispels drunkenness,
Sharpens the eyes and ears,
Relaxes the body and brings benefit to men.
This is what is called the hero wind of Your Majesty."

"How well you have described it" said the king. "But now may
I hear about the wind of the common people?" And Sung Yu
replied:

"The wind of the common people
Comes whirling from the lanes and alleys,
Poking in the rubbish, stirring up the dust,
Fretting and worrying its way along,
It creeps into holes and knocks on doors,
Scatters sand, blows ashes about,
Muddles in dirt and tosses up bits of filth.
It sidles through hovel windows
And slips into cottage rooms.
When this wind blows on a man,
At once he feels confused and downcast.
Pounded by heat, smothered in dampness,
His heart grows sick and heavy,
And he falls ill and breaks out in a fever.
Where it brushes his lips, sores appear;
It strikes his eyes with blindness.
He stammers and cries out,
Not knowing if he is dead or alive.
That is what is called the lowly wind of the common people."

(Sung Yu, Chinese, 3rd c. B.C., tr. Burton Watson.)

[Religious buildings, open to all, made inspiring beauty available
to most of the population. The creation of beauty is in itself an act
of offering and devotion. As God is more and more abolished we
see fewer and fewer objects of beauty on earth. The next poem
praises the lavishing of time and wealth on the creation of a
wonderful building; such spending, the poet says, is not 'vain
expense'. 'Tax with', in the first line, has the same meaning as
'accuse of'.]

Tax not the royal Saint with vain expense,
With ill-matched aims the Architect who planned –

Albeit labouring for a scanty band
Of white-robed Scholars only – this immense
And glorious Work of fine intelligence!
Give all thou canst; high Heaven rejects the lore
Of nicely calculated less or more;
So deemed the man who fashioned for the sense
These lofty pillars, spread that branching roof
Self-poised, and scooped into ten thousand cells,
Where light and shade repose, where music dwells
Lingering – and wandering on as loth to die;
Like thoughts whose very sweetness yieldeth proof
That they were born for immortality.

(William Wordsworth, English, 1770–1850.)

[However, too much civilisation can lose for us the intense joy
that comes from living close to Nature.]

O warmth of summer
gliding over the land in waves!
Not a gust of wind,
not a cloud –
And in the mountains,
the belling reindeer,
the sweet reindeer
in the bluish distance!
O, how it pulls me,
O, how it fills me with delight!
Sobbing with emotion,
I lie down on the earth.

(Anon., Eskimo, 1920's, tr. Rasmussen and Lowenstein.)

Clearing the Fields

We clear the grasses and trees,
We plough and carve the land,

Two thousand men and women scrabbling weeds
Along the low wet lands, along the dyke walls.
The masters, the eldest sons,
The labourers, the hired servants,
They mark out the fields, they ply their colters,
Overflowing food baskets are brought to them,
They gaze on their fair wives
And press close to them.
They have sharp ploughshares,
They have set to work on the south acres,
They sow the many kinds of grain.
Each seed holds a moist germ;
Splendidly, splendidly the young grain shoots forth,
Sleekly, sleekly the young plants rise,
Tenderly, tenderly comes the young grain.
Thousands of weeders scrabbling among the weeds!
Host upon host of reapers!
Close-huddled stooks arranged in due order!
Myriads, many hundred thousands and millions of grains!
From them come wine and sweet liquor,
Offering to the ancestors, the male and the female,
In fulfilment of sacrifices.
So glory shall come to the land.
They will have a sharp smell of pepper,
They will give comfort to the aged.
It is not only here that it is so,
It is not only now that it is so:
But in most ancient times ever and ever.

(Anon, Chinese, from 'Book of Songs', 7th century B.C., tr. Payne.)

[Tribal peoples live for the most part fairly peacefully, with laws
and customs favouring stability and continuity. Unless they are
nomadic, their prosperity depends on their looking after the land
and not abusing it. The myth of Eden is about leaving primitive
conditions for the gains and sacrifices of civilisation (not for
nothing is New York called the Big Apple).

The 'primitive' peoples of the world are gradually being swallowed up in Western civilisation. We and our pollution are destroying their environments, and so also their ways of life. In many cases they have no option but to join our jamboree. Some peoples hold out against the process as best they can, but find themselves gradually disinherited. Those that join in all too often find the fruits of their labour taken away from them to be enjoyed elsewhere.

Civilisation draws people and resources to its cities, draining outlying communities of human and material resources. Industrialisation demands a substantial workforce that will do repetitive work for low pay. Then, as technology swallows up their jobs, many are out of work. The next poem tells of the anger which builds up in people whose dream is never realised.]

Harlem

What happens to a dream deferred?

Does it dry up
like a raisin in the sun?
Or fester like a sore –
And then run?
Does it stink like rotten meat?
Or crust and sugar over –
like a syrupy sweet?

Maybe it just sags
like a heavy load.

Or does it explode?

(Langston Hughes, American, 1902–1967.)

[Forugh Farrokhzad took the garden as a metaphor for civilisation, which needs care and thought in its cultivation. Her poem of a neglected garden prophesies violence for a society that abandons looking after itself.]

I Pity the Garden

No one cares about the flowers
No one cares about the fish
No one wants
to believe the garden's dying
the garden's heart bloating beneath the sun
the garden's mind slowly slowly
being drained of its green memories
And it's as though the garden's feelings
are a solitary something decaying in the garden's solitude.

The courtyard of our house is lonely
the courtyard of our house
yawns
waiting for some unknown cloud to rain
and the pool of our house is empty
From the treetops, innocent little stars
fall to earth
and the sound of coughing comes at night
through the wan windows of the fishes' house
The courtyard of our house is lonely

Father says
" It's beyond me now
It's beyond me now
I lugged my load
and did my work"
And sits in his room from sunup to sundown
reading either the old epic poems
or the *History of Histories*
Father says to Mother
"To hell with the birds and the fish
What do I care
if there's a garden or not
when I'm dead
My pension's good enough for me"

All her life
Mother's been a prayer rug
spread at the gate of hell's terrors
Mother hunts for sin's footprints
under everything
and believes the garden's been fouled
by some sin's blaspheming
Mother prays all day long
Mother sins naturally
and blows[6] on all the flowers
and blows on all the fish
and blows on herself
Mother awaits the coming of heaven
and the descent of forgiveness

My brother calls the garden a graveyard
My brother laughs at the rioting weeds
and counts the corpses of the fish
rotting away to atoms
beneath the water's turbid skin
My brother's addicted to philosophy
My brother thinks the garden's healed
by its destruction
He gets drunk
and beats his fists on doors and walls
and mumbles
about his aches and tired hopelessness
He takes his pessimism out
to the street and the bazaar
along with his I.D. and pocket calendar and handkerchief
                    and lighter and fountain pen
And his pessimism's
so tiny he loses it each night
in the crowd at the bar

And my sister, once a friend to flowers
who used to gather them silently, lovingly
with her heart's simple words

---

[6] To bless them.

when Mother had punished her
and treat the family of fish
with tidbits and the sun too now and then -
she's in her house across town
She's in her phony house
with her phony goldfish
and in her phony husband's lovenest
singing phony songs
beneath the branches of phony apple trees
and making real children
She
showers herself with eau de cologne
whenever she visits us
and smudges the hem of her skirt with the garden's
poverty
Every time she visits us she's
pregnant

The courtyard of our house is lonely
The courtyard of our house is lonely
All day long
sounds of shattering
and explosions can be heard
Instead of flowers our neighbours are planting
machine guns and mortars in their garden grounds
Our neighbours are covering
their tiled pools
and the tiled pools
becoming ammunition caches
without ever being asked
And the kids on our street
have loaded their briefcases
with little bombs
The courtyard of our house feels sick
I fear the time
that is heartless
I fear the image of all these futile hands
and the sight of all these strange faces
I'm lonely as a pupil

who's crazy
about her geometry class
I imagine that the garden could be taken to the hospital
I imagine...
I imagine...
I imagine...
And the garden's heart lies bloating beneath the sun
and the garden's mind is slowly slowly
drained of its green memories

(Forugh Farrokhzhad, Persian, 1934–67, tr. J. Kessler and A. Banani.)

[We fill our immediate surroundings with roads and ugly architecture, then destroy what's left of the world by crowding it out
as tourists. If we looked after our own back yards, streets, towns,
cities and countrysides, and made sure they were beautiful, we
wouldn't have such a relentless appetite for travel. Human beings
and beauty are not incompatible. We lived on the earth for
hundreds of thousands of years before we began turning it into a
giant cess-pool afloat with islands of garbage.

   The next two poems are about love of native place.]

Happy is he who, like Ulysses, has made a good journey
Or like that other who won the golden fleece,
And then returned, used well by the world and wise,
To live among his kin and thereby end his days!

When will I see again, alas! my little village,
Smoke rising from its chimneys, and in what season
Will I see again the plot round my poor house
Which is a province to me, and much else besides?

More pleasing to me is the abode built by my forebears
Than Roman palaces with their brilliant facades;
More than by hard marble I'm pleased by the fineness of slate,

More by my Gaulish Loire than by the Latin Tiber,
More by my little Lire than by the Palatine Hill;
And more than sea air, I love the softness of Anjou.

(Joachim du Bellay, French, 1522–60, tr. I.M.)

In the month of June the grass grows high
And round my cottage thick-leaved branches sway.
There is not a bird but delights in the place where it rests:
And I too – love my thatched cottage.
I have done my ploughing:
I have sown my seed.
Again I have time to sit and read my books.
In the narrow lane there are no deep ruts:
Often my friends' carriages turn back.
In high spirits I pour out my spring wine
And pluck the lettuce growing in my garden.
A gentle rain comes stealing from the east
And a sweet wind bears it company.
My thoughts float idly over the story of the King of Chou,
My eyes wander over the pictures of Hills and Seas.
At a single glance I survey the whole Universe.
He will never be happy, whom such pleasures fail to please!

(Tao Yuan-Ming, aka Tao Ch'ien, Chinese, 372–427, tr. Arthur Waley.)

[The human spirit can survive poverty and hardship, but can it survive affluence and power? The answer is it can, but only by exercising extreme care. In the next poem, Boethius argues that no amount of good fortune can slake greed.]

Rapid blowing stirs up in the sea
   How many grains of sand?
Clear and starry nights allow
   How many stars to shine?
Should in such numbers goods be given
   From fortune's plenteous horn,
Not for a second would humankind
   Stop its misersable moans.
However freely God meets desires –
   Showering spendthrifts in gold,
Adorning the greedy with eminent honours –
   It all seems soon as nothing;
Raging greed devours the gains,
   And opens fresh jaws for more.

What can rein in headlong greed
   And keep it in reasonable bounds?
Do floods of gifts, more upon more,
   Just parch the thirst for possession?
People aren't rich who anxiously sigh
   And think they're in need of more.

(Boethius, Roman, c.480–524, tr. from Latin by I.M.)

[Poverty and hardship often make people generous even with the little they have. Mandelstam wrote joyous poetry in utter destitution, knowing the State would soon destroy him.]

Still I have not died, and still am not alone,
while with my beggarwoman friend
I take my pleasure from the grandeur of the plain
and from its gloom, its hunger and its hurricanes.

In splendid poverty, luxurious beggardom
I live alone – both peaceful and resigned –
blessed are those days and nights
and blameless is the sweetly sounding work.

Unhappy the man who like his shadow
quivers at a bark, is scythed down by the wind,
and poor the man who, half alive himself,
from a shadow begs for charity.

(Osip Mandelstam, Russian, 1891–1938, tr. D. McDuff.)

[If we never feel intense need, we never feel intense satisfaction. But the option of comfort is hard to resist. Who would voluntarily undergo the hunger of the children in the next poem – or wish the experience on their own children?]

The Transfixed

Black in the snow and in the fog
Against a vent all glowing and warm
Their backsides in a circle

Five little urchins squat – pitiful! –
Watching the baker as he makes
His bread, heavy and white.

They watch the strong white arm knead
The grey dough, then put it in to bake
In the bright hole.

They listen as the good bread cooks.
The baker, with his fat smile,
Hums an old tune.

Huddled together, none of them budge
In the air from the glowing red vent
Hot like a breast.

When, for some midnight breakfast,
Round and bulging like a brioche
The bread comes out

When, under black and smoky beams,
The fragrant crusts hiss, singing
Along with the house-crickets,

How the warm hole breathes life!
Their soul is in such delight
Underneath the rags

That suddenly they're feeling life is good,
Poor little Jesuses, full of frost,
And there they stay

Pressing small and pink noses
Against the trellis, mumbling things
In between the holes,

Stupefied, and saying their prayer,
Bent over towards the lights of
Heaven re-opened before them,

Straining so much their trousers rip
And their shirt tails flutter free
In the winter wind.

(Artur Rimbaud, French, 1854–91, tr. I.M.)

[With so much technology at our disposal it should be possible to
build a civilisation that can be shared by all. Are we experiencing
the teething pains of a new phase in civilisation, or are we
engaged in a final orgy of feasting and violence at the expense of a
dying Earth? Time alone will give us the answer.

We should proceed with more caution. Reckless and cynical
arrogance will only lead to our own destruction. The poet
Ma'arri wrote almost a thousand years ago:]

We laughed; our laughing betrayed scorn.
People on this earth should live in fear.
When men shake hands with time, time crushes
Them like tumblers; little pieces of glass.

(Ma'arri, Arabic (Syrian), 973–1057, tr. al-Udhari and Wightman.)

[Once on a bandwagon, it's hard to get off. Human nature takes
the blame for squandering the potential which technology lays
before us. Restraint and sacrifice are out; glimmers of hope are
few in the prevailing darkness.]

God help us, we have sold our souls, all that was best,
To an enterprise in the hands of the Receiver.
We've no dividends, or rights, for the price we paid.
Yet should our wills choose between this corrupt business
And a paradise to come, rest assured they'd want

The world we have now.

(Ma'arri, Arabic (Syrian), 973–1057, tr. al-Udhari and Wightman.)

[Holderlin provides a more optimistic view of human life. It's a poem written in his madness, which explains the date and signature attached.]

People find themselves on this world to live
As the years are, as the times strive higher;
So, as change rolls on, a lot of truth is left.
Permanence enters into the different years;
Perfection joins to life in such a way
That life accomodates people's high-aimed striving.

Humbly, Scardanelli.   17 May 1748.

(Holderlin, German, 1770–1843, tr. I.M.)

6. Birds, Beasts, Blossoms, Bugs, Trees . . . and People

[A miscellany of poems, mostly without commentary, illustrating some of the different ways we experience our fellow living creatures.]

A Song

A widow bird sat mourning for her love
  Upon a wintry bough;
The frozen wind crept on above,
  The freezing stream below.

There was no leaf upon the forest bare,
  No flower upon the ground,
And little motion in the air
  Except the mill-wheel's sound.

(P.B. Shelley, English, 1792–1822.)

Sparrows

Snow in hair, winter in my bones,
The eyes weary, loyal, I greet
The sparrows like friends, this gang
That, in March, is already in my yard.
In a wide band, chirping, clamorous
They come and (hop!) are scattered
Like grain on the thawing snow:
Then call – and they are gone.
Longingly, the eyes follow. My heart wakens.

I recall my friends: my crowd
So noisy, like the sparrows in their dance.
They could not reach the joy of winter.
In summer, they left – before harvest,
The joy of their summer unable to sustain them.

(Mani Leib, Yiddish, 1883–1953, tr. Nathan Helper.)

The Twa Corbies

As I was walking all alane   two crows or ravens
I heard twa corbies making a mane
The tane unto the t'ither did say   one to the other
'Where shall we gang and dine this day?'   go

'– In behint yon auld fail dyke   turf wall
I wot there lies a new-slain knight;
And naebody kens that he lies there   knows
But his hawk, his hound, and his lady fair.

'His hound is to the hunting gane,
His hawk to fetch the wild-fowl hame
His lady's ta'en anither mate,
So we may mak our dinner sweet.

'Ye'll sit on his white hause-bane   neck-bone
And I'll pike out his bonny blue e'en: pick eyes
Wi ae lock o' his gowden hair   one
We'll theek our nest when it grows bare.   thatch

'Mony a one for him maks mone,   makes moan
But nane shall ken whar he is gane;
O'er his white bones, when they are bare,
The wind sall blaw for evermair.'

(Anon, Scottish Ballad.)

To a Goldfinch

O crimson zither who, at break of day,
Trilling laments for your beloved spouse,
And pasturing on the amber of the rose,
Tints with coral the tip of your golden beak.

Sweet golden linnet, sad small bird,
As soon as you looked out on lovely dawn,
At the first improvised note of your song
Death entered your domain and stilled your voice.

There is in life no certainty of dying;
Your own voice led the hunter to you,
Making sure his shot released was good.

Oh Fortune most desired, and yet most feared!
Who would think, accomplice in your dying
Would be your own life, not keeping silence?

(Juana de Asbaje, Mexican, 1651–95, tr. I.M.)

Ode to Salted Mutton Birds

Mutton birds! I like 'em I'll eat 'em any way.
Skin 'em 'n braise 'em and serve 'em on a tray.
Stuff 'em 'n bake 'em, and serve 'em with sauce.
Or put 'em over the coals, on a spit of course.
I like 'em grilled, I like 'em fried.
And there's plenty of other ways I've tried.
But salted birds, just scar and boil.
With carrots, spuds and swedes as well.
It's the best way known to man or beast
To eat mutton birds and have a feast.

(Jim Everett, Aboriginal Australian, b. 1942.)

The Caged Bird

This bird was happy once in the high trees.
You cage it in your cellar, bring it seed,
Honey to sip, all that its heart can need
Or human love can think of: till it sees,
Leaping too high within its narrow room
The old familiar shadow of the leaves,
And spurns the seed with tiny desperate claws.
Naught but the woods despairing pleads,
The woods, the woods again, it grieves, it grieves.

(Boethius, Roman, c. 480–524; tr. from Latin by Helen Waddell.)

Night Herons

It was after a day's rain:
the street facing the west
was lit with growing yellow;
the black road gleamed.

First one child looked and saw
and told another.
Face after face, the windows
flowered with eyes.

It was like a long fuse lighted,
the news travelling.
No one called out loudly;
everyone said "Hush."

the light deepened; the wet road
answered in daffodil colours,
and down its centre
walked the two tall herons.

Stranger than wild birds, even,
what happened on those faces:
suddenly believing in something,
they smiled and opened.

Children thought of fountains,
circuses, swans feeding:
women remembered words
spoken when they were young.

Everyone said "Hush;"
no one spoke loudly;
but suddenly the herons
rose and were gone. The light faded.

(Judith Wright, Australian, b. 1915.)

A Bird, Just a Bird

"What fragrance," the bird said, "what sunlight, oh
Spring's come
and I'll go find my mate."

Off the porch sill flew
the bird, flitting like some messenger, and was gone

A little bird
a thoughtless bird
a bird who never reads the news
a bird free from debt
a bird unacquainted with us

The bird flew through the air
above the red lights
unaware in the heights
and deliriously living
moments of blue

The bird was oh, just a bird

(Farogh Farrokhzad, Persian, 1934–67; tr. Kessler and Banani.)

The Song of the Savage Tiger

Dark are the mountain forests to north and south
The savage tiger prowls in daylight around the village
At dusk he appears in person on the highways looking for food
And the mountain deer and antelope hold their breath
Yearly he bears his offspring in the deserted valleys
Male and female, big and small, there's no telling
Near his mountain lair is a little village
And often from the farmers there he'll steal a newborn calf
The local youths don't dare to shoot at him
In the forest helplessly they stare at his tracks.

(Zhang Ji, Chinese, 768–830, tr. John Scott.)

What She Said (to her friend)

The colours on the elephant's body
shine, as he grazes
with his herd
on bamboo shoots,
breaking down the branches;
then, in thirst,
he goes to a watering place,
kills a crouching tiger
poised for attack.
Pouring rains
clean the tusks, wash down the blood on their tips,
as he walks slowly along slopes
of jagged rock.
He's arrogant
after finishing off a vicious enemy,
and with six-legged bees making lute-music
over the juices of his lust
he mounts his female,
then goes to sleep
in our man's banana groves.

Friend,
  comforting me once, you said lovingly,
  "The man is just right
  for your rank and nature."
Sweet words those, bless you,
they've come true:
  garlands smell on him
like nectar to people who crave it,
  his chest's embrace so tight
there's no place
  even for the waist of a bee,
and love
  is tireless still
  as on the very first day.

(Kapilar, Tamil, ?1stC. A.D., tr. A.K. Ramanujan.)

On Seeing a Wounded Hare Limp by me, which a Fellow had just shot at

Inhuman man! curse on thy barb'rous art,
  And blasted be thy murder-aiming eye;
  May pity never soothe thee with a sigh,
Nor pleasure glad thy cruel heart!

Go live, poor wanderer of the wood and field,
  The bitter little that of life remains!
  No more the thickening brakes and verdant plains
To thee shall home, or food, or pasture yield.

Seek, mangled wretch, some place of wonted rest,
  No more of rest, but now thy dying bed!
  The sheltering rushes whistling o'er thy head,
The cold earth with thy bloody bosom prest.

Oft as by winding Nith I musing, wait
The sober eve, or hail the cheerful dawn,
I'll miss thee sporting o'er the dewy lawn,
And curse the ruffian's aim, and mourn thy hapless fate.

(Robert Burns, Scottish, 1759–1796.)

Putu

It was a long-drawn Chaitra noon;
the earth was thirsty, burnt by the day.
Suddenly I heard someone calling
somewhere outside, 'Puturani come!'
The river-bank's deserted in the midday,
so the voice of affection made me curious.
Closing my book, I slowly got up,
opened the door a little and looked outside.
A huge buffalo, covered in mud,
tender-eyed, was standing on the bank.
A young man was in the water, calling her
to give her a bath, 'Puturani, come!'
When I saw the young man and his Puturani,
gentle tears mingled with my smiles.

(Rabindranath Tagore, 1861–1941, Bengali, tr. Ketaki Kushari Dyson.)

The Death and Dying Words of Poor Mailie

(the author's only pet ewe – an unco mournfu' tale)

As Mailie, an' her lambs thegither,	together
Was ae day nibblin on the tether,	one
Upon her cloot she coost a hitch,	hoof; looped; knot
An' owre she warsl'd in the ditch:	floundered
There, groanin, dying, she did lie,	
When Hughoc he came doytin by.	doddering

Wi' glowrin een, an' lifted han's   *staring eyes*
Poor Hughoc like a statue stan's;
He saw her days were near-hand ended,
But, wae's my heart! he nae could mend it!   *woe's*
He gaped wide, but naething spak.
At length poor Mailie silence brak: -

'O thou, whase lamentable face
Appears to mourn my woefu' case!
My dying words attentive hear,
An' bear them to my Master dear.

'Tell him, if e'er again he keep   *have*
As muckle gear as buy a sheep –   *enough money*
O, bid him never tie them mair,
Wi' wicked strings o' hemp or hair!
But ca' them out to park or hill,   *drive*
An' let them wander at their will:
So may his flock increase, an' grow
To scores o' lambs, an' packs o' woo'!   *wool*

'Tell him, he was a Master kin',   *kind*
An' ay was guid to me an' mine;   *always*
An' now my dying charge I gie him,
My helpless lambs, I trust them wi' him.

'O, bid him save their harmless lives,
Frae dogs, an' tods, an butchers' knives!   *foxes*
But gie them good cow-milk their fill,   *give*
Till they be fit to fend themsel;   *look after*
An' tent them duly, e'en an' morn,   *tend*
Wi' teats o' hay an' ripps o' corn.   *bits; handfuls*

'An' may they never learn the gaets,   *bad ways*
Of ither vile, wanrestfu' pets –   *restless*
To slink thro' slaps, an' reave an' steal,   *holes in the hedge; rob*
At stacks o' pease, or stocks o' kail!   *cabbages*

So may they, like their great forebears,   ancestors
For monie a year come thro' the sheers:
So wives will gie them bits o' bread,
An' bairns greet for them when they're dead.

 'My poor toop-lamb, my son an' heir,
O, bid him breed him up wi' care!
An' if he live to be a beast,
To pit some havins in his breast!   manners
An' warn him – what I winna name –
To stay content wi' yowes at hame;   ewes at home
An' no to rin an wear his cloots,   run; hoofs
Like other menseless, graceless, brutes.   mannerless

 'An' niest, my yowie, silly thing;   next; girl-lamb
Gude keep thee frae a tether string!   God
O, may thou ne'er forgather up,   take up with
Wi' onie blastit, moorland toop;   blasted; ram
But ay keep mind to moop an' mell, always remember to
Wi' sheep o' credit like thysel!   nibble and mate

 'And now, my bairns, wi' my last breath,
I lea'e my blessin' wi' you baith:
An' when you think upo' your mither,
Mind to be kind to ane anither.

 'Now, honest Hughoc, dinna fail,
To tell my master a' my tale;
An' bid him burn this cursed tether,
An' for thy pains thou'se get my blether.' bladder

 This said, poor Mailie turn'd her head,
An' clos'd her een amang the dead!

(Robert Burns, Scottish, 1759–96.)

The Man Who Encountered a Bear

Rumbling down the slope
something blackly black came sliding along
poised on its haunches front paws raised....
A bear! The moment I realized it
he tumbled sideways into the cover of some bamboo bushes
- - - - - I'd no sooner thought he was gone than I saw him
again scurrying away from me up the mountain trail

I had set out walking again
Resolved not to look back
I moved deliberately
but told myself I didn't need to walk so calculatedly slow
I took a cigarette from my pocket
finally found a match and lit up
Half a kilometer down the mountain I met a woodcutter
He badgered me about my pale face
'A bear!' I told him
'Frightening?' After consideration I replied
'It was certainly uncanny'

Indeed no deception there
Quite an eerie sensation
When the beast looked at me with those eyes
innocent yet burning brightly deep within
I immediately sensed reality fade
No no not exactly I sensed rather that
Time from an entirely other dimension
had crossed the Time where I'd existed
        in which I continue to exist
an unknown time breathing and pulsing wildly like the wind
Unexpectedly absolutely unexpectedly
I stood at their intersection

Instantly the mountain stream stood still
In response to the hush the forest the grass the earth the rocks
briefly echoed a shriek
resounding even now within my head

(Maruyama Kaoru, Japanese, 1899–1974, tr. Robert Epp.)

Untitled

Today I feel bearish
I've just climbed out of
A stream with a jerking
Trout in my paw

Anyone who messes with
Me today will be hugged
And dispatched

(Ishmael Reed, American, contemporary.)

Song of the Lemming

(On a cold winter's day, a little lemming came out of his
warm hole. He looked about him, shivered, shook himself
and sang:)

The sky,
like a vast belly,
arches itself
around my burrow.
The air is clear,
no clouds in sight:
icy weather! Aiee!
I'm freezing! freezing!

(Anon, Eskimo, written down 1920's, tr. Rasmussen and Löwenstein.)

Is it boiled barley
or love that's making you scrawny,
wife-cat?

(Matsuo Basho, 1644–94, Japanese, tr. I.M.)

Pangur Ban

I and Pangur Ban, my cat,
'Tis a like task we are at;
Hunting mice is his delight,
Hunting words I sit all night.

Better far than praise of men
'Tis to sit with book and pen;
Pangur bears me no ill will,
He too plies his simple skill.

'Tis a merry thing to see
At our tasks how glad are we,
When at home we sit and find
Entertainment to our mind.

Oftentimes a mouse will stray
In the hero Pangur's way;
Oftentimes my keen thought set
Takes a meaning in its net.

'Gainst the wall he sets his eye
Full and fierce and sharp and sly;
'Gainst the wall of knowledge I
All my little wisdom try.

When a mouse darts from its den,
O how glad is Pangur then!
O what gladness do I prove
When I solve the doubts I love!

So in peace our tasks we ply,
Pangur Ban, my cat and I;
In our hearts we find our bliss,
I have mine and he has his.

Practice every day has made
Pangur perfect in his trade;
I get wisdom day and night
Turning darkness into light.

(Anon., Irish, 8th C., tr. Robin Flower.)

Giving Rabbit to my Cat Bonnie

Pretty Bonnie, you are quick as a rabbit,
though your tail's longer,
emphasizing suppressed disapproval,
and your ears are shorter – two
radar detectors set on swivels
either side of your skull, and your yawn
is a view of distant white spires – not
the graveyard jaw of this poor dead naked pink

rabbit, who like you, was a
technological success, inheriting a snazzy
fur coat, pepper-and-salt coloured, cosy,
and beautiful fur shoes with spiked toes.
You're both of you
better dressed than I am for most occasions.
Take off your shoes and suits, though,
what have you got?

Look, puss, I've brought us a rabbit for supper.
I bought it in a shop.
The butcher was haggis-shaped, ham-coloured,
not a bit like you. His ears
were two fungi on the slab of his head.
He had a fat, flat face.
But he took your brother rabbit off a hook
and spread him on the counter like a rug,

and slice, slice, scarcely looking,
pulled the lovely skin off like a bag.
So, Bonnie, all I've brought us is food
in this silly pink shape – more like me, really.
I'll make a wine sauce with mushrooms, but will
you want this precious broken heart? this perfect liver?
See, protected in these back pockets, jewels?
Bonnie. What are you eating? Dear Bonnie, consider!

(Anne Stevenson, English, b. 1933.)

[The first of the following two poems was famous for three
centuries before the poet of the second answered it – with another
question.]

1.   Under a broad sky,
          In the peaceful light
          Of a spring day,
          Why so restlessly
          Do blossoms scatter down?

2.   How is it,
          The restless spirit
          Of scattering blossoms
          Itself reveals
          The peaceful colour of spring?

(1st by Tomonori, fl. c. 890; 2nd by Teika, 1162–1241; Japanese, tr. I.M.)

The Sick Rose

O rose thou art sick.
The invisible worm,
That flies in the night
In the howling storm:

Has found out thy bed
Of crimson joy:
And his dark secret love
Does thy life destroy.

(William Blake, English, 1757–1827.)

Half of Life

With yellow pears it hangs
And full of wild roses
The land down into the lake,
You dear and lovely swans;
And drunk from kisses
You dip your heads
In the sacred clarity of water.

Poor me! Where shall I get, when
Winter comes, flowers; and where
The sunshine and
The shadows of the earth?
The walls stand
Speechless and cold; in the wind
Flags are cracking.

(Friedrich Holderlin, German, 1770–1843, tr. I.M.)

The Rain at Night

The good rain knows when to fall,
Coming in this spring to help the seeds,
Choosing to fall by night with a friendly wind,
Silently moistening the whole earth.
Over this silent wilderness the clouds are dark.
The only light shines from a river boat.
Tomorrow morning everything will be red and wet,
And all Chengtu will be covered with blossoming flowers.

(Tu Fu, Chinese, 713–70, tr. Nee Wen-yei.)

1921

Everything has been plundered, betrayed, sold out,
The wing of black death has flashed,
Everything has been devoured by starving anguish,
Why, then, is it so bright?

From fantastic woods near the town
Wafts the scent of cherry blossoms by day,
At night new constellations shine
In the transparent depths of the skies of July -

And how near the miraculous draws
To the dirty, tumbledown huts...
No one, no one knows what it is,
But for centuries we have longed for it.

(Anna Akhmatova, Russian, 1889–1966, tr. Judith Hemschemeyer.)

[Robert Burns delights as he watches the antics of a louse in a smart lady's bonnet in church. Pretending to berate the louse, he comments on the the fragility of our human airs and affectations.]

To a Louse

(On Seeing One on a Lady's Bonnet at Church)

Ha! whare ye gaun, ye crowlin ferlie?	going; crawling marvel
Your impudence protects you sairly,	
I canna say but ye strunt rarely	strut
Owre gauze and lace,	
Tho' faith! I fear ye dine but sparely	
On sic a place.	

Ye ugly, creepin, blastit wonner	wonder
Detested, shunn'd by saunt an' sinner,	

How dare ye set your fit upon her –   *foot*
    Sae fine a lady!
Gae somewhere else and seek your dinner
    On some poor body.

Swith! in some beggar's hauffet squattle: *Away!; temples squat*
There ye may creep, and sprawl, and sprattle,   *scramble*
Wi' other kindred, jumpin' cattle,
    In shoals and nations;
Whare horn nor bane ne'er daur unsettle   *comb; poison*
    Your thick plantations.

Now haud ye there! ye're out o' sight,   *hold on*
Below the fatt'rils, snug an' tight;   *ribbons*
Na, faith ye yet! ye'll no be right,
    Till ye've got on it -
The vera tapmost, tow'ring height
    O' Miss's bonnet.

My sooth! right bauld ye set your nose out,   *bold*
As plump an' grey as onie grozet: *gooseberry*
O for some rank, mercurial rozet,   *smelly; resin*
    Or fell, red smeddum,   *deadly; powder*
I'd gie ye sic a hearty dose o't   *such*
    Wad dress your droddum!   *punish; offence*

I wad na been surprised to spy   *wouldn't have been*
You on an auld wife's flainen toy;   *flannel cap*
Or aiblens some bit duddie boy,   *maybe; ragged*
    On's wyliecoat;   *vest*
But Miss's fine Lunardi! fye!   *balloon bonnet*
    How dare ye do't?

O Jenny, dinna toss your head,
An' set your beauties a' abroad!   *spread; abroad*
Ye little ken what cursed speed
    The blastie's makin'!
Those winks an' finger-ends, I dread,   *pointing fingers*
    Are notice takin'!

O wad some power the giftie gie us   little gift
To see oursels as ithers see us!
It wad frae monie a blunder free us,
        An foolish notion:
What airs in dress an' gait wad lea'e us,
        An' ev'n devotion!

(Robert Burns, Scottish, 1759–96.)

[Written at a mountain temple –]

    Such stillness!
    Into the rocks sink
    Cicadas' cries.

(Matsuo Basho, Japanese, 1644–94, tr. I.M.)

The Fly

    She sat on a willow-trunk
    watching
    part of the battle of Crecy,
    the shouts,
    the gasps, the groans,
    the tramping and the tumbling.

    During the fourteenth charge
    of the French cavalry
    she mated
    with a brown-eyed male fly
    from Vadincourt.

    She rubbed her legs together
    as she sat on a disembowelled horse
    meditating
    on the immortality of flies.

With relief she alighted
on the blue tongue
of the Duke of Clervaux.

When silence settled
and only the whisper of decay
softly circled the bodies

and only
a few arms and legs
still twitched jerkily under the trees,

she began to lay her eggs
on the single eye
of Johann Uhr,
the Royal Armourer.

And thus it was
that she was eaten by a swift
fleeing
from the fires of Estrees.

(Miroslab Holub, Czech, b. 1923, tr. George Theiner.)

Encounter

Knowing too much altogether about beetles:
Latin names, classifications, numbers – six legs, four wings,
thorax, antennae, eyes, segmented abdomen,
I stoop, cut off his light like a thunderstorm
or bird of prey. My interfering finger
chases this hurrying black-clad person,
turns him over. Earthquake. This beetle can scream!
Heaving and bellowing, world turned upside-down,
he begs and curses. Given a stick to fasten
on, he clasps it, click, like a pocket-knife,
a mechanical clown.

After that mutual surprise
suddenly his whole shape turns to blur and buzz,
he's off, wholly at home in air, in life.

I've no idea what beetle is.
Beetle never recognised me. Nevertheless,
it was a double event, a wild encounter.

(Judith Wright, Australian, b. 1915.)

Earwig

Maligned, the earwig. Unlikely he'd take shelter
Within the labyrinth of your ear, still more improbable
He'd penetrate the brain and start to eat it.
He's safer refuges – dry hedgerow kexes
More appetising fare than that grey soggy blob
Inside your skull, that's stuffed with indigestible
And useless information. He'll devour
The pink and overblown hearts of dahlias,
The golden mop-heads of chrysanthemums,
And the last roses that the summer leaves.

(John Heath-Stubbs, English, b. 1918.)

Willow

To understand
A little of how a shaken love
May be sustained

Consider
The giant stillness
Of a willow

After a storm.
This morning it is more than peaceful
But last night that great form

Was tossed and hit
By what seemed to me
A kind of cosmic hate,

An infernal desire
To harass and confuse,
Mangle and bewilder

Each leaf and limb
With every vicious
Stratagem
So that now I cannot grasp
The death of nightmare,
How it has passed away

Or changed to this
Stillness,
This clean peace

That seems unshakeable.
A branch beyond my reach says
'It is well

For me to feel
The transfiguring breath
Of evil

Because yesterday
The roots by which I live
Lodged in apathetic clay.

But for that fury
How should I be rid of the slow death?
How should I know

That what a storm can do
Is to terrify my roots
And make me new?

(Brendan Kennelly, Irish, b. 1936.)

Trees

When the soul, incensed,
Has drunk its fill of insult,
When it has seven times vowed to cease
Battle with the demons -

Not with those who are cast down into the abyss
By showers of fire:
With the earthly lowliness of days,
With human stagnation -

Trees! I come to you! To save myself
From the roar of the marketplace.
How my heart breathes out
Through your flights upward!

Theomachist oak! Striding into battles
With all your roots!
My willow-prophetesses!
Virginal birches!

Elm – fierce Absalom,
Pine – racked
In torture – thou, psalm of my lips:
Bitter taste of rowan.

To you! To the alive-plashing mercury
Of the leaves – what if they are falling!
For the first time to throw open my arms!
To abandon my manuscripts!

A swarm of green reflections
As into applauding hands...
My bare-headed ones,
My trembling ones!

(Marina Tsvetayeva, Russian, tr. Jane A. Taubmann.)

[There follow three poems on the death of trees. A second one on the same subject by Charlotte Mew is in the section 'Man and Woman'.]

Domus Caedet Arborem [1]

Ever since the great planes were murdered at the end of the gardens
The city, to me, at night has the look of a Spirit brooding crime;
As if the dark houses watching the trees from dark windows
      Were simply biding their time.

(Charlotte Mew, English, 1869–1928.)

The Poplar-Field

The poplars are fell'd, farewell to the shade
And the whispering sound of the cool colonnade,
The winds play no longer, and sing in the leaves,
Nor Ouse on his bosom their image receives.

Twelve years have elapsed since I last took a view
Of my favourite field and the bank where they grew,
And now in the grass behold they are laid,
And the tree is my seat that once lent me a shade.

The blackbird has fled to another retreat
Where the hazels afford him a screen form the heat,
And the scene where his melody charm'd me before,
Resounds with his sweet-flowing ditty no more.

My fugitive years are all hasting away,
And I must ere long lie as lowly as they,
With a turf on my breast, and a stone at my head,
Ere another such grove shall arise in its stead.

[1] 'House kills tree.'

'Tis a sight to engage me, if anything can,
To muse on the perishing pleasures of man;
Though his life be a dream, his enjoyments, I see,
Have a being less durable even than he.

(William Cowper, English, 1731–1800.)

Binsey Poplars

felled 1879

My aspens dear, whose airy cages quelled,
Quelled or quenched in leaves the leaping sun,
All felled, felled, are all felled;
   Of a fresh and following folded rank
       Not spared, not one
       That dandled a sandalled
     Shadow that swam or sank
On meadow and river and wind-wandering weed-winding bank.

O if we but knew what we do
   When we delve or hew -
Hack and rack the growing green!
   Since country is so tender
To touch, her being so slender,
That, like this seek and seeing ball
But a prick will make no eye at all,
Where we, even where we mean
       To mend her we end her,
    When we hew or delve:

After-comers cannot guess the beauty been.
   Ten or twelve, only ten or twelve
     Strokes of havoc unselve
       The sweet especial scene,
    Rural scene, a rural scene,
    Sweet especial rural scene.

(G.M. Hopkins, English, 1844–89.)

[Four short poems written in middle age.]

1.   On the river shallows too
              Rain is falling.
              From within the palace
              I hear plovers crying,
              Never a place to settle.

2.   Across spring fields
              Mist is trailing.
              Sad and lonely
              In the evening shadows
              A bush-warbler sings.

3.   Close to my house,
              Small clusters of bamboo
              Blown in the wind
              Rustle indistinctly
              This spring evening.

4.   Soft and gentle
              Shines the spring sun.
              A lark rises,
              My heart is sad,
              I'm alone with my thoughts.

(Otomo Yakamochi, Japanese, 718–785, tr. I.M..)

Two Riddles:

1.   My clothes are silent as I walk the earth
              Or stir the waters. Sometimes that which
              Makes me beautiful raises me high
              Above men's heads, and powerful clouds
              Hold me, carry me far and wide.
              The loveliness spread on my back rustles
              And sings, bright, clear songs,

And loud, whenever I leave lakes
And earth, floating in the air like a spirit. [2]

2. A worm ate words. I thought that wonderfully
Strange – a miracle – when they told me a crawling
Insect had swallowed noble songs,
A night-time thief had stolen writing
So famous, so weighty. But the bug was foolish
Still, though its belly was full of thought. [3]

(Anon, Old English, 11th C., tr. Burton Raffel.)

from 'The Romance of the Rose'

Without fail, all dumb beasts
Naked and empty of understanding
By nature have no knowledge of themselves.
For if they had communication,
And reason enough to understand,
They could learn from one another,
And no good would come to us from it!
Never would fine battle-chargers
Allow themselves to be tamed by men
Or knights to ride astride them!
Never the ox his horn-crowned head
Would submit to be put to yoke and plough!
Asses, mules and camels all
Would deny their help as beasts of burden –
Indeed, they'd give not a damn for man!
To carry a castle on his back
An elephant would never agree,
Who's used to trumpeting out of his nose,
And who eats through it too, night and morning,
Just as a man does with his hands.
Dogs or cats wouldn't serve man,
For they can get on fine without him.

[2] Swan.
[3] Bookworm.

Bears, wolves, lions, leopards and boars
Would all like to bite man to death;
Even rats would bite him to death
As he lies small, in his cradle.
Never would birds, however instructed,
Put their skins in peril for man;
Indeed, they could do him much harm
By pecking open his eyes as he sleeps.
And if man's reply to all this
Is that he could confound them all
By making such things for himself as armour,
And helmets, and halberds, and sharp swords;
By making bows, and crossbows too;
Why then, so too could the beasts!
Haven't they monkeys, and marmosets,
Who'd make strong coats for them
Of leather, of iron – and jackets too?
Nor would they be at a loss over stitching,
They're perfectly able to use their hands,
They'd be as good at it as man;
And monkeys could also be their scribes.
Truly, they wouldn't be such fools
As to overlook gathering skills
With which to fight off armed attack;
Some kind of engine they'd probably make
By which to hurt man grievously.
Even fleas, and earwigs too,
Once they manage to worm their way in –
Through the ear, while he's asleep –
Could do wondrous damage to man.
Lice also, and crabs, and nits
Often pay man such close attention
That he has to leave off work
And bend over, grovel down,
Writhe, twist, jump and leap,
Scratch himself and rub his clothes –
Finally tearing off clothes and shoes
So badly they harass him.

Even flies, while man is eating,
Often bring him great peril
And attack him in the face
Not bothering if he's king or page.
Ants and other nasty pests
Could trouble man far too much
If they realised their powers;
But, you see, their ignorance
Comes to them from their own natures.
But, for creatures possessed of reason –
Be they mortal men or angels
All of whom owe praise to God –
If they fail to know themselves,
The fault in their case comes from vice
Which troubles and makes drunk their sense.
Because they're able to understand reason
And exercise freedom of choice,
Nothing can excuse their failure.

(Jean de Meung, French, d. 1305?, tr. I.M.)

7. Men and Women

[The questions explored in this section are, does the domination of society by men promote our destrucion of the planet, and would more female influence make things any better?

   The first poem, by a woman, clearly implies it would and will.]

The Pan, the Pot, the Burning Fire I Have in Front of Me

For a long time
these things have always been placed
in front of us women:

a pan of reasonable size
suited to one's strength,
a pot in which it's convenient for rice
to begin to swell and shine, grain by grain,
the heat of the fire inherited since the very beginning –
in front of them there have always been mothers, grandmothers,
                                                and their mothers.

What measures of love and sincerity
they must have poured
into these utensils –
sometimes red carrots,
sometimes black seaweed,
sometimes crushed fish

in the kitchen, always accurately
for morning, noon and evening, preparations have been made
and in front of the preparations, in a row, there have always been
some pairs of warm knees and hands.

Ah without those persons waiting
how could women have gone on
cooking so happily?
their unflagging care,
so daily a service they became unconscious of it.

Cooking was assigned oddly
as the woman's role,
but I don't think that was unfortunate;
because of that, her knowledge and position in society
may have lagged behind the times
but it isn't too late:
the things we have in front of us,
the pan and the pot and the burning fire,

in front of these familiar utensils
let us also study government, economy, literature
as sincerely
as we cook potatoes and meat,

not for vanity and promotion
but so everyone
may be served for mankind
so everyone may work for love.

(Ishigaki Rin, Japanese, b. 1920, tr. Hiroaki Sato.)

[The next poem is the despairing cry of a young man looking at the work in progress of his own sex's domination. He committed suicide shortly after the poem was written.]

Untitled Poem (him to her)

I'll show you
I'll give you
a ruined world

I'll give you lonely people
I'll give you
dark streets
where thin dogs walk
and steal the bread from beggars
I'll give you
old and sooty buildings
where families live
without a father
without a decent mother
I'll give you
thieves aged 14
and murderers aged 18

And you, girl, give me your body
and your hair
give me your breath
close, close to my face
give me your eyes
and the smell of your skin

I'll give you
plundered continents
exterminated nations
burned bodies
and beheaded children
I'll give you
hunger and wanderings
fear and sufferings
I'll give you
wars, exterminations,
genocides
and concentration camps.

And you give me...
... ...
...

I'll give you
garbage heaps in city streets
rivers of sewage streaming to the sea
cats, hungry and ferreting,
mice carrying diseases
and black plagues
which spread mercilessly,
taking their victims
from all of woman born
I'll give you madmen
who lead nations
to destruction

And you give me...
... ...
...

I'll give you a God
who's cruel and cold
I'll give you
suffering prophets
and crucified apostles
I'll give you Jobs
and Abrahams and Moses
I'll give you promises
written on tablets of stone

And you, give me...
... ...
...

I'll give you
obelisks and pyramids
built on the bodies of thousands of slaves
I'll give you flourishing gardens
and green groves
which have sprouted over vales of slaughter

I'll give you charred earth
green earth
I'll give you snows
which one day will melt
and will flood our land
and your people.
I'll give you black clouds
carrying terror and fear
I'll give you Inquisitors
I'll give you creatures of Satan

And you, give me...
... ...
...

I'll give you oil wells
which sprouted in place of teepees
I'll give you blocks of houses
which sprouted in the place of sloping vineyards
I'll give you fenced-in camps
which sprang up in the wilderness of ice
I'll give you crematoriums
which were born out of the young green grass
I'll give you tanks and planes
fire machines and bombs
created to glorify the names of
leaders and victors
at the expense of the pure souls
who are no more

And you, give me...
... ...
...

I'll give you
the polished offices
where are buried alive
your parents, your acquaintances and your friends

I'll give you
the murderous mechanism
which leads us all
to a future that's frozen,
mechanical, inconsiderate,
of computers and machines
sophisticated bombs
and pilotless planes

But you, keep for me your body
and your hair
keep for me your breath
close, close to my face
keep for me your eyes
and the smell of your skin.
Keep for me this pure corner,
the last in the world:
give me
give me your smile

That is all I can give you now

And you won't want me this way.
Will you want me?

(Ron Adler, Israeli, 1957–1976, tr. Richard Flantz.)

[Anthropologists male and female write that nowhere on earth is a society where women hold more power than men. In the history of human societies, women have most influence at the time when hunter-gatherers settle down to cultivate crops and live in larger communities. Marija Gimbutas[1] argues that a golden age existed in Old Europe at just such a time, between 6500 and 3500 BC, when peaceful cities flourished where women had public influence and the Mother Goddess was chief deity. Their written records are indecipherable.

Later on, when populations began to come into conflict over living space, communities dominated by warrior men could (and did)

[1] In her books 'Goddesses and Gods of Old Europe' and 'The Civilisation of the Goddess'.

overwhelm communities attuned to peace. Human evolution thus favoured male-dominated war-like tribes that bred with no restraint. After five or more thousand years, these two characteristics – unrestrained population growth and the mentality of conquest – have ceased to be useful for the human species; on the contrary, they threaten our survival.

Restraint is obviously the key to living in harmony, no matter how big or small the community. It has been said, 'The supreme achievment of civilisation is the domestication of the human male'. Our civilisation has rather channelled the aggression of the human male into corporations where it can plunder whole countries.

The first of the two poems that follow praises an object of natural beauty. The second describes the reaction to it of the kind of small-minded inadequate man whose exercised power is ruining our planet.]

The Wattle-Tree

The tree knows four truths –
earth, water, air and the fire of the sun.
The tree holds four truths in one.
Root, limb and leaf unfold
out of the seed, and these rejoice
till the tree dreams it has a voice
to join four truths in one great word of gold.

– Oh, that I knew that word!
I should cry loud, louder than any bird.
O let me live for ever, I would cry.
For that word makes immortal what would wordless die;
and perfectly, and passionately,
welds love and time into the seed,
till tree renews itself and is for ever tree –

Then upward from the earth
        and from the water
then inward from the air
        and the cascading light
poured gold, till the tree trembled with its flood.

Now from the world's four elements I make
my immortality; it shapes within the bud.
Yes, now I bud, and now at last I break
into the truth I had no voice to speak:
into a million images of the Sun, my God.

...and Mr. Ferritt

But now Mr Ferrit
with his troublesome nose,
with his shaven chin
and his voice like a grief
that grates in dark corners,
moves in his house
and scrapes his dry skin
and sees it is morning.

O day, you sly thief,
now what have you taken
of all the small things
I tie on my life?
The radio serial
whines in the kitchen,
caught in a box,
and cannot get out.
The finch in his cage,
the border of phlox

as straight as a string
drawn up in my garden,
the potted geranium,
all are there.
But day from his cranium
twitches one hair;
and never again
will a hair grow there.
– O day, you sly thief,
how you pluck at my life,
frets Mr Ferritt;
but there, he must bear it.

Outside the fence
the wattle-tree grows.
It tosses; it shines;
it speaks its one word.
Beware! beware!
Mr Ferritt has heard.
– What are axes for?
What are fences for?
Who planted the wattle-tree
right at my door?
God only knows.
All over the garden
its dust is shaken.
No wonder I sneeze
as soon as I waken.

O world, you sly thief;
my youth you have taken,
and what have you given
who promised me heaven,
but a nagging wife
and a chronic catarrh,
and a blonde on the pictures
as far as a star?

And wild and gold
as a film-star's hair
that tree stands there,
blocking the view
from my twenty-perch block.
What are axes for,
what are fences for
but to keep this tree
away from my door?

And down came the tree.
But poor Mr Ferritt
still has hay-fever.
Nothing will cure it.

(Judith Wright, Australian, b. 1915.)

[The difference between men and women is argued about more in ideological terms than in terms of what we know. Ideology is the modern name for superstition, and it's adherents cling to it strongly whether or not truth and reason are on their side. When truth is ignored in favour of fanaticism there's normally a high price to pay. In this case, pretending that men and women are the same except in a few physical details means that any special contribution women are able to make is abolished. In effect, women are encouraged to join in the rape of the Earth that corporate competitive capitalism has become.

When Ghenghis Khan had conquered almost half the earth he was told 'You cannot rule from the horse what you have conquered from the horse'. The success of his conquest had made his conqueror's role redundant; what was needed after it was able and just administration. We can say something similar about competitive capitalism; what we need now is careful and loving concern for Nature, not more rape and pillage from the seats of machines.

The geneticist C.D. Darlington wrote, the two sexes are 'genetically as different as two species; sometimes two very remote species'.[2] These genetic differences are reflected in the different values held by men and women. Values are the priorities we give to qualities; instinctively, men seem to give more priority to their aggressive and managing side, and women to their nurturing and protective side.

The next six poems offer some examples of the values, held more by women than by men, which could restrain humans from destruction of our world.

In the first, Anna Akhmatova takes the familiar tale of Lot's wife — in which God the Father punishes her for looking back on his destruction of Sodom — and makes it into a defence of woman's love of place and home.]

Lot's Wife

And the righteous man followed the envoy of God,
Huge and bright, over the black mountain.
But anguish spoke loudly to his wife:
It is not too late, you can still gaze

---

[2] 'The Evolution of Man and Society', p. 56.

At the red towers of your native Sodom,
At the square where you sang, at the courtyard where you spun,
At the empty windows of the tall house
Where you bore children to your beloved husband.

She glanced, and, paralyzed by deadly pain,
Her eyes no longer saw anything;
And her body became transparent salt
And her quick feet were rooted to the spot.

Who will weep for this woman?
Isn't her death the least significant?
But my heart will never forget the one
Who gave her life for a single glance.

(Anna Akhmatova, Russian, 1889–1966, tr. Judith Hemschemeyer.)

[The next poem is almost the only fragment by its (woman) author to
survive. It survived in text-books written by men, as an example of
how not to write poetry. In its love of simple objects it must have
undermined the male value of creating very important things – like
armies, philosophy and progress.]

> Loveliest of what I leave
>   is the sun himself
> Next to that the bright stars
>   and the face of mother moon
> Oh yes, and cucumbers in season,
>   and apples, and pears.

(Praxilla, Greek, c. 450 B.C., tr. John Dillon.)

[The next poem defends the sanctity of the family and of sexual fidelity.
It also, in the last few lines, seems to call for legislation against sexual
harassment.]

An Answer to a Love-Letter in Verse

Is it to me, this sad lamenting strain?
Are heaven's choicest gifts bestowed in vain?
A plenteous fortune, and a beauteous bride,
Your love rewarded, and content your pride:
Yet leaving her − 'tis me that you pursue,
Without one single charm but being new.

How vile is man! how I detest the ways
Of artful falsehood, and designing praise!
Tasteless, and easy happiness you slight,
Ruin your joy, and mischief your delight.
Why should poor pug★ (the mimic of your kind)   ★pet ape
Wear a rough chain, and be to box confined?
Some cup, perhaps, he breaks, or tears a fan,
While moves unpunished the destroyer, man.
Not bound by vows, and unrestrained by shame,
In sport you break the heart, and rend the fame.
Not that your art can be successful here,
Th'already plundered need no robber fear:
Nor sighs, nor charms, nor flattery can move,
Too well secured against a second love.
Once, and but once, that devil charmed my mind;
To reason deaf, to observation blind,
I idly hoped (what cannot love persuade?)
My fondness equalled, and my troth repaid:
Slow to distrust, and willing to believe,
Long hushed my doubts, and would myself deceive;
But oh! too soon − this tale would ever last;
Sleep, sleep my wrongs, and let me think 'em past.

But you, who mourn with counterfeited grief,
And ask so boldly like a begging thief,
May soon on other nymph inflict the pain
You know so well with cruel art to feign.
Though long you've sported with Dan Cupid's dart,
You may see eyes, and you may feel a heart.

So the brisk wits, who stop the evening coach,
Laugh at the fear which follows their approach;
With idle mirth, and haughty scorn, despise

The passenger's pale cheek and staring eyes:
But, seized by Justice, find a fright no jest,
And all the terror doubled in their breast.

(Lady Montague, English, 1689–1762.)

[The often-commented-upon difficulty men have in expressing
emotion is the subject of the next poem]

Ancestral Burden

You told me: My father did not weep;
You told me: My grandfather did not weep;
They have never wept, the men of my race;
They were of steel.

Speaking thus, a tear welled from you
And fell upon my mouth... More venom
Have I never drunk from any other glass
As small as that.

Weak woman, poor woman who understands,
Sorrow of centuries I knew in the drinking of it:
Ah, this soul of mine can not support
All of its weight!

(Alfonsina Storni, Argentinian, 1892–1938, tr. R. O'Connell.)

[The next poem looks at boys and girls. The boys take after their
fathers.]

The Secret Life of Frogs

Mr Gabriel Fur, my Siamese,
brings to the hearth a Common Toadlet,
Crinia tasmaniensis.
Mice are permitted, frogs forbidden.
It will live. I carry it outside.

Its heartbeat troubles my warm hand
and as I set it down I see
two small girls in a warmer land.

My friend Alice and I would sit
cradling our frogs behind the tankstand.
Our fathers would talk about
the Great War. Mine would only say,
"I used to be a stretcher-bearer."
Not seen, not heard, in childhood's earshot
of the women on the back veranda,
we knew about atrocities.
Some syllables we used as charms;
Passchendale Mons Gallipoli.
We knew about Poor George, who cried
if any woman touched her hair.
He'd been inside a brothel when
the Jerries came and started shooting.
(We thought a brothel was a French
hotel that served hot broth to diggers.)
The girl that he'd been with was scalped.
Every Frog in the house was killed.

Well, that was life for frogs. At school
the big boys blew them up and spiked them.
One bully had the very knife
with which his father killed ten Germans -
twenty - a hundred - numbers blossomed.
Dad the Impaler! making work
for the more humble stretcher-bearers.

In safety by the dripping tankstand
our frogs with matchstick hands as pale
as the violet stems they lived among
cuddled their vulnerable bellies
in hands that would not do them wrong.

(Gwen Harwood, Australian, b. 1920.)

[In 1731 women in the Bishnoi community of North-West India hugged trees that were to be axed for timber; 360 were killed by axemen before the felling was stopped. Now, the Bishnoi area is a green oasis in a barren landscape.[3] In the next poem, Charlotte Mew watches men cutting down trees.]

The Trees are Down

– and he cried with a loud voice;
Hurt not the earth, neither the sea, nor the trees

They are cutting down the great plane-trees at the end of the
  gardens.
For days there has been the grate of the saw, the swish of the
  branches as they fall,
The crash of the trunks, the rustle of trodden leaves,
With the "Whoops'and the "Whoas," the loud common talk,
  the loud common laughs of the men, above it all.

I remember one evening of a long past Spring
Turning in at a gate, getting out of a cart, and finding a large dead
  rat in the mud of a drive.
I remember thinking: alive or dead, a rat was a god-forsaken
  thing,
But at least, in May, that even a rat should be alive.

The week's work here is as good as done. There is just one
  bough
On the roped bole, in the fine grey rain,
      Green and high
      And lonely against the sky.
          (Down now!–)
      And but for that,
      If an old dead rat
Did once, for a moment, unmake the Spring, I might never have
  thought of him again.

It is not for a moment the Spring is unmade today;
These were great trees, it was in them from root to stem:
When the men with the "Whoops" and the "Whoas" have
    carted the whole
        of the whispering loveliness away
Half the Spring, for me, will have gone with them.
It is going now, and my heart has been struck with the hearts of
    the planes;
Half my life it has beat with these, in the sun, in the rains,
    In the March wind, the May breeze,
In the great gales that came over to them across the roofs
            from the great seas.
    There was only a quiet rain when they were dying;
    They must have heard the sparrows flying,
And the small creeping creatures in the earth where they were
    lying -
        But I, all day, I heard an angel crying:
            "Hurt not the trees."

(Charlotte Mew, English, 1869–1928.)

[A society takes on the colour of its dominant members. But
logically, can the values of non-dominance dominate? This
problem pre-occupies one of the earliest philosophical works to
come down to us, the Tao Te Ching. Three extracts from it
follow.]

1.   The spirit of the Fountain never dies:
     It is called the Mysterious Female.
     The entrance to the Mysterious Female
     Is the root of all Heaven and Earth.
     Frail, frail it is, hardly existing,
     But touch it; it will never run dry.

2.   Know the male,
     Cleave to the female,
     Be the abyss of all things under heaven:
     He who is the abyss of all things under heaven

Knows a power that is never exhausted,
Returns again to a state of infancy.
Know the white,
Cleave to the black,
Follow the design of all things under heaven:
He who follows the design of all things under heaven
Knows a power that is effortless,
Returns again to the unbounded.
Know glory,
Cleave to ignominy,
Become the fountain of all things under heaven.
He who becomes the fountain of all things under heaven
Knows a power that is limitless,
Returns again to the uncarved block.
A block may be shaped into vessels,
But when the Sage uses it
He makes leaders of men:
"The great carver does not cut."

3.   In the world there is nothing more submissive and weak
     than water. Yet for attacking that which is hard and strong
     nothing can surpass it. This is because there is nothing that
     can take its place.
          That the weak overcomes the strong,
          And the submissive overcomes the hard,
          Everyone in the world knows yet no one can put into
             practice.

     Therefore the sage says,
          One who takes upon himself the humiliation of the state
          Is called a ruler worthy of offering sacrifices
             to the gods of earth and millet;
          One who takes upon himself the calamity of the state
          Is called a king worthy of dominion over the whole
             empire.

     Straightforward words
     Seem paradoxical.

(from Tao Te Ching, anon. Chinese, 4th C. B.C.; compiled from various
translations.)

[For most of recorded history, women have been denied any substantial public role in society. The next poem expresses the frustration of a poet denied public office because of her sex.]

On a Visit to Ch'ung Chen Temple I see the List of Successful Candidates in the Imperial Examinations

Cloud capped peaks fill the eyes
In the Spring sunshine.
Their names are written in beautiful characters
And posted in order of merit.
How I hate this silk dress
That conceals a poet.
I lift my head and read their names
In powerless envy.

(Yu Hsuan-Chi, Chinese, mid 9th C., tr. K. Rexroth and Ling Chung.)

[Some women undertake the task of revenge.]

Siren Song

This is the one song everyone
would like to learn: the song
that is irresistible:

the song that forces men
to leap overboard in squadrons
even though they see the beached skulls

the song nobody knows
because anyone who has heard it
is dead, and the others can't remember.

Shall I tell you the secret
and if I do, will you get me
out of this bird suit?

I don't enjoy it here
squatting on this island
looking picturesque and mythical

with these two feathery maniacs,
I don't enjoy singing
this trio, fatal and valuable.

I will tell the secret to you,
to you, only to you.
Come closer. This song

is a cry for help: Help me!
Only you, only you can,
you are unique

at last. Alas
it is a boring song
but it works every time.

(Margaret Atwood, Canadian, b. 1939.)

[The stifling boredom of middle class suburbia is blamed on men:]

Nervous Prostration

I married a man of the Croydon class
When I was twenty-two.
And I vex him, and he bores me
Till we don't know what to do!
It isn't good form in the Croydon class
To say you love your wife,
So I spend my days with the tradesmen's books
And pray for the end of my life.

In green fields are blossoming trees
And a golden wealth of gorse,
And young birds sing for joy of worms:
It's perfectly clear, of course,

That it wouldn't be taste in the Croydon class
To sing over dinner or tea:
But I sometimes wish the gentleman
Would turn and talk to me!

But every man of the Croydon class
Lives in terror of joy and speech,
'Words are betrayers', 'Joys are brief'
The maxims their wise ones teach.
And for all my labour of love and life
I shall be clothed and fed,
And they'll give me an orderly funeral
When I'm still enough to be dead.

I married a man of the Croydon class
When I was twenty-two.
And I vex him and he bores me
Till we don't know what to do!
And as I sit in his ordered house,
I feel I must sob or shriek,
To force a man of the Croydon class
To live, or to love, or to speak.

(Anna Wickham, English, 1884–1947.)

[Since we've in the area of abuse, here's a bit from the other side –
though here, abuse is outweighed by affection.]

In Praise of Small Women

For your sake I'd like to keep my sermon short
Because, for me, what pays in preaching is conciseness;
In women, smallness; in arguments, succinctness;
For what's small and well-made sticks in the heart.

Great talking's mocked; great laughter means a fool;
In little women you'll find great love, not small;
There are very big women I'd not swap for small;
A swap the other way I'd not regret at all.

Cold on the outside, inside they burn with love;
In bed they're a solace; useful, laughing, gay;
At home, sensible, witty, full of good things;
Much more you'll discover, if you're of a mind to learn.

A lark's a small bird, and so's a nightingale;
But both sing sweeter than birds a great deal bigger;
A woman, by being small, is none the worse for that;
Affection makes her sweeter than roses or sugar.

So always choose small over big, or bigger;
To run from great terror is no outrage;
Of evils choose the lesser, says the sage;
Therefore, among women, the smaller the better.

(Juan Ruiz, Spanish, 14th c., tr. I.M.)

[The condition of women under men's domination has varied
from abject slavery to exalted elevation. Two extracts from a
poem by Dante reveal how women could be worshipped without
being given power. For Dante, woman's role was to be the
embodiment of divine beauty, here on earth to inspire virtue in
men. Love brings these qualities together, creating perfection on
Earth. In Dante's scheme of things, women have no place
exercising power in public; their place is to influence men to
behave properly in the exercise of power.

The extracts are from a poem against avarice in men. Dante,
addressing women, says men are behaving so badly that women
should withhold or destroy their own beauty.]

I say, to you women in love,
If virtue to us men
Is granted, and beauty to you;
And to Love, the power to make one out of two;
Then you should no longer love,
But cover the beauty that's given you;
For Virtue, which was Beauty's goal, is dead.
Alas! What am I led to say?

I say, a beautiful disdain
It would be in Woman,
And praised by Reason,
To send beauty away, by her own decision.

[After many lines attacking the avarice of men, Dante returns to
his opening theme; beauty rooted in goodness inspires love and
virtue, but beauty which has deserted goodness inspires only
lust.]

I have revealed, Ladies, in some of its parts,
The vileness of those who admire you,
So you may treat them with anger.
But much and more than this I've left hidden;
To notice it, even, is ugly.
In each of men is every vice assembled;
Through this, the amity of the world is lost.
You see, the leaves of Love,
Rooted in goodness, need other good to draw them out;
So, like is attracted to like.
Now see what conclusion I reach;
That she should not believe (she
To whom beauty seems good)
Herself *loved* by men such as these –
Unless we choose to enumerate beauty
Among the *evils*; then she can believe,
In which case Love becomes the appetite of Beasts!
But may such women perish
Who set their beauty apart
From natural goodness, and, for such a cause,
Believe that love is outside the garden of Reason!

(Dante, Italian, 1265–1321; tr. I.M.)

[The long poem 'Sir Gawain and The Green Knight' concerns
man's attitudes to both women and nature. At the New Year a
mighty Green Man challenges the men of Arthur's court; one of
them can strike him with an axe, but in return must be struck
back a year later. Gawain volunteers to accept the challenge, and

strikes the giant's head off. Plant-like, the giant does not die. He tucks his head under his arm and leaves.

The year passes, drawing the day closer when Gawain must present himself for the return blow.]

Then comes the season of summer, with its soft winds,
When the west wind breathes himself on seeds and grasses;
A source of great joy is the growth that springs from them,
While the dampening dew is dropping from the leaves
To bide a blissful blush of the bright sun.
But then the harvest hastens, hardening the green shoot,
Warning of winter's approach, to grow quite ripe;
Drought dries the dust; driven by wind, it rises
From the face of the earth, flying full high;
Wild winds from heaven wrestle with the sun,
Leaves fall from lime-trees, lighting on the ground.
Grass grows now in greys, that once was green;
Then all ripens and rots, which first was sprung,
And so the year grows old, with many yesterdays,
And winter's winds are here again, as is the way of the world,
      no lie,
      Till Michaelmas moon
      Came with winter's pledge
      Reminding Gawain all a-sudden
      Of his troublesome quest.

[Gawain, after a long journey, comes across a wonderful castle surrounded by mighty trees. The owner of this castle is actually the Green Knight, but he's no longer green and Gawain doesn't recognise him. Gawain accepts his hospitality.

The Green Knight – a masculine embodiment of Nature which thrusts its spears of growth through earth and air – has a wife who is beautiful. Early in the morning, while her husband is out hunting, she tries to seduce Gawain, who is still in bed asleep.]

The lady, for love's sake, allowed herself no sleep,
Nor respite to the purpose planted in her heart;
She got herself up early, to make her way to him,

In a merry mantle, that reached right to the ground.
Fine furs lined it, made of pelts well trimmed;
No gaudy colour in her hair, but well-cut jewels
Interlaced her tresses, twenty to each cluster.
Her lively face and throat lay naked to the air
Her breast bare before her, her back naked too.
She comes within his chamber door and closes it behind her
Opens wide a window, calling to the knight
Right away regaling him with her rich words
   and cheer;
   "Ah! friend, how can you sleep?
   The morning is so clear!"
   He had been deep in troubled sleep
   But then knew he she was there.

[The Green Man's seductive wife tempts Gawain to go further
than he feels he should. But Gawain behaves honourably. His
only offence is to conceal from her husband the gift of a green
girdle, which the lady assured him had life-preserving properties.
This deception is later punished by the Green Knight, who
wounds him in the neck on the return stroke.

 Returning to Arthur's court, Gawain relates his adventure
and shows everyone the wound in his neck and the lace girdle.]

"Look, Lord!" says Gawain, handling the lace,
"This is the cloth, whose blame I bear in my neck,
This is the wrong, and this the wound, reward
For covetous cowardice, which caught me in its snare.
This tokens the untruth in which I was discovered,
And I must wear it now, until the day I die.
For none may hide his harm without courting mishap;
For once it's stuck to him it will leave him never."
The king comforts the knight, and all the court join in;
Laughing loudly over it, they lovingly agree
That all the lords and ladies belonging to the Table, [4]
Each member of the brotherhood, should as a token wear

---

[4] The Round Table, symbol of the fellowship of Arthur's court.

A band cross-wise about him, made of bright green,
And wear it, for Gawain's sake, following his example.
By this was reconciled the renown of the Round Table
And honour was accorded its wearers evermore,
As it is written, in the best books of romance.

(Anon, English, late 14th C., version I.M.)

[In 'Sir Gawain and the Green Knight', Nature and Woman are not to be taken advantage of. The trouble is, people find it difficult not to abuse their power, especially if they think life or livelihood is at stake. Confusion is added when the pursuit of livelihood is itself damaging life.

In the poem, Nature – in the person of the Green Knight – is strong enough to punish any man who takes excessive advantage. Then, Nature was obviously stronger than homo sapiens. Nowadays, Nature may seem weaker; but we may be sure that if we destroy it we will destroy ourselves too, and by damaging it we damage our children.

The principle of sexual selection (as important in evolution as natural selection) is that over the generations each sex chooses the kind of other sex it wants. One sex is responsible for how the other sex develops. Men are stronger because for thousands of years women have found strong men sexy. Looking the other way, Darlington writes, 'We know how Adam complained of Eve's enticing and deceptive arts. Yet it is now clear that these arts are themselves the effect of man's preference over the last ten thousand years for those women who enticed and deceived him more successfully'. The Mexican (woman) poet Juana Asbaje made the same point three hundred years earlier:]

Verses against the Inconsistency of Men

(9 verses out of 17)

Foolish men, who accuse
Woman without reason
Not seeing you're the cause
Of the very thing you blame!

If your unequalled craving
Is inspired by her disdain,
Why demand good behaviour
While inciting her to wrong?

You combat her resistance
Then later gravely blame
Her fickleness in giving
What your persistence won.

You resemble, in the bravery
Of your insane behaviour,
A child inventing a monster
Then holding it in fear!

Could anything be odder than
Such lack of common sense,
Which breathes upon a mirror
Then fumes when it's not clear?

No woman's well-reputed,
Even the most discreet;
If she won't let you in she's cold,
And if she does she's loose.

Of what should she be made,
She who would win your love,
When if she's cold she offends you,
And if she's easy she's boring?

Between the boredom and pain
You throw in our direction
Good luck to her who rejects you -
And welcome your complaints!

Why are you so appalled
By a blame of your own making?
Either like her as you've made her,
Or make her as you'd like her!

(Juana Asbaje, Mexican, 1651–95, tr. I.M.)

[Looking the other way, men's strength and capacity for aggression has for centuries been a valuable asset to women needing protection for their families, as well as meat and other toiled-for food. Two poems by women follow that give us an idea of how women appreciated in men the qualities of strength and ability at war. They are by sisters and mothers; poems appreciating warriors as lovers are (as far as I know) by other men. The first poem, by a woman, describes a mother finding her son dead on the battle-field.]

There, in the very middle
of battle-camps
    that heaved like the seas,

pointing at the enemy
    the tongues of lances,
new-forged and whetted,

urging soldiers forward
    with himself at the head
in a skirmish of arrow and spear,

cleaving through
    an oncoming wave of foes,
forcing a clearing,

he had fallen
in that space
    between armies,
his body hacked to pieces:

    when she saw him there
    in all his greatness,
    mother's milk flowed again
    in the withered breasts
    of this mother
    for her warrior son
    who had no thought of retreat.

(Auvaiyar, Tamil, ?1st C. A.D., tr. A.K. Ramanujan.)

[The next poem is a woman's lament for her brother slain in battle. Al-Khansa wrote many laments for her brother Sahr; this one witnesses yet another day of slaughter, as she watches other sisters and mothers mourning their dead. Al-Khansa was a pre-Islamic Arab poet. Islam united the various Arab tribes and turned their war-like habits against the outside world.]

Evening brings memories, which banish sleep from my eyes;
Morning breaks me with a fresh assault of anguish.
I weep for Sahr; what warrior is equal to Sahr,
When the time comes to fight a valiant chief,
To hold the head high in face of unjust aggressors,
To vindicate by arms the rights of the oppressed?
No, never before has misery struck like this,
Not in the realm of the angels, nor of humankind.
Unflinching, he fought the onslaughts of the age;
Without equivocation, he solved insoluble problems.
If at night a guest knocked on the door,
Heart trembling, alarmed at the slightest noise,
Sahr would welcome him and give him safety
Banishing from his heart all thought of fear.
The rising sun brings Sahr before my eyes;
The setting sun leaves Sahr still in my heart.
Were not a crowd of mourners at my side
Lamenting their brothers too, grief would have killed me.
How many mothers I see, lamenting their sons!
How many eyes cry for the day to turn back!
A sister weeps for her brother taken this day,
Weeps for the day that brought misery to her life.
The dead they mourn are not my brother Sahr,
And I command in my soul the strength of patience.
God be my witness! No, I will not forget you!
Not when my blood is dry and my grave is dug!
The day I lost Sahr Abu Hassan,
I said farewell to joy and lightness of heart.
I weep for him, my mother weeps with me —
How else, when morning and evening he sleeps in the tomb!

(Al-Khansa, Arab, 7th. C.; version I.M. from 1889 French translation of Le P. de Coppier.)

[Men's and women's roles have changed greatly over the centuries, adapting in response to new circumstances. Conflict and cooperation between the sexes are part of our struggle to flourish. The aggression of men has helped our species become dominant all over the earth; perhaps the care of women will help us survive the attrition that has followed.

The next poem, like 'Gawain and the Green Knight', deals with relations between men, women, and the world. Written from a man's point of view, it says the world depends on how we treat it. If we abuse it, it becomes an abused world, and we have to live in an abused world. Further, the world stays beautiful to the extent that we allow it to reject us and the advances we can't help making. Those advances which injure the world, we must accept as rejected.]

> If the intellect is unstable
> It is overwhelmed by the world,
> A weak man embraced by a whore.
>
> If the mind becomes disciplined,
> The world is a distinguished woman
> Who rejects her lover's advances.

(Al-Ma'arri, Arabic, 973–1057, tr. Wightman and al-Udhari.)

[A short poem by a man challenges women to get on top of things:]

> Me, horizontally above her.
> Action: perfect strokes downward oblique.
> Hence, man dominates because of limitation.
> Or, so it shall be until women learn their stuff.

(Jean Toomer, American, 1894–1967, from 'Cane'.)

[The challenge is taken up in the next poem, which provides a sequel to the story of the expulsion from the Garden of Eden. In

the Book of Genesis Eve, Woman, is blamed for the expulsion.
Judith Wright takes up the story from Eve's point of view.]

Eve to Her Daughters

It was not I who began it.
Turned out into draughty caves,
hungry so often, having to work for our bread,
hearing the children whining,
I was nevertheless not unhappy.
Where Adam went I was fairly contented to go.
I adapted myself to the punishment; it was my life.

But Adam, you know...!
He kept on brooding over the insult,
over the trick They had played on us, over the scolding.
He had discovered a flaw in himself
and he had to make up for it.

Outside Eden the Earth was imperfect,
the seasons changed, the game was fleet-footed,
he had to work for our living, and he didn't like it.
He even complained of my cooking
(it was hard to compete with Heaven).

So he set to work.
The earth must be made a new Eden
with central heating, domesticated animals,
mechanical harvesters, combustion engines,
escalators, refrigerators,
and modern means of communication
and multiplied opportunities for safe investment
and higher education for Abel and Cain
and the rest of the family.
You can see how his pride had been hurt.

In the process he had to unravel everything,
because he believed that mechanism

was the whole secret – he was always mechanical-minded.
He got to the very inside of the whole machine
exclaiming as he went, So this is how it works!
And now that I know how it works, why, I must have invented it.
As for God and the Other, they cannot be demonstrated,
and what cannot be demonstrated
doesn't exist.
You see, he had always been jealous.

Yes, he got to the centre
where nothing at all can be demonstrated
And clearly he doesn't exist; but he refuses
to accept the conclusion.
You see, he was always an egotist.

It was warmer than this in the cave;
there was none of this fall-out.
I would suggest, for the sake of the children,
that it's time you took over.

But you are my daughters, you inherit my own faults of character;
you are submissive, following Adam
even beyond existence.
Faults of character have their own logic
and it always works out.
I observed this with Cain and Abel.

Perhaps the whole elaborate fable
right from the beginning
is meant to demonstrate this; perhaps it's the whole secret.
Perhaps nothing exists but our faults?
At least they can be demonstrated.

But it's useless to make
such a suggestion to Adam.
He has turned himself into God,
who is faultless, and doesn't exist.

(Judith Wright, Australian, b. 1915.)

8. Poetry Itself

[The word 'poet' comes from the Greek for maker, creator. A sense of mystery surrounds the making of creative art, suggesting that sacred communion with a muse, or patron god, is taking place. Some poets have a reputation that it's the devil they're communing with. There is in any case a sense of truth – 'inspiration' – coming from a divine source to the poet. Truth is being pursued by instinct as much as by reason.

This section looks at the way poetry has influenced our lives. All forms of art can bring to our attention ways of being and behaving of which we were previously unaware. Poetry is credited with the birth of Romanticism in Europe, which profoundly changed peoples' values and expectations. Social order, personal sacrifice, conventional morality and authority were out; individual experience, liberty, wild nature and social progress were in. Blame for life's inadequacies was taken away from God and the natural order, and placed on the shoulders of humanity.

Today, we are reaping both the benefits and the banes of this shift. An awareness that our whims can be satisfied has become an expectation that they will be. Two centuries of slaking human appetites has left the planet badly bruised.

Poetry's credentials as guardian spirit of nature are well established. Basho's feeling was that poetry was born out of our relationship with nature:]

> Poetry's source –
> In the far north,
> Rice-planting songs.

(Basho, Japanese, 1644–94, tr. I.M.)

[According to Sanskrit tradition, poetry began as a way for humans to converse with gods. Secular poetry had its origins later, about two and a half thousand years ago, when Valmiki, author of the Ramayana, was out walking in the forest. He heard the anguished cry of a bird whose mate, while in the act of love, had been shot by a hunter. Valmiki was moved to compose a poem as an elegy for the bird and a rebuke to the hunter.]

Prologue to the 'Ramayana'

Once, not far from the river Tamasa,
The ascetic Valmiki was wandering in a forest,
Meditating on the beauty of nature.
Nearby, unafraid,
Two sweet-voiced krauncha birds were mating
Savouring the delights of spontaneous love.
An ill-minded fowler of the Nishada tribe,
With deliberate malice,
In Valmiki's presence,
Killed the male bird.
Pierced by an arrow in the act of love,
The pink-tufted crane, wings outspread,
Toppled.
Wrenched from under her lover
The female, seeing blood gush out,
Screamed.
She screamed piteously.
Compassion stirred in Valmiki's heart
When he saw the bird die.
More compassion stirred in him
When he heard the screams of the female.
Horrified by the act of transgression
He cursed the fowler:

'Fowler! Listen to my words.
May peace of mind never be yours!
For you have killed this innocent bird
In his act of innocent love.'

Even as the words issued from his mouth,
He felt uneasy, and he thought:
What is this that I have said
In the intensity of my grief?
For some time wise Valmiki brooded;
Then, turning to his disciple Bharadvaja,
He said:

'Four lines of eight syllables each!
From my sorrow came this song!
From grief comes the making of verse:
There is no poetry without compassion.'

(Valmiki, Sanskrit, ? between 8th and 2nd c. B.C., tr. P. Lal.)

[Nature's need of protection increased dramatically with the Industrial Revolution. Wordsworth opened many peoples' eyes to the beauty of nature, but when he became respectably successful he was accused of trading in his 'storm-cloud's thunderous melody' for the bleat of 'an old half-witted sheep'[1]. In the next two poems we see these two voices in poetic action. First, in a poem of 1833, the half-witted sheep approves human progress though it mars nature. Eleven years later Wordsworth changes his mind and shows the 'storm-cloud's thunderous melody' is not entirely dead in him.]

Steamboats, Viaducts and Railways (1833)

Motions and Means, on land and sea at war
With old poetic feeling, not for this,
Shall ye, by Poets even, be judged amiss!
Nor shall your presence, howsoe'er it mar
The loveliness of Nature, prove a bar
To the Mind's gaining that prophetic sense
Of future change, that point of vision, whence
May be discovered what in soul ye are.
In spite of all that beauty may disown

[1] From a poem by J.K. Stephen.

In your harsh features, Nature doth embrace
Her lawful offspring in Man's art; and Time,
Pleased with your triumphs oe'r his brother Space,
Accepts from your bold hands the proffered crown
Of hope, and smiles on you with cheer sublime.

On the Projected Kendal and Windermere Railway (1844)

Is then no nook of English ground secure
From rash assault? Schemes of retirement sown
In youth, and mid' the busy world kept pure
As when the earliest flowers of hope were blown,
Must perish;– how can they this blight endure?
And must he too the ruthless change bemoan
Who scorns a false utilitarian lure
'Mid his paternal fields at random thrown?
Baffle the threat, bright Scene, from Orrest-head
Given to the pausing traveller's rapturous glance:
Plead for thy peace, thou beautiful romance
Of nature; and, if human hearts be dead,
Speak, passing winds; ye torrents, with your strong
And constant voice, protest against the wrong.

(William Wordsworth, English, 1770–1850.)

[George Eliot's 'In a London drawingroom' was not published until after her death. The grey alienation it describes has spread a long way since 1865, when it was written.]

In a London Drawingroom

The sky is cloudy, yellowed by the smoke.
For view there are the houses opposite
Cutting the sky with one long line of wall
Like solid fog: far as the eye can stretch

Monotony of surface and of form
Without a break to hang a guess upon.
No bird can make a shadow as it flies,
For all is shadow, as in ways o'erhung
By thickest canvass, where the golden rays
Are clothed in hemp. No figure lingering
Pauses to feed the hunger of the eye
Or rest a little on the lap of life.
All hurry on and look upon the ground,
Or glance unmarking at the passers by.
The wheels are hurrying too, cabs, carriages
All closed, in multiplied identity.
The world seems one huge prison-house and court
Where men are punished at the slightest cost,
With lowest rate of colour, warmth and joy.

(George Eliot (Mary Anne Evans), English, 1819–80.)

[Alfonsina Storni could not have read Eliot's poem, but her 'Street' is like a twentieth-century version of the above, complete with the image of 'multiplied identity', only this time in a psychological, nightmarish and surreal guise.]

Street

An alley open
between high gray walls.
At any moment: the dark mouth of the doors,
the tunnels of the entries,
traps that lead
to human catacombs.
Isn't there a shudder
in the entrance halls?
A bit of terror
in the rising whiteness
of a stairway?
I pass by hastily.
Every eye that looks at me

doubles me and scatters me
through the city.

A forest of legs,
a whirlwind
of rolling circles,
a cloud of shouts and sounds,
separate my head from my body,
my hands from my arms,
my heart from my chest,
my feet from my legs,
my will from its source.
Up above
the blue sky
calms its transparent water:
cities of gold
sail across it.

(Alfonsina Storni, Argentinian, 1892–1938, tr. M. Freeman.)

[A poem by Judith Wright brings the theme of poetry as nature's guardian angel up to date. Passenger pigeons were once so numerous that flocks of them blackened the sky. This lament for them becomes a protest against our human besmirching of the natural world as we turn it all to our use. And it re-affirms the role of poetry, which by singing celebrates and recreates the value and meaning of life.]

Lament for Passenger Pigeons

("Don't ask for the meaning, ask for the use." – Wittgenstein)

The voice of water as it flows and falls,
the noise air makes against earth-surfaces
have changed; are changing to the tunes we choose.

What wooed and echoed in the pigeon's voice?
We have not heard the bird. How reinvent
that passenger, its million wings and hues,

when we have lost the bird, the thing itself,
the sheen of life on flashing long migrations?
Might human musics hold it, could we hear?

Trapped in the fouling nests of time and space,
we turn the music on; but it is man,
and it is man who lends a deafening ear.

And it is man we eat and man we drink
and man who thickens round us like a stain.
Ice at the polar axis smells of men.

A word, a class, a formula, a use:
that is the rhythm, the cycle we impose.
The sirens sang us to the ends of sea,

and changed to us; their voices were our own,
jug-jug to dirty ears in dirtied brine.
Pigeons and angels sang us to the sky

and turned to metal and a dirty need.
The height of sky, the depth of sea we are,
sick with a yellow stain, a fouling dye.

Whatever Being is, that formula,
it dies as we pursue it past the word.
We have not asked the meaning, but the use.

What is the use of water when it dims?
The use of air that whines in emptiness?
The use of glass-eyed pigeons caged in glass?

We listen to the sea, that old machine,
to air that hoarsens on earth-surfaces
and has no angel, no migrating cry.

What is the being and the end of man?
Blank surfaces reverb a human voice
whose echo tells us that we choose to die:

or else, against the blank of everything,
to reinvent that passenger, that bird-
siren-and-angel image we contain
essential in a constellating word.
To sing of Being, its escaping wing,
to utter absence in a human chord
and recreate the meaning as we sing.

(Judith Wright, Australian, b. 1915.)

[Many poets have suffered for following their art with conviction. Long stretches of poverty, even persecution, torture and death have awaited them. Today, in the democratic West, being ignored is the widespread fate of poets, as poetry seems irrelevant in the struggle for wealth.

During times when poets are widely read, there's always the danger of annoying those in power. The fourteenth century Persian poet Hafiz wrote that he would gladly give two great cities for a mole on his beloved's cheek. The psychopathic conqueror Tamburlane, to whom the cities in question belonged, summoned Hafiz to account for his impudence. Hafiz explained, 'Because I can't help giving things away, that's why I'm as poor as you see'. He survived.

Poets have wandered far and wide in search of audiences and remuneration. The following lines describe a poet's life in Anglo-Saxon times.]

Thus wandering, they who shape songs for men
Pass over many lands, and tell their need,
And speak their thanks, and ever, south or north,
Meet someone skilled in songs and free in gifts,
Who would be raised among his friends to fame,
And do brave deeds till light and life are gone;
He who has thus wrought himself praise shall have
A settled glory underneath the stars.

(Anon., Anglo-Saxon, 7th C.; final lines of 'Widsith', tr. H. Morley.)

[The poet as wanderer appears in many traditions.]

Light Rain on the Road to Sword Gate

Wine stains and mud mottle my coat.
As I travel on, my heart breaks with every scene.
It looks as if I'm a poet at last,
Riding my donkey through Sword Gate in the drizzling rain.

(Lu Yu, Chinese, 1125–1209, tr. J.Chaves.)

[A similar image comes across in the next poem – with the added
complaint of poverty.]

> he sees me
> as nothing
> but a useless poet –
> I owe the man money

(Takuboku, Japanese, 1885–1912, tr. Carl Sesar.)

[The Chinese poet Chu Yuan became a wanderer because he
would not compromise his integrity. He was a statesman, whose
advice was ignored by his sovereign. Leaving court, he wrote a
long poem called 'Encountering Sorrow', then drowned himself
in a river. In this excerpt, he laments the takeover of his country
by greedy and unscupulous men.]

They go stampeding in search of money and grain.
Surfeited, they are not afraid to come for more.
Alas, they forgive themselves and blame only others.
Their fret their hearts away, swayed by envy and greed.

They ride roughshod in pursuit of their ends.
My heart does not hunger after such things.
Gradually old age will fall about me;
Perhaps I shall never establish my good fame.

At dawn I drink the dropping dews of magnolias,
At dusk I eat fallen chrysanthemum petals.
If I respect only the good and the virtuous,
Why should I grieve over their interminably hungry jaws?

(Chu Yuan, Chinese, 340–278 BC; tr. Robert Payne.)

[When a tyrant wanted to rule justly, poets and philosophers would find themselves welcome at court. The poet Sa'di, at the end of his long life (he is supposed to have lived to one hundred and eight), wrote books of poetry and prose desribing the principles of good government, from which the following extract is taken.]

There is a story that while some game was being roasted for Nushirvan the Just during a hunting party, no salt could be found. A boy was sent to a nearby village to bring some. Nushirvan said, 'Pay for the salt lest it should become a custom and the village be ruined.' When asked what harm could come from such a trifling demand, Nushirvan replied, 'The foundation of oppression was small in the world; but those coming later have added to it, so it reached its present size.'

If a king eats an apple from the garden of a subject,
His slayes will uproot the whole tree for him.

Should a king allow the theft of five eggs,
His soldiers will steal and roast a thousand fowls.

A tyrant does not stay long in this world,
But the curse on his name rests for ever!

(Sa'di, Persian, story 19 from the Gulistan, from 19th century translations.)

[When government is less benevolent, poets find themselves voicing the discontents of the people. Popular poets keep the spirit of the people alive. The next two poems, complete with story, concern a wandering Irish poet resenting the yoke of foreign domination.]

A Reminiscence of Egan O'Rahilly

A splendid yew-tree had long been growing above a well of pure water beside a church that Cromwell had plundered, and that stood on a grassy plain which a greedy Protestant minister had seized from an Irish nobleman... This pleasant fellow now wished to cut off a fine long branch of it to make furniture for his house: but none of the carpenters or other workmen would touch the branch, as it provided a lovely shade for them... "I'll cut it down," declared the minister's skinny bandy-legged son, "so get me an axe at once!"

The reckless boy scrambled up the tree like a terrified cat fleeing from a pack of dogs, and reached a point where two branches were growing one across the other. He made an attempt at separating them with his hands; but in a flash they sprang back again from his grasp, gripped him by the windpipe, and hung him high between heaven and hell. And so the wretched Sassenach was left to dangle his legs from the swaying branches, with his feet touching nothing and his tongue protruding as if to taunt his father.

The minister was yelling and screaming like a pig in a bag or a goose caught under a gate – and no wonder! – as the workmen put up a ladder to rescue his son. Now Egan O'Rahilly from Slieve Luachra happened to be there, and he addressed the tree in the following lines composed on the spot:

> "What a glorious fruit you do bear!
> May every branch do as well!
> My sorrow not to see such fruit
> on each tree in Innisfail!"

"What is the poor wild Irish devil saying?" the minister asked, in English of course. "Och, he's lamenting your darling son," replied, also in English, a local wit who was standing beside

him. "Here is twopence for you to buy tobacco". "Thank'ee"
said Egan in English, adding, in Irish, "you servant of Satan!"
He then uttered the following lines:

> "Hurroo for the minister who gave me
> Twopence for lamenting his brat!
> May every single one of them
> suffer a fate such as that!"

(Egan O'Rahilly, Irish, 1670–1726, tr. S.D.P. Clough.)

[While Russia was under totalitarian rule, there was a hunger for
poetry, which was in scarce supply because most of what was
good was banned. The poet Akhmatova describes an event that
happened while she waited day after day outside prison gates for
news of her son, who had been taken away by the secret
police.]

In the terrible years of the Yezhov terror, I spent
seventeen months in the prison lines of Leningrad. Once,
someone recognised me. Then a woman with bluish lips
standing behind me, who, of course, had never heard me called
by name before, woke up from the stupour to which everyone
had succumbed and whispered in my ear (everyone spoke in
whispers there):
"Can you describe this?"
And I answered: "Yes, I can."
Then something that looked like a smile passed over
what had once been her face.

[The long poem 'Requiem' which this story prefaces describes the
Yezhov terror. It ends as follows.]

Epilogue 1

I learned how faces fall,
How terror darts from under eyelids,

How suffering traces lines
Of stiff cuneiform on cheeks,
How locks of ashen-blonde or black
Turn silver suddenly,
Smiles fade on submissive lips
And fear trembles in a dry laugh.
And I pray not for myself alone,
But for all those who stood there with me
In cruel cold, and in July's heat,
At that blind, red wall.

Epilogue 2

Once more the day of remembrance draws near.
I see, I hear, I feel you:

The one they almost had to drag at the end,
And the one who tramps her native land no more,

And the one who, tossing her beautiful head,
Said: "Coming here's like coming home."

I'd like to name them all by name,
But the list is confiscated and nowhere to be found.

I have woven a wide mantle for them
From their meagre, overheard words.

I will remember them always and everywhere
I will never forget them no matter what comes.

And if they gag my exhausted mouth
Through which a hundred million scream,

Then may the people remember me
On the eve of my remembrance day.

And if ever in this country
They decide to erect a monument to me,

I consent to that honour
Under these conditions – that it stand

Neither by the sea, where I was born:
My last tie with the sea is broken,

Nor in the tsar's garden near the cherished pine stump,
Where an inconsolable shade looks for me

But here, where I stood for three hundred hours,
And where they never unbolted the door for me.

This, lest in blissful death
I forget the rumbling of the Black Marias,

Forget how that detested door slammed shut
And an old woman howled like a wounded animal.

And may the melting snow stream like tears
From my motionless lids of bronze,

And a prison dove coo in the distance,
And the ships of the Neva sail calmly on.

(Anna Akhmatova, Russian, 1889–1966, tr. Judith Hemschemeyer.)

[The American prose-writer and humorist Mark Twain resorted
to poetry to express his bad conscience. In the interests of keeping
his popularity, he let himself be persuaded (by his publishers) not
to publish work critical of the direction his country had taken.

Twain felt the U.S. government had abandoned its role as
'defender of the weak' and become instead an 'extinguisher of
struggling liberties'. The poem that follows was written in secret

in 1901, and not published until 1966. The poem is written in the
voice of an imaginary American President, who has overseen the
betrayal of values and is filled with remorse.]

My Last Thought

I meant my country well –
God is my witness, this is true. In the beginning
I did not waver in my trust, but gave her loyal service –
The fair and just, when they reflect, will grant me this.
They know I was not bad at heart,
Though now they think my heart has changed...
And so it has – but not as *they* conceive! They think
It black and hard – whereas it only bleeds! Bleeds
For the widows it has made, the orphans it has starved,
The freedom it has crushed, the humble friends
It turned against, the faiths it broke,
The treacheries it devised, the freed slaves
It chained again,
The land it took by fraud and keeps by force,
The praise it won from sceptred thieves
For stooping to their ways,
The dirt it put upon our flag and name!

Lord God, forgive! For I was only weak,
Not bad. And I was out of place –
A lost and wandering atom in that vast Seat
Which only Lincolns and their like compactly fill.
I loved my country, and I meant it well:
I say it with my dying breath...
Pearl of the Antilles, speak!
I broke your chains, I set you free; I raised
My country's honour to the skies; I won
The Old World's scorn and hate, the New World's
'Well done, thou faithful son!'

O *then* I was myself! Grant me that!
Remember only that, dear land of my nativity,
Which I have brought to shame – forget the rest!

I erred through weakness, not intent. For I
Was overborne by sordid counsels,
Base ambitions, and from my head I took
The precious laurel I had earned, and in its place
I set this poor tin glory, now my wear,
Of World-Power, Conqueror of helpless tribes,
Extinguisher of struggling liberties!

Forget? Thou? No – that is a dream.
Thou canst not. The memory of treasons such as mine
Remains. They make a bartered nation blush;
And the wise know that only deeds
That lift a people's pride, and deeds
That make it hang its head,
Abide forever in its heart.

Arnold![2] How they crimson at his name! And yet -
Why, his meditated treason but concerned a garrison -
Mine – accomplished – peddled out a Nation and its honour:
And sold them for a song!

Upon my fading sight a holy vision rises
Our flag of snow and flame far-flashing in the sky!
And toward it the oppressed of every clime
Uplifting their poor fettered hands
In hope and trust and worship.....

It is gone.....How blest am I
That the last office of my dying eyes should be
To show it me as once it was: protector of the wronged,
Defender of the weak, friend of the homeless and forlorn!

....But there! – is not this the Flag again?
The dimness grows. It is the Flag, I think, but changed....
The twilight mellows....
Now the picture clears....It is the Flag, but -
O, not as it was in its great old days!

[2] Celebrated traitor who, during the American War of Independence, attempted
to hand over his garrison to the British.

The Stars are gone, a Skull and Bones
Are in their place; the Red Bars are there,
But soaked with guiltless blood;
The White Bars are Black –
Hide it from my sight!

The night of Death is come:
Its shadows deepen – let me sleep....
Sleep and forget, sleep and be forgotten –
If that dear boon might but be mine!
Farewell, my country –
So beloved by me, and so betrayed! I have sinned,
And I repent – have charity!
Teach the flowers that spring where I am hid,
And wandering summer airs that blow above my grave,
To speak for my dumb lips
And say to any that would search me out, 'Pass on –
Naught can ye learn of him:
Give him of your peace, forgive him and forget –
Pass on!'
(written May, 1901)

(Mark Twain (Samuel Langhorne Clemens), American, 1835–1910.)

[Poetry of the conscience is followed by poetry as the guardian
angel of words. The ancient sanctity of words is recalled by the
Russian poet Gumilev, who was Akhmatova's husband. He
argues that when words are only used about worldly things they
die.]

It is written that the Word is God.
But we have limited Its range
To the paltry boundaries of this world,
And like dead bees in an empty hive
Dead words emit a foul odour.

(N. Gumilev, Russian, 1886–1921, tr. J. Harris and C. Link.)

[Kennelly describes the same process eighty years on. Ozzie wonders what use words are.]

Words

what's words ozzie assed me
sounds dat kum outa peepul's mouths i said
where dey kum from first sez ozzie
dunno i replied

fukken fish have no words ozzie went on
but dey enjoy de fukken sea
and fukken tigers have no words
but dey enjoy eatin you and me

only peepul has words ozzie said
an luk at de shit dey talk
if i kud reed i'd say buks are shit as well

words are to kummynikate sez i

like shit sez ozzie won good bomm
blow de whole fukken world ta hell

(Brendan Kennelly, Irish, b. 1936; from 'Book of Judas'.)

[Ozzie never thought about words making pleasure and beauty. Eskimos used to expect each other to be poets, some good some bad. For them, words were part of the magic of the world, its harshness and its beauty.]

Delight in Singing

It's wonderful
to make up songs:
but all too many of them fail.

It's wonderful
to have your wishes granted:
but all too often
they slip by.

It's wonderful
to hunt reindeer:
but all too seldom
you succeed,
standing like a bright fire
on the plain.

(Anon., Eskimo, 1920's, tr. Rasmussen and Lowenstein.)

[A similar poem from another culture:]

It's a pleasure
When, after a hundred days
Of twisting my words
Without success,
Suddenly
A poem turns out nicely.

(Tachibana Akemi, Japanese, 1812–68, tr. D. Keene.)

[Using words, poets fashion visions to entrance us. The next three poems concern visions of harmony and peace. Humans have a deep-rooted and haunting conception, almost like a memory, of what it's like to live in harmony and peace. The myth of the Garden of Eden is just one of many stories recording a memory that became a vision — or is it the other way round? High expectations lead to bitter disappointment when they are not fulfilled.]

If only I could live
In the shade of spring leaves
Instead of in a world
Of disillusion and despair.

(Higuchi Ichiyo, Japanese, 1872–1896, tr. R. Danley.)

[A vision of happiness and harmony is the subject of the next poem, which is prefaced by a story. The story became known to all educated Chinese.]

During the T'ai-yuan period of the Chin dynasty a fisherman of Wu-ling once rowed upstream, unmindful of the distance he had gone, when he suddenly came to a grove of peach trees in bloom. For several hundred paces on both banks of the stream there was no other kind of tree. The wild flowers growing under them were fresh and lovely, and fallen petals covered the ground – it made a great impression on the fisherman. He went on for a while with the idea of finding out how far the grove extended. It came to an end at the foot of a mountain whence issued the spring that supplied the stream. There was a small opening in the mountain and it seemed as though light was coming through it. The fisherman left his boat and entered the cave, which at first was extremely narrow, barely admitting his body; after a few dozen steps it suddenly opened out onto a broad and level plain on which well-built houses were surrounded by rich fields and pretty ponds. Mulberry, bamboo and other trees and plants grew there, and criss-cross paths skirted the fields. The sounds of cocks crowing and dogs barking could be heard from one courtyard to the next. Men and women were coming and going about their work in the fields. The clothes they wore were like those of ordinary people. Old men and boys were carefree and happy.

When they caught sight of the fisherman, they asked in surprise how he had got there. The fisherman told the whole story, and was invited to go to their house, where he was served wine while they killed a chicken for a feast. When the other villagers heard about the fisherman's arrival they all came to pay him a visit. They told him that their ancestors had fled the disorders of Ch'in times and, having taken refuge there with wives and children and neighbours, had never ventured out again; consequently they had lost all contact with the outside world. They asked what the present ruling dynasty was, for they had never heard of the Han, let alone the Wei and the Chin. They sighed unhappily as the fisherman enumerated the dynasties one by one and recounted the vicissitudes of each. The visitors all asked him to come to their houses in turn, and at every house he had wine and food. He stayed several days. As he was about to go away, the people said, 'There's no need to mention our existence to outsiders.'

After the fisherman had gone out and recovered his boat, he carefully marked the route. On reaching the city, he reported what he had found to the magistrate, who at once sent a man to follow him back to the place. They proceeded according to the marks he had made, but went astray and were unable to find the cave again.

A high-minded gentleman of Nan-yang named Liu Tzu-chi heard the story and happily made preparations to go there, but before he could leave he fell sick and died. Since then there has been no one interested in trying to find such a place.

> The Ying clan disrupted heaven's ordinance
> And good men withdrew from such a world.
> Huang and Ch'i went off to Shang Mountain
> And these people too fled into hiding.
> Little by little their tracks were obliterated
> The paths they followed overgrown at last.
> By agreement they set about farming the land;
> When the sun went down each rested from his toil.
> Bamboo and mulberry provided shade enough,
> They planted beans and millet, each in season.
> From spring silkworms came the long silk thread,
> On the fall harvest no king's tax was paid.
> No sign of traffic on overgrown roads,

Cockcrow and dogsbark within each other's earshot.
Their ritual vessels were of old design,
And no new fashions in the clothes they wore.
Children wandered about singing songs,
Greybeards went paying one another calls.
When grass grew thick they saw the time was mild,
As trees went bare they knew the wind was sharp.
Although they had no calendar to tell,
The four seasons still filled out a year.
Joyous in their ample happiness
They had no need of clever contrivance.
Five hundred years this rare event stayed hid,
Then one day the fay retreat was found.
The pure and the shallow belong to separate worlds:
In a little while they were hidden again.
Let me ask you who are convention-bound,
Can you fathom those outside the dirt and noise?
I want to tread on the thin thin air
And rise up high to find my own kind.

(Tao Yuan Ming (T'ao Ch'ien), Chinese, 372–427, tr. J.R Hightower.)

[Gwen Harwood presents a modern-day vision of harmony in which people, sailing boats and engines are not incompatible with peace on earth.]

Threshold

Know that a peaceful harbour
framed by low hills, a refuge
that might be glimpsed one moment
in a happy dream, exists:
a marina spiky with masts;
salt glitter, boat-brightness rocking
in grey-green shallows, and gulls
reading in deeper sea-gleam
the text of wind and tide.

Some genius of earth
devised this generous place,
this charm of light compacting
sea, sky, the hills of Bruny,
the birds with airfilled bones,
the clouds like ghosts of sails,
into one form, one presence
whose guests we are, and welcome.
The ferry's engines throb

among water's ancient voices.
Children's and seabirds' cries
fade at the fringe of language
as the road leads gently upwards
to a gate where casuarinas
crosshatch the shining water.
The road leads on. But pause:
lift clear from time's refractions,
from the mind's reflective tricks,

this day; see its true shape.
Look how a lizard skims
from leaf-shade, and is basking
stone-still on stone, a finger-length
creature absorbing sunlight.
A crow with steel-bright eye
testing the pitch of silence
flaps to a neighbouring pine,
settles his dark voice down;

pause for a moment here.
These gums that fracture light
are home to the intricate compound
eyes of the insect kingdom,
and birds, whose eyes can read
the to-us invisible pattern
of the polarized sky, are singing
what is real but still unnamed.
Our words and thoughts are polished

like pebbles ground in the stream
of time, but here's an enclave,
land held in arms of water,
where the plover and their young
are safe in feathery grasses
stirred by the seawind breathing
a prayer of peace and healing
in the pure, authentic speech
that earth alone can teach.

(Gwen Harwood, Australian, b. 1920.)

[By holding out these expectations poets remind us of what life
could be like and what is worth striving for. But the yearning for
harmony and order can lead to dangerous ground. The poet
d'Annunzio invented fascism[3] and Yeats followed it. Mao
Tse-tung loved and wrote poetry while devising the deaths of
millions. Heaven-on-earth is a fine ideal, but life is cruel and we
should not use cruelty of our own in trying to outwit it. Jean
Ingelow wrote of the difference between the afflictions of
Providence and the inflictions of our fellow human beings:]

When troubles come of God,
When men are frozen out of work, when wives
Are sick, when working fathers fail and die,
When boats go down at sea – then nought behoves
Like patience; but for troubles wrought of men
Patience is hard – I tell you it is hard.

(Jean Ingelow, English, 1820–97.)

[From visions of harmony we move to dissent. The voice of
dissent is strong in Islamic poetry, which was given much freedom by the Prophet's statement that all poets are liars. This gave
poets protection from criticism – who gives serious attention to

[3] In 1921 he invaded the disputed port of Fiume with some Nationalist friends,
and he ruled it for 16 months as Fascist leader.

liars? − and many of them devoted themselves to celebrating drunkenness, a sin in Islam. Furthermore, because simple belief in God protects an individual from persecution under Islamic law, poets were free to be critical of religious hypocrisy. The poet al-Ma'arri freely criticised the orthodox religious thinking of his time:]

> You said we've a wise creator
> And I replied you're right, but look,
> You claim he's timeless and nowhere.
> Such terms, for all we know, could be
> A secret language: which amounts
> To saying we cannot think straight.

(al-Ma'arri, Arabic (Syria), 973–1053, tr. Wightman and al-Udhari.)

[Poets can be like pipers, piping a tune for the world to dance to, and they can lead us to new ideas of how life can be lived. In 1955, the Persian poet Farrokhzhad shocked readers by writing of female sexual desire.]

> I sinned a sin full of pleasure,
> in an embrace that was warm and fiery,
> I sinned surrounded by arms
> that were hot and avenging and iron.
>
> In that dark and silent seclusion,
> I looked into his secret-full eyes.
> My heart impatiently shook in my breast
> in response to the request of his needful eyes.
>
> In that dark and silent seclusion,
> I sat dishevelled at his side.
> His lips poured passion on my lips,
> I escaped from the sorrow of my crazed heart.

I whispered in his ear the tale of love:
I want you, o life of mine,
I want you, o life-giving embrace,
o crazed lover of mine, you.

Desire sparked a flame in his eyes;
the red wine danced in the cup.
In the soft bed, my body
drunkenly quivered on his chest.

I sinned a sin full of pleasure,
next to a shaking, stupefied form.
O god, who knows what I did,
In that dark and quiet seclusion.

(Farogh Farrokhzhad, Persian, 1934–67, tr. M. Hillman.)

[Pushkin was in trouble with authority for most of his short life.
In the next poem he defends the poet's instinct to follow what he
knows is right and not what others tell him. The lines about
Desdemona and the Moor have a personal relevance; Pushkin was
the great grandson of a Moor employed by Peter the Great, and
Pushkin was proud of the black element in his ancestry.]

Eyes open wide, the poet weaves,
Blind as a bat, his urgent way;
But feels a tug upon his sleeve,
And hears a passing stranger say:
'Why do you betray the Muse
By wandering aimlessly, my friend?
Before you reach the heights, you choose
To gaze beneath you, and descend.
Blind to the great harmonious scheme
Of creation, you become possessed,
Too often, by some trivial theme,
And sterile fevers rack your breast.

A genius should look up – the duty
Of a true poet is to rise;
His dwelling place should be the skies;
His theme and inspiration, beauty.'
– Why does a wind swirl through a dusty
Ravine and shake its stunted trees,
And yet a ship spread out its thirsty
Canvas in vain for a light breeze?
Why does an eagle leave the peak,
And, gliding past the church-spire, seek
The miserable tree-stump? Why
Did youthful Desdemona swoon
In the Moor's spasm, as the moon
In the night's shadow loves to lie?
Because for wind, and eagle's claws,
And a girl's heart, there are no laws.
The poet too, like Aquilon★,   ★the north wind
Lifts what he wants, and bears it on –
Flies like an eagle, heeds no voice
Directing him, spurns all control,
And clasps the idol of his choice,
Like Desdemona, to his soul.

(Alexander Pushkin, Russian, 1799–1837, tr. D.M. Thomas.)

[Poets take their calling seriously. Sometimes bitter insults are cast
to and fro concerning who is true to the muse and who isn't.
Faludy complains to a friend who has won Hungary's chief
literary award:]

They'll never give me such a medal,
Not in a thousand years they won't!
Not me, because of what I write;
But you, because of what you don't.

[and Auden said of poets who betray their calling:]

'abhorred in the heavens are all
self-proclaimed poets who, to wow an
audience, utter some resonant lie'.

[Truth can be uncomfortable. Western civilisation, while
admirably rejecting old-fashioned censorship, has found other
methods of suppressing uncomfortable truths, methods which are
all the more successful for involving no coercion. Rewarding
conformity is an obvious one; more insidious is the pervasive
admiration of what is commercially successful, which banishes
dissenting minority voices to a lunatic fringe. Novelty takes on
the role and even the name of art, and it must grow more and
more bizarre to satisfy more and more jaded appetites. Purveyors
of popular culture fall back on tried and tested fascinations like sex
and violence. The next poem describes the kind of stuff a modern
'professional' writer is expected to churn out. A scriptwriter is
being told by a film producer to get down to basics, forget about
his love of islands and give people 'what they want'.]

The Man Who Loved Islands

A Two-Page Outline

A man is leaning on a cold iron rail
watching an islet from an island and so on,
say, Charlotte Amalie facing St. John,
which begins the concept of infinity
uninterrupted by any mortal sail,
only the thin ghost of a tanker drawing the horizon
behind it with the silvery slick of a snail,
and that's the first shot of this forthcoming film
starring James Coburn and his tanned, leathery, frail
resilience and his now whitening hair,
and his white, vicious grin. Now, we were where?
On this island, one of the Virgins, the prota-
gonist established. Now comes the second shot,

and chaos of artifice still called the plot,
which has to get the hero off somewhere
else, 'cause there's no kick in contemplation
of silvery light upon wind-worried water
between here and the islet of St. John,
and how they are linked like any silver chain
glinting against the hero's leather chest,
sold in the free gift ports, like noon-bright water.
The hero's momentary rest on the high rail
can be a good beginning. To start with rest
is good – the tanker can come later.
But we can't call it 'The Man Who Loved Islands'
any more than some Zen-Karate film
would draw them with 'The Hero Who Loves Water'.
No soap. There must be something with diamonds,
emeralds, emeralds the color of the shallows there,
or sapphires, like blue unambiguous air,
sapphires for Sophia, but we'll come to that.
Coburn looks great with or without a hat,
and there must be some minimum of slaughter
that brings in rubies, but you cannot hover
over that first shot like a painting. Action
is all of art, the thoughtless pace
of lying with style, so that when it's over,
that first great shot of Coburn's leathery face,
crinkled like the water which he contemplates,
could be superfluous, in the first place,
since that tired artifice called history,
which in its motion is as false as fiction,
requires an outline, a summary. I can think of none,
quite honestly. I'm no photographer; this
could be a movie. I mean things are moving,
the water for example, the light on the man's hair
that has gone white, even those crescent sands
are just as moving as his love of islands;
the tanker that seems still is moving, even
the clouds like galleons anchored in heaven,
and what is moving most of all of course

is the violent man lulled into this inaction
by the wide sea. Let's hold it on the sea
as we establish their ancient interaction,
a hint of the Homeric, a little poetry
before the whole mess hits the bloody fan.
All these islands that you love, I guaran-
tee we'll work them in as background, with
generous establishing shots from Jim's car and
even a few harbours and villages, *if*
we blow the tanker up and get the flames
blazing with oil, and Sophia, if she's free,
daintily smudged, with her slip daintily torn,
is climbing down this rope ladder, and we shoot up
from Coburn's P.O.V. – he's got the gems –
that's where we throw in Charlotte Amalie
and the waterfront bars, and this Danish alley
with the heavies chasing, and we can keep all the
business of Jim on the rail; that lyric stuff
goes with the credits if you insist on keeping it tender; I can see it, but things must get rough
pretty damn fast, or else you lose them, pally,
or tell you what, let's save it for THE END.

(Derek Walcott, St Lucia, b. 1930.)

[In an economy where the emphasis is on turnover, poetry is a product to be ignored. It's cheap to reproduce, it doesn't lose its meaning, and a book of it can give pleasure to generations.

The next poem presents a very different idea of what society wants from its writers.]

The wisdom of the scribe depends on the opportunity of leisure;
    only the one who has little business can become wise.
How can one become wise who handles the plough,
    and who glories in the shaft of a goad,
who drives oxen and is occupied with their work,
    and whose talk is about bulls?

He sets his heart on ploughing furrows,
    and he is careful about fodder for the heifers.
So too is every artisan and master artisan
    who labours by night as well as by day;
those who cut the signets of seals,
    each is diligent in making a great variety;
they set their heart on painting a lifelike image,
    and they are careful to finish their work.
So too is the smith, sitting by the anvil,
    intent on his iron-work;
the breath of fire melts his flesh,
    and he struggles with the heat of the furnace;
the sound of the hammer deafens his ears,
    and his eyes are on the pattern of the object.
He sets his heart on finishing his handiwork,
    and he is careful to complete its decoration.
So too is the potter sitting at his work
    and turning the wheel with his feet;
he is always deeply concerned over his products,
    and he produces them in quantity.
He moulds the clay with his arm
    and makes it pliable with his feet;
he sets his heart to finish the glazing,
    and he takes care in firing the kiln.

All these rely on their hands,
    and all are skillful in their own work.
Without them no city is inhabited,
    and wherever they live, they will not go hungry.
Yet they are not sought out for the council of the people,
    nor do they attain eminence in the public assembly.
They do not sit in the judge's seat,
    nor do they understand the decisions of the courts;
they cannot expound discipline or judgement,
    and they are not found among the rulers.
But they maintain the fabric of the world,
    and their concern is for the exercise of their trade.

How different the one who devotes himself
  to the study of the law of the Most High!
He seeks out the wisdom of all the ancients,
  and is concerned with prophecies;
he preserves the sayings of the famous
  and penetrates the subtleties of parables;
he seeks out the hidden meanings of proverbs
  and is at home with the obscurites of parables.
He serves among the great
  and appears before rulers;
he travels in foreign lands
  and learns what is good and evil in the human lot.
He sets his heart to rise early
  to seek the Lord who made him,
and to petition the Most High;
  he opens his mouth in prayer
and asks pardon for his sins.

(Jesus Ben Sira, Jewish Egyptian, fl. c. 180 BC. The Bible, New Revised Standard Version, Sirach 38.24 – 39.5.)

[The next poem celebrates the struggle to hope when there seems little justification for hope, to understand when understanding seems impossible, and to be happy when cause for misery is all around.]

Testament

To the youngest prostitute
In the oldest and darkest barrio*   *town district
I leave my earrings
Cut in crystal, limpid and pure...

And to that forgotten virgin
Girl without tenderness
Dreaming somewhere of a happy story
I leave my white dress
My wedding dress
Trimmed with lace...

I offer my old rosary
To that old friend of mine
Who does not believe in God...

And my books – rosaries
That tell of a different suffering –
Are for humble folk
Who never learned to read.

As for my crazy poems
Those that echo sincerely
The confusion and sadness in my heart
Those that sing of hope
Where none can be found
Those I give to you my love...

So that in a moment of peace
When my soul comes from afar
To kiss your eyes

You will go into the night
Accompanied by the moon
To read them to children
That you meet along each street...

(Alda Lara, Angolan, contemporary, tr. D. Burness.)

[Poetry is born of our experience of living, its intense joys and
sorrows. 'Who knows what horrors go to make a song?' writes
Brendan Kennelly. In the next poem Oswald Mtshali describes
beautiful singing coming from the hearts of degraded mine
workers. Those who are degrading them lose such beauty as
surely as they gain luxury.]

Amagoduka at Glencoe Station

We travelled a long journey
through the wattle forests of Vryheid,
crossed the low-levelled Blood River

whose water flowed languidly
as if dispirited for the
shattered glory of my ancestors.

We passed the coalfields of Dundee –
blackheads in the wrinkled face
of Northern Zululand –
until our train ultimately came
to a hissing stop at Glencoe.

Many people got off
leaving the enraged train
to snort and charge at the night
on its way to Durban.

The time was 8 pm.

I picked up my suitcase,
sagging under the weight of a heavy overcoat
I shambled to the "non-European Males" waiting room.

The room was crowded
the air hung, a pall of choking odour,
rotten meat, tobacco and sour beer.

Windows were shut tight
against the sharp bite of winter.

Amagoduka* sat on bare floor   *mine labour recruits
their faces sucking the warmth
of the coal fire crackling in the corner.

They chewed dried bread
scooped corned beef with rusty knives,
and drank mqombothi from the plastic can
which they passed from mouth to mouth.

They spoke animatedly
and laughed in thunderous peals.

A girl peeped through the door,
they shuddered at the sudden cold blast,
jumped up to fondle and leer at her
"Hau! ngena Sisi! – Oh! come in sister!"

She shied like a frightened filly
banged the door and bolted.
They broke into tumultuous laughter.

One of them picked up a guitar
plucked it with broken finger nails
caressed its strings with a castor oil bottle -

it sighed like a jilted girl.
"You play down! Phansi! Play D" he whispered.

Another joined in with concertina,
its sound fluttered in flowery notes
like a butterfly picking pollen from flower to flower.

The two began to sing,
their voices crying for the mountains
and the hills of Msinga, stripped naked of
their green garment.

They crossed rivers and streams,
gouged dry by the sun rays,
where lowing cattle genuflected
for a blade of grass and a drop of water
on riverbeds littered with carcasses and bones.

They spoke of hollow-cheeked maidens
heaving drums of brackish water
from a far away fountain.

They told of big-bellied babies
sucking festering fingers
instead of their mothers' shrivelled breasts.

Two cockroaches
as big as my overcoat buttons
jived across the floor
snatched meat and breadcrumbs
and scurried back to their hideout.

The whole group joined in unison:
curious eyes peered through frosted windows
"Ekhaya bafowethu! – Home brothers!"

We come from across the Tugela river,
we are going to EGoli! EGoli! EGoli!*   *Johannesburg
where they'll turn us into moles
that eat the gold dust
and spit out blood.

We'll live in compounds
where young men are pampered
into partners for older men.

We'll visit shebeens
where a whore waits for a fee
to leave your balls burning
with syphilitic fire.

If the gods are with us –
Oh! beloved black gods of our forefathers
What have we done to you
Why have you forsaken us –
We'll return home
to find our wives nursing babies –
unknown to us
but only to their mothers and loafers.

(Oswald Mbuyiseni Mtshali, South African, b. 1940.)

[Simone Weil comments on our human need for poetry, 'Slavery is work without any light from eternity, without poetry, without religion'.[1] The more poetry of all sorts is ignored by society, the grimmer people's lives become. In the next poem, the poet says that however unhappy her life has been, at least she has 'lived' in the fullest sense of the word.]

Life

When I have watched the people crawling by
So haggard-visaged, and so wrinkled-browed,
With eyes that see naught save the greedy ground,
With ears that hear naught save their toiling feet,
To whom there can exist no other world
Besides the one of Commonplace and Real,
Where Fancy's idle beams ne'er fleck the gloom
With dancing, changing, lights of flitted dreams,
I do rejoice, for I, with all my woes
May see the sights and hear the sounds they miss,
For I may see the beauty in a cloud
Or tiny flower or slender blade of grass,
May watch the tree-tops whispering with the winds,
The slanting rain drops greyed by solemn skies,
And find insistent joyousness in all;
May speechless stand before some landscape grand,
Where mountains lift their regal heads in peace,
Enwrapped at morn in frail, sheer, robes of mist,
Enwrapped at even in voluptuous garb,
For I may hear the songs of little things,
The cricket, locust, tree-toad, and the bird
That sings within the woods at summer dawns
And twitters sleepily at summer dusks;
For I may hear the yearnings of the soul
Within the voice or throbbing violin
Until the ear so wrung by chords of joy
Comes nigh to bursting in delicious pain;
For I may feel the fierceness of great love

[1] Simone Weil: An Anthology, ed. Sian Miles (Virago, 1986) p. 180.

With all its agony and rare delights,
Its dire despair and lightning heights of joy.
What though I die mid racking pain,
And heart seared through and through by grief,
I still rejoice for I, at least, have lived.

(Angelina Weld Grimke, American, 1880–1958.)

[In the following poem Mandelstam, surrounded by the carnage
of the Stalin era, prophesies the survival of the values he lives
by.]

Into the distance go the mounds of people's heads.
I am growing smaller here – no one notices me any more,
but in caressing books and children's games
I will rise from the dead to say the sun is shining.

(Osip Mandelstam, Russian, 1891–1938, tr. D. McDuff.)

9. The End?

[The Twentieth Century isn't the first historical age to be racked by anxiety and despair about the future. The first poem was written in Germany during the Thirty Years War, when Christians were tearing each other to pieces (literally) over points of doctrine. Ruminations on these events give us hope; there's nothing like looking back on another time when hope seemed the property of idiots.]

All is Vanity

Whichever way we look, only vanity on earth.
What one man builds today, another destroys tomorrow.
The land where cities stand will soon again be meadows;
On them, peasant children, playing among the flocks.
Blooms, luxurious now, are soon trodden down;
What boasts defiantly now is just tomorrow's ashes.
Nothing on earth can last; not of stone or bronze.
Should fortune shine today, hardships soon will thunder.
The fame of lofty deeds vanishes like a dream,
Can Time's plaything, Man, be expected then to last?
Ah! What is everything dear to us, everything we value
But wretched triviality; like shadow, dust, and wind,
Like a flower in a meadow found once but never more.
Yet – not a single person wants to think on the eternal.

(Gryphius, German, 1616–1664, tr. I.M.)

[Petronius saw the greedy decadence of Rome from the inside. Helen Waddell, the translator of the next poem, notes 'He was an aristocrat who had been an admirable provincial governor in the old tradition, and then came back to Rome, recording the

civilization that he relished and sickened at.' Despite the
decadence of the time he observed, it was another four centuries
before Rome finally collapsed.]

The Roman was the victor of the world.
All seas, all lands, the journeys of the sun,
Aye, and the moon,
He owned them all and was not satisfied.
The fretted seas he sent this way and that
With his great-bellied keels: if round yon headland
A little bay hid, or distant land
That cropped with gold, she was the enemy;
The obedient oracles for war stood ready,
The hunt for wealth was up.
He had no pleasure in familiar things
That please the common folk: the well-worn joys
That poor men's hands have handled. Out at sea
Soldiers would prate about the bronze of Corinth;
The purple that was once got from the shellfish
Is dull stuff now beside their chemicals.
The men of Africa have cause to curse them.
China's despoiled of silk, Arabia
Hath stripped her incense fields.
Always fresh killing and new wounds of peace...
They hew the citron tree in Africa
And make their tables of its gold-flecked surface,
And round that barren and ignoble wood
Gather a crowd of men sodden with drink,
And yon mercenary swills the wealth of the world,
Rust on his idle sword.

Your gluttony is an ingenious rascal.
Sea-water keeps your wrasse★ alive,   ★a type of fish.
Come all the way to your plate from Sicily.
The Lucrine oysters are extravagance,
But most reviving to a dulled appetite.
Silent, O Phasis, are thy waters now,
Silent the shore.

A solitary wind sighs through the boughs,
Where the birds nest no more.
The selfsame madness is in politics:
Easy to buy a Roman citizen:
He'll sell you his vote any day for a bucket-shop share
Or a spot of cash. The man in the street's for sale,
And so is the man in the House: they all have their price.
The pristine liberal virtue of the old men
Has dropt away, the power they had they lost
Scrambling for gold, their ancient dignity
Rotted by money, trodden underfoot.
They set the mob on Cato, drove him out,
And now they are more sick at heart than he.
The man's abashed that took his office from him.
Here is the symbol of a people's shame,
The ruin of their standards:
When they beat the old man up, sent him to exile,
It was no man they banished,
It was the honour and the power of Rome.

Lost, lost is Rome, her own self her own prey.
She hath made herself a spoil and there is none
That will avenge her.
This flooding sewer of money out at interest
Has caught the common folk in a double whirlpool,
Their usury has choked them.
Not a house but is mortgaged, not a man but in pawn.
Like a disease hatched in the silent cells
This madness rages through their harried bodies,
Baying them down.
Men ruined think of robbery in arms:
The good things luxury has spent and spoiled
They'll win again by wounds.
Your beggar dare be bold: he has naught to lose.
There's Rome asleep in the gutter, snoring fast.
And what's to wake her?
Sound reason or the arts?

Or naught but war and madness and the lust
That's wakened by the sword?

(Petronius, Roman, died A.D. 66; tr. Helen Waddell.)

[After the Roman Empire's final collapse, its provinces were left
at the mercy of marauders to re-establish a more primitive order.
A poem survives from Britain telling of these times. Appro-
priately, it is partly lost; the two pages on which it was written are
damaged by fire.]

Fate has smashed these wonderful walls,
This broken city, has crumbled the work
Of giants. The roofs are gutted, the towers
Fallen, the gates ripped off, frost
In the mortar, everything moulded, gaping,
Collapsed. The earth has clutched at rulers
And builders, a hundred generations rotting
In its rigid hands. These red-stained stones,
Streaked with grey, stood while governors
And kingdoms dissolved into dust, and storms
Crashed over them; they were broad and high, and they fell.
....
....
.... strong-hearted men hung
The walls together with beaten wire.
It was a shining city, filled with bath-houses,
With towering gables, with the shouts of soldiers,
With dozens of rousing drinking-halls,
Until Fate's strength was swung against it.
The riches died away, pestilence
Came, the crowds of soldiers were dead;
Their forts and camps crumbled to the ground,
And the city, with all its idols and temples,
Decayed to these ruins, its buildings rotted,
Its red-stoned arches splitting brick
From brick. And the ruined site sank

To a heap of tumbled stones, where once
Cheerful, strutting warriors flocked,
Golden armour gleaming, giddy
With wine; here was wealth, silver,
Gems, cattle, land, in the crowning
City of a far-flung kingdom. There were buildings
Of stone, where steaming currents threw up
Surging heat; a wall encircled
That brightness, with the baths inside at the glowing
Heart. Life was easy and lush.
They'd make the warm streams pour over
Old grey stones.....................
.... until
The rounded pools grew hot...........
....
....
.... a kingly thing,
A house ....a city.......

(Anon., Anglo-Saxon, ? before 940 A.D., tr. Burton Raffel.)

[Since our destiny is physical extinction, it's often argued that we
should eat, drink and be merry while we are able. However,
many poets respond to mortality in a different vein. The existence
of death makes a mockery of our constructions of wealth and
glory, and we should take life seriously while we are able.]

> The glories of our blood and state
> Are shadows, not substantial things;
> There is no armour against fate;
> Death lays his icy hand on kings..... (James Shirley)

> Our pleasure here is all vainglory
> This false world is transitory,
> The flesh is brittle, the Fiend is sly:-
> Timor Mortis conturbat me...[1]   (William Dunbar)

---

[1] 'Fear of Death confounds me'.

[The poet Gongora uses images of imminent mortality to urge his friend Licio to take life seriously.]

On Life's Deceptive Brevity

Solicitous, the swift arrow speeds
Towards its destined mark, in which it bites;
Silent in the mute sand, the chariot
Turns in victory round the winning post;
Yet swifter, and more secretly, our life
Hurries us to our end. For those that doubt –
Beasts bereft of reason though they be –
Day by day the sun is a warning comet.
Has Carthage[2] learned this, Licio, yet you doubt?
You live dangerously, Licio, persisting
In chasing shadows and holding to deceptions.
The hours will hardly forgive you your folly;
The hours, which are filing away at the days,
The days, which are gnawing away at the years.

(Gongora, Spanish, 1561–1625, tr. I.M.)

[Baudelaire relishes mortality, which mocks the pretensions of humanity that disgust him.]

The Lid

Wherever he may go, on land or sea,
Under a climate of flame or a white sky,
Be he a servant of Jesus, or courtier of Venus,
A beggar lost in darkness or glittering Croesus,

City– or country-dweller, vagrant or in a chair,
Whether his little brain is active or slow, –
Everywhere man submits to the terror of mystery,
And looks above him only with trembling eye.

[2] City destroyed by Rome in A.D. 146.

Above him, the Heavens! – the wall of his stifling tomb,
A ceiling lit by a comic opera's glare
Where each buffoon stomps the blood-soaked earth;

Terror of the libertine, hope of the mad hermit;
The Sky! Blackened lid of the great stew-pot
Where humanity boils, imperceptible and vast!

(Baudelaire, French, 1821–67, tr. I.M.)

[Another contemplation of mortality, this time from Tao Yuan-Ming.]

Returning to my Home in the Country

So long since I've enjoyed the hills and ponds,
the boundless pleasures of woods and fields –
I take my sons and nephews in hand;
parting brushwood, we walk through the tangled site of a village,
strolling among the knolls and grave mounds,
lingering lingering where people lived long ago.
Here and there are traces of their wells and cooking ranges,
rotting stumps of mulberry and bamboo still remaining.
We asked someone gathering firewood,
"Where are all these people now?"
The wood gatherer turned to us and said,
"They're dead and gone, none of them left!"
In one generation both court and city change –
be assured, that's no idle saying.
Man's life is a phantom affair,
and he returns at last to the empty void.

(Tao Yuan Ming, Chinese, 372–427, tr. Burton Watson.)

[Wallowing in despair can make our own human destructiveness seem less bad – if life's like that, how can we be otherwise? The reasonable voice of Goethe speaks out against such a view of life,

observing that life's beauty is the flourishing of mortal
creatures.]

"It alarms me, the insidiousness
Of all this worthless talk
In which nothing lasts, all is fugitive
And what one sees is already gone;
And it entangles me, the fearsome
Grey-knit ensnaring net." -
Take comfort! What perishes not
Is the everlasting law, by which
Flourish and bloom the lily, and the rose.

(Goethe, German, 1749–1832, tr. I.M.)

[Macbeth, in Shakespeare's play, having ruined his personal
prospects of survival utters one of the great speeches of despair. It
expresses an attitude fashionable in contemporary art and
literature (as our own culture moves us close to self-destruction)
that life signifies nothing.]

To-morrow, and to-morrow, and to-morrow,
Creeps in this petty pace from day to day,
To the last syllable of recorded time;
And all our yesterdays have lighted fools
The way to dusty death. Out, out, brief candle!
Life's but a walking shadow, a poor player,
That struts and frets his hour upon the stage,
And then is heard no more; it is a tale
Told by an idiot, full of sound and fury,
Signifying nothing.

(William Shakespeare, English, 1564–1616.)

[Should we as a species die out, or lose our dominance, other
species will eventually gain at our expense. Maybe in time
another species will dominate the Earth as the dinosaurs once did

and as we do now. Something like a horror of this displacement haunts Yeats' poem, written in the shadow of war. As civilised values collapse a mythical beast, 'vexed to nighmare' by the image of the gentle Christ-child, makes its second coming in the town where Jesus was born.]

The Second Coming

Turning and turning in the widening gyre
The falcon cannot hear the falconer;
Things fall apart; the centre cannot hold;
Mere anarchy is loosed upon the world,
The blood-dimmed tide is loosed, and everywhere
The ceremony of innocence is drowned;
The best lack all conviction, while the worst
Are full of passionate intensity.

Surely some revelation is at hand;
Surely the Second Coming is at hand.
The Second Coming! Hardly are those words out
When a vast image out of *Spiritus Mundi* [3]
Troubles my sight: somewhere in sands of the desert
A shape with lion body and the head of a man,
A gaze blank and pitiless as the sun,
Is moving its slow thighs, while all about it
Reel shadows of the indignant desert birds.
The darkness drops again; but now I know
That twenty centuries of stony sleep
Were vexed to nightmare by a rocking cradle,
And what rough beast, its hour come round at last,
Slouches towards Bethlehem to be born?

(W.B. Yeats, Irish, 1865–1939.)

[The subject is treated more humourously and optimistically by Gwen Harwood. The grim rationality of science destroys the

---

[3] A term use by Yeats for a kind of corporate imagination, similar to Jung's collective unconscious.

values of humanity and then, unintentionally, humanity itself.
But humanity's wondering, questing spirit is reborn when the
blob created in the laboratory evolves into an 'airy, merman
race'.]

Hesperian

"The old philosophy's dead and finished.
Dazzled by positivistic light
it lay while Wittgenstein dispatched it
and Russell kicked it out of sight.
A few old men in musty studies
study the dead brute's photograph."
So the young scientist in his laboratory
said to his keen, admiring staff.

(At: "Essence is expressed by *grammar*"
an aged philosopher sighed, "My God!")
From a jar of amnion in the laboratory
a cytoplasmic pseudopod,
past apparatus set up that morning
to find if headless dogs could bark,
crept to the garden and told by texture
the white from the red rose in the dark.

Captured next day, returned to its fluid
apparently dead, it escaped and curled
round the switch that fired the fuse that exploded
the secret bomb that wrecked the world.
Blown past the debris of men and cities
it might have circled infinity,
but by chance this morsel of deathless jelly
fell in the vast Venusian sea.

On luminous waves half cloud, half water,
translucent tissue conceived the sun;
pulsed in his dim, refracted ardour;
grew eyebuds; divided itself from one

to two, and pursuing its *alter ego*
spread billowing wings, assumed a face
of lustrous, dolphin-curving beauty,
fathered an airy-merman race

air-boned, sea-smooth, of flawless bearing
trimmed to their watery element,
who in their liquid-rolling language
questioned the truth of their descent:
"What is the God whose fiat ordered
genesis in our cloudy sphere?
What is this flux we call becoming?
What secret force sustains us here?

"What is the true, eternal essence
we apprehend, but cannot see?
What is this stuff that rains from nowhere,
broken, and heavier than we?
Our origin? Our end? The substance
of some lost alien world, in truth?
(One fingered as he spoke, unknowing,
a fragment of a human tooth.)

"What is our archetypal being?
What is the good? the true? the right?"
So they discoursed, while deepening shadows
involved the long Venusian night,
When, rising through their cloudy stratum,
they watched the constellations thrust
their quivering shafts, diffused in splendour
through wandering tellurian dust.

(Gwen Harwood, Australian, b. 1920.)

[Though Nature is 'red in tooth and claw' and life within it
'nasty, brutish and short', there is nevertheless an innocent joy in

most of Nature's proceedings. To Wordsworth, our human species looks bad in comparison.]

Lines Written in Early Spring

I heard a thousand blended notes
While in a grove I sat reclined
In that sweet mood when pleasant thoughts
Bring sad thoughts to the mind.

To her fair works did Nature link
The human soul that through me ran;
And much it grieved my heart to think
What man has made of man.

Through primrose tufts, in that green bower,
The periwinkle trailed its wreaths;
And 'tis my faith that every flower
Enjoys the air it breathes.

The birds around me hopped and played,
Their thoughts I cannot measure:-
But the least motion that they made,
It seemed a thrill of pleasure.

The budding twigs spread out their fan,
To catch the breezy air;
And I must think, do all I can,
That there was pleasure there.

If this belief from heaven be sent,
If such be Nature's holy plan,
Have I not reason to lament
What man has made of man?

(William Wordsworth, English, 1770–1850.)

[Tagore was nearly eighty when the Second World War began. Reading of the slaughter in the West he despaired, almost wishing that his own species should suffer extinction for its crimes.]

When the god of death gave the command for annihilation,
men took on themselves the task of self-destruction.
Depressed, I've thought: why doesn't a sudden disaster
hit this errant planet which has veered from its course,
so we all die together, in one big blazing pyre?
But then I reflect: if through suffering on suffering
sin hasn't rotted, its seed will surely sleep
in the ashes of the holocaust, and on the breast
of a new creation
once more raise its thorns.

(Tagore, Bengali, 1861–1941, tr. Ketaki Kushari Dyson.)

[Timon of Athens, in Shakespeare's play of the same name, prayed in bitterness for humankind to lose its dominion. He speaks as he digs with his hands for roots to eat, addressing earth as 'mother'.]

      Common mother, thou,
Whose womb unmeasurable and infinite breast
Teems, and feeds all; whose selfsame mettle,
Whereof thy proud child, arrogant man, is puffed,
Engenders the black toad and adder blue,
The gilded newt and eyeless venomed worm,
With all th'abhorred births below crisp heaven
Whereon Hyperion's quick'ning fire doth shine;
Yield him, who all thy human sons doth hate,
From forth thy plenteous bosom one poor root!
Ensear* thy fertile and conceptious womb,   *dry up, or
Let it no more bring out ingrateful man!   close by burning
Go great with tigers, dragons, wolves and bears;
Teem with new monsters, whom thy upward face

Hath to the marbled mansion all above
Never presented! – O, a root! dear thanks! -
Dry up thy marrows, vines, and plough-torn leas;
Whereof ingrateful man, with liquorish draughts
And morsels unctuous, greases his pure mind,
That from it all consideration slips!
(*Enter Apemantus*)
More man? Plague, plague!

(Shakespeare, English, 1564–1616: Timon, 4, 3, 175–195.)

[Despair at the behaviour of human towards human is an old
subject for poetry. The poem that follows was written four
thousand years ago. It is from the 'Dispute over suicide'. A man is
talking to his soul, arguing that it's right for him to end his own
life.]

To whom shall I speak today?
    Brothers are evil,
    The companions of yesterday do not love.
To whom shall I speak today?
    Hearts are rapacious,
    Every man seizes the goods of his neighbour...
To whom shall I speak today?
    Men are contented with evil,
    Goodness is neglected everywhere.
To whom shall I speak today?
    One who should make a man enraged by his evil behaviour
    Makes everyone laugh, though his iniquity is grievous...
To whom shall I speak today?
    The wrongdoer is an intimate,
    The brother with whom one should act is become an enemy.
To whom shall I speak today?
    Yesterday is not remembered,
    No one now helps him that hath done good.
To whom shall I speak today?
    Faces are averted,

Every man has his face downcast towards his brethren.
To whom shall I speak today?
  Hearts are rapacious,
  No man has a heart upon which one can rely.
To whom shall I speak today?
  There are no righteous men.
  The land is given over to workers of iniquity...
To whom shall I speak today?
  I am laden with misery
  Through lack of an intimate.
To whom shall I speak today?
  The sin that roams the land,
  It has no end.
Death is in my sight today,
  Like the recovery of a sick man,
  Like going abroad after detention.
Death is in my sight today
  Like the smell of myrrh,
  Like sitting under an awning on a windy day.
Death is in my sight today
  Like the scent of lotus flowers,
  Like sitting on the bank of drunkenness.
Death is in my sight today
  Like a well-trodden path,
  As when a man returns home from an expedition.
Death is in my sight today
  Like the clearing of the sky,
  Like a man attracted thereby to what he knows not.
Death is in my sight today
  Like the longing of a man to see home,
  When he has spent many years held in captivity.
Surely he who is yonder shall
  Be a living god,
  Punishing the sin of him who commits it.
Surely he who is yonder shall
  Stand in the barque of the sun,
  Causing the choicest things to be given therefrom to the
    temples.
Surely he who is yonder shall

Be a man of knowledge,
Who cannot be prevented from petitioning Re when he
    speaks.

(The Soul replies)

Put care aside, my comrade and brother. Make an offering on
the brazier and cling to life. Desire me here and reject the
West,[4] but desire to reach the West when the body goes into
the earth, that I may alight when you grow weary. Then let
us make an abode together.

(Anon., Old Egyptian, c. 2000 B.C., tr. T.W. Thacker.)

[The soul at the end of the last poem seems to be saying; don't
hurry things, death will come to you soon enough.

    Despair at humanity's treatment of Nature is a newer pheno-
menon than despair at 'what man has made of man.' In the next
poem, Judith Wright praises the justice that in killing Nature we
ourselves must die.]

Australia 1970

Die, wild country, like the eaglehawk,
dangerous till the last breath's gone,
clawing and striking. Die
cursing your captor through a raging eye.

Die like the tigersnake
that hisses such pure hatred from its pain
as fills the killer's dreams
with fear like suicide's invading stain.

Suffer, wild country, like the ironwood
that gaps the dozer-blade.
I see your living soil ebb with the tree
to naked poverty.

[4] In the West is the land of the dead.

Die like the soldier-ant
mindless and faithful to your million years.
Though we corrupt you with our torturing mind,
stay obstinate; stay blind.

For we are conquerors and self-poisoners
more than scorpion or snake
and dying of the venoms that we make
even while you die of us.

I praise the scoring drought, the flying dust,
the drying creek, the furious animal,
that they oppose us still;
that we are ruined by the thing we kill.

(Judith Wright, Australian, b. 1915.)

[We are bequeathing our children a broken world. Is that why
Western children are so spoiled with material goods – from guilt? or
to make them accomplices in crime?

A recent theory suggests dinosaurs became extinct as a result of
their flatulence, which created massive global warming. Our
mechanical and chemical flatulences are well on the way to doing the
same for us.]

Dinosauria, we

born like this
into this
as the chalk faces smile
as Mrs. Death laughs
as the elevators break
as political landscapes dissolve
as the supermarket bag boy holds a college degree
as the oily fish spit out their oily prey
as the sun is masked

we are
born like this
into this
into these carefully mad wars
into the sight of broken factory windows of emptiness
into bars where people no longer speak to each other
into fist fights that end as shootings and knifings

born into this
into hospitals which are so expensive that it's cheaper to die
into lawyers who charge so much it's cheaper to plead guilty
into a country where the jails are full and the madhouses closed
into a place where the masses elevate fools into rich heroes

born into this
walking and living through this
dying because of this
muted because of this
castrated
debauched
disinherited
because of this
fooled by this
used by this
pissed on by this
made crazy and sick by this
made violent
made inhuman
by this

the heart is blackened
the fingers reach for the throat
the gun
the knife
the bomb
the fingers reach toward an unresponsive god

the fingers reach for the bottle
the pill
the powder

we are born into this sorrowful deadliness
we are born into a government 60 years in debt
that soon will be unable even to pay the interest on that debt
and the banks will burn
money will be useless
there will be open and unpunished murder on the streets
it will be guns and roving mobs
land will be useless
food will become a diminishing return
nuclear power will be taken over by the many
explosions will continually shake the earth
radiated robot men will stalk each other
the rich and the chosen will watch from space platforms
Dante's Inferno will be made to look like a children's playground

the sun will not be seen and it will always be night
trees will die
all vegetation will die
radiated men will eat the flesh of radiated men
the sea will be poisoned
the lakes and rivers will vanish
rain will be the new gold

the rotting bodies of men and animals will stink in the dark wind

the last few survivors will be overtaken by new and hideous diseases
and the space platforms will be destroyed by attrition
the petering out of supplies
the natural effect of general decay

and there will be the most beautiful silence never heard

born out of that.

the sun still hidden there

awaiting the next chapter.

(Charles Bukowski, American, b. 1920.)

[Most people now live in towns. They have little awareness of the creeping death that is stifling the planet. Even many who live in the country insulate themselves from such knowledge.]

The Fish are all Sick

The fish are all sick, the great whales dead,
the villages stranded in stone on the coast,
ornamental, like pearls on the fringe of a coat.
Sea men, who knew what the ocean did,
turned their low houses away from the surf.
But new men, who come to be rural and safe,
add big glass views and begonia beds.

Water keeps to itself.
White lip after lip
curls to a close on the littered beach.
Something is sicker and blacker than fish.
And closing its grip, and closing its grip.

(Anne Stevenson, English, b. 1933.)

[Western scientists, observing the slowness of some races to pick up and manage the new technology, deem them less intelligent. But this lesser intelligence begins to seem the greater, as our pursuit of mercurial inventiveness brings the world to disaster.

Only disaster seems to focus the mind of homo sapiens on its limitations. In the next poem, Edwin Muir finds hope in looking beyond catastrophe, seeing even a gain in the destruction of the 'old bad world that swallowed its children quick'.]

The Horses

Barely a twelvemonth after
The seven days war that put the world to sleep,
Late in the evening the strange horses came.
By then we had made our covenant with silence,
But in the first few days it was so still
We listened to our breathing and were afraid.
On the second day
The radios failed; we turned the knobs; no answer.
On the third day a warship passed us, heading north,
Dead bodies piled on the deck. On the sixth day
A plane plunged over us into the sea. Thereafter
Nothing. The radios dumb;
And still they stand in corners of our kitchens,
And stand, perhaps, turned on, in a million rooms
All over the world. But now if they should speak,
If on a sudden they should speak again,
If on the stroke of noon a voice should speak,
We would not listen, we would not let it bring
That old bad world that swallowed its children quick
At one great gulp. We would not have it again.
Sometimes we think of the nations lying asleep,
Curled blindly in impenetrable sorrow,
And then the thought confounds us with its strangeness.
The tractors lie about our fields; at evening
They look like dank sea-monsters couched and waiting.
We leave them where they are and let them rust;
'They'll moulder away and be like other loam'.
We make our oxen drag our rusty ploughs,
Long laid aside. We have gone back
Far past our fathers' land.
And then, that evening,
Late in the summer the strange horses came.
We heard a distant tapping on the road,
A deepening drumming; it stopped, went on again
And at the corner changed to hollow thunder.

We saw the heads
Like a wild wave charging and were afraid.
We had sold our horses in our fathers' time
To buy new tractors. Now they were strange to us
As fabulous steeds set on an ancient shield
Or illustrations in a book of knights.
We did not dare go near them. Yet they waited,
Stubborn and shy, as if they had been sent
By an old command to find our whereabouts
And that long-lost archaic companionship.
In the first moment we had never a thought
That they were creatures to be owned and used.
Among them were some half-a-dozen colts
Dropped in some wilderness of the broken world,
Yet new as if they had come from their own Eden.
Since then they have pulled our ploughs and borne our loads
But that free servitude still can pierce our hearts.
Our life is changed; their coming our beginning.

(Edwin Muir, Scottish, 1887–1959.)

[Pao Chao's view is different. Nature's rule is harsh, and we must
work hard, intelligently and in an ordered fashion to establish our
dominion within it.]

The Ruined City

The immense plain
   runs south to the foamy waves of the sea
   and north to the purple passes of the Great Wall.
In it
   canals are cut through the valleys;
And rivers and roads
   lead to every corner.

In its golden past,
   axles of chariots and carts

often rubbed against each other
  like men's shoulders.
Shops and houses stood row upon row
And laughter and songs rose up from them.
Glittering and white were the salt fields;
Gloomy and blue were the copper mines.
Wealth and talents
And cavalry and infantry
Reinforced the strict and elaborate
Regulations and laws.
Winding moats and lofty walls
Were dug and built, to ensure
That prosperity would long endure.
People were busy working
On palaces and battlements
And ships and beacon stations
Up and down, far and wide
At all places.
Magnets[5] were installed at mountain passes;
Red lacquer was applied to doors and gates.
The strongholds and fortresses
  would see to it
That for a myriad generations
  the family's rule should last.
But after five centuries or three dynasties
The land was divided like a melon
Or shared like beans.

Duckweed flourishes in the wells
And brambles block the roads.
Skunks and snakes dwell on sacred altars
While muskdeer and squirrels quarrel on marble steps.
In rain and wind,
Wood elves, mountain ghosts,
Wild rats and foxes
  yawp and scream from dusk to dawn.
Hungry hawks grind their beaks
As cold owls frighten the chicks in their nests.

[5] To attract enemy arrows.

Tigers and leopards hide and wait
   for a drink of blood
   and a feast of flesh.
Fallen tree-trunks lie lifelessly across
Those once busy highways.
Aspens have long ceased to rustle
And grass dies yellow
In this harsh frosty air
Which grows into a cruelly cold wind.
A solitary reed shakes and twists,
And grains of sand, like startled birds,
   are looking for a safe place to settle.
Bushes and creepers, confused and tangled,
   seem to know no boundaries.
They pull down walls
And fill up moats.
And beyond a thousand miles
Only brown dust flies.
Deep in my thoughts, I sit down and listen
To this awesome silence.

Behind the painted doors and embroidered curtains
There used to be music and dancing.
Hunting and fishing parties were held
In the emerald forests or beside the marble pools.
The melodies from various states
And works of art and rare fish and horses
Are all now dead and buried.
The young girls from east and south
Smooth as silk, fragrant as orchids,
White as jade with their lips red,
Now lie beneath the dreary stones and barren earth.

The greatest displeasure of the largest number
Is the law of nature.
For this ruined city,
I play the lute and sing:
"As the north wind hurries on,
   the battlements freeze.

They tower over the plain
  where there are neither roads nor field-paths.
For a thousand years and a myriad generations,
  I shall watch you to the end in silence.''

(Pao Chao, Chinese, 414–466, tr. Jerome Ch'en and Michael Bullock.)

[Whatever the future holds, while there is life there is joy to be
found in the innocence of being alive.]

A Fable

Resting by the water-side
the plane tree and I.
Our reflections are thrown on the water
the plane tree's and mine.
The sparkle of the water hits us
the plane tree and me.

Resting by the water-side
the plane tree, I and the cat.
Our reflections are thrown on the water
the plane tree's, mine and the cat's.
The sparkle of the water hits us
the plane tree, me and the cat.

Resting by the water-side
the plane tree, I, the cat and the sun.
Our reflections are thrown on the water
the plane tree's, mine, the cat's and the sun's.
The sparkle of the water hits us
the plane tree, me, the cat and the sun.

Resting by the water-side
the plane tree, I, the cat, the sun and our life.
Our reflections are thrown on the water
the plane tree's, mine, the cat's, the sun's and our life's.

The sparkle of the water hits us
the plane tree, me, the cat, the sun and our life.

Resting by the water-side.

First the cat will go
its reflection will be lost on the water.
Then I will go
my reflection will be lost on the water.
Then the plane tree will go
its reflection will be lost on the water.
Then the water will go
the sun will remain
then it will go too.

Resting by the water-side
the plane tree, I, the cat, the sun and our life.
The water is cool
the plane tree spreading
I am writing a poem
the sun is warm
it's great to be alive.
The sparkle of the water hits us
the plane tree, me, the cat, the sun and our life.

(Nazim Hikmet, Turkish, 1902–1963, tr. R. McKane.)

[If our civilisation fails, the power of our technology is such that it may take the rest of human life with it. Individually, what can we do? If we strive to understand, and attempt to live by more life-sustaining values, then we can also hope that others will make those efforts too.

Concerning innocence and the value of a clear conscience, the poet Muriel Rukeyser relates a vision of Saint Fursey, taken up into the sky by angels.]

Saint Fursey on high, and earth far below him a dark valley. Despair, gloom on earth, and around him in the air four

streaming flames, fires kindled separate in the four directions.
One to burn the souls of those forsworn and untruthful.
Two, to burn those given up to greed.
Three, those who stir up strife and discord.
Four, those who find it no crime to deceive the helpless.
Then the fires swept together; they coalesced, and threatened him. Fursey cried out. A voice answered him; the angel said, "That which you did not kindle shall not burn within you." Fursey drew breath, and a great voice could be heard, saying, *Respice mundum.* [6]

RESPECT THE WORLD.

[The three motors speeding us into ecological disaster are population growth, economics driven by waste and ever higher expectations of consumption. Whatever safeguards are put on the environment, it seems only disaster will halt these motors.

Is it just human nature or is it in the nature of life itself, to be wise only after the event? Memory of disaster is the source of wisdom, whether for a tree deciding when to flower or for humans learning restraint. Such ecological wisdom as we now have is only after the event of much destruction. The question is not 'will there be a disaster?' but 'how all-embracing and acute will the disaster become?'

Population growth is an interesting example of the operation of learning and self-interest. Stable primitive communities carry the wisdom of survival, and population is curtailed by methods that are not attractive to civilised expectations; enforced restrictions on intercourse, sexual deviance, abortion and infanticide. As soon as a community abandons its traditional ways its population rockets. Disease, war and starvation then take the place of more voluntary restraints. Much of the world's population is now subject only to these controls, and is increasing faster than ever before.

In the most civilised countries, however, as the burden of rearing children gets more exhausting, as pensions reduce people's

[6] From 'The Orgy' by Muriel Rukeyser, 1965.

dependence on their children in old age, as more women expect a career, and as birth control methods become less difficult, population growth is vanishing.

Societies where wisdom is out and novelty is in will pursue indulgence to the bitter end. All over the world, study and knowledge of human culture, which reveals the unpalatable facts of how we came to be in such a mess, are scarce commodities. Nowhere are they a part of mainstream education. We assume dinosaurs weren't intelligent enough to avoid their fate. We know we are; it's just a question of when and how we choose to use our intelligence.]

Acknowledgements

I would like to thank my mother-in-law Helen Oppenheimer, my wife Xanthe and Richard Barnes of Frontier Publishing for the help they gave in the making of this book.

The following three books were particularly formative of ideas in the prose which links the poems: C.D. Darlington, 'The Evolution of Man and Society'. Nadezhda Mandelstam, 'Hope against Hope' and 'Hope Abandoned'.

Regarding the poems, acknowledgement is due to all copyright holders on material used. We have tried in each case to contact copyright holders. The publishers and the editor apologise where material has been used without permission, and would be glad to hear from copyright holders who have not been consulted.

To facilitate reference by readers, poets' names are in capitals.

1. REPRINTED FROM BOOKS ON INDIVIDUAL POETS: ALPHABETICALLY BY POET.

'After the wind and the frost', 'Lot's Wife', 'Everything has been plundered, betrayed, sold out...', 'Instead of a Preface' and Epilogues 1 and 2 from 'Requiem' are translated by Judith Hemschemeyer, and are reprinted from 'The Complete Poems of Anna AKHMATOVA' (second edition, 1992) with the permission of Zephyr Press. Translations copoyright 1990, 1992 by Judith Hemschemeyer.

'Siren Song' is reprinted from 'Poems' by Margaret ATWOOD, Virago Press.

'Ode to Terminus' and 'The Shield of Achilles' are reprinted from 'W.H. AUDEN: Selected Poems', ed. E. Mendelson. Faber and Faber Limited, 1979.
'The Last Word', tr. A.A. Steinbach, is reprinted from 'Selected Poems of Hayyim Nahman BIALIK' ed. Israel Efros. Bloch Publishing Co., New York, 1965. Copyright Histadruth Ivrith, 1965.

'Dinosauria, we' Copyright 1992 by Charles BUKOWSKI is reprinted from 'The Last Night of the Earth Poems' with the permission of Black Sparrow Press.

'Nocturnal'is reprinted from 'Luis de CAMOES: Epic and Lyric' by Keith Bosley. Carcanet Press Limited, 1990.

'Death Fugue' is reprinted from 'Poems of Paul CELAN' translated by Michael Hamburger. Anvil Press Poetry, 1988.

'Vergissmeinnicht' and 'How to Kill' are reprinted by permission of Oxford University Press from 'Keith DOUGLAS: The Complete Poems' ed. Desmond Graham 1978. Poems copyright Marie J. Douglas 1978.

'The window-frame shakes. What is below?', 'John Calvin', 'Monsieur Majora, Technocrat', 'To a Friend on his Acceptance of Hungary's Chief Literary Award' and 'Draktulf' are reprinted from 'George FALUDY: Selected Poems' ed. and tr. Robin Skelton. McClelland and Stewart, Toronto, Canada 1985.

'I Pity the Garden' and 'A Bird, Just a Bird' are reprinted from 'Bride of Acacias: Selected Poems of Forugh FARROKHZHAD' tr. Jascha Kessler with Amin Banani. Copyright Bibliotheca Persica 1982.

'I sinned a sin full of pleasure' is reprinted from 'A Lonely Woman: Forugh FARROKHZHAD and Her Poetry' by Michael C. Hillman. Mage Publishers, 1032 29th St. NW, Washington DC 20007.

'The man whose heart's desires are gratified' is reprinted from Chapter 4 of 'Sutta Nipata' by GOTAMA, tr. Lord Chalmers. Harvard University Press, 1932.

'Give me your eyes', and 'Life' are reprinted from 'Selected Works of Angelina Weld GRIMKE', Oxford University Press, 1991.

'The dawn is breaking...' and 'I went into the garden...' are reprinted from 'HAFIZ of Shiraz: Thirty Poems' tr. Peter Avery and John Heath-Stubbs. John Murray (Publishers), 1952.

'Life on Cold Mountain', 'The clear water sparkles like crystal', and 'Man, living in the dust...' are reprinted from 'Cold Mountain; 100 Poems by the T'ang Poet HAN SHAN', by Burton Watson. Published by Jonathan Cape.

'Threshold', 'Andante', 'The Secret Life of Frogs', and 'Hesperian' are reprinted by permission of Oxford University Press from 'Collected Poems' by Gwen HARWOOD. Copyright Gwen Harwood, 1991.

'Earwig' and 'The Green Man's Last Will and Testament' are reprinted from 'Selected Poems' by John HEATH-STUBBS, Carcanet Press 1990.

'And little knowledge but much pleasure...' by HOLDERLIN is reprinted from 'Holderlin's Madness' by David Gascoyne. J.M. Dent and Sons, 1938.

'The Fly', is reprinted by permission of Bloodaxe Books from 'The Fly' by Miroslav HOLUB, translated by Ewald Osers, George Theiner and Jarmila Milner (Bloodaxe Books, 1987).

The excerpt from The Iliad is reprinted from 'The Iliad of HOMER' tr. Ennis Rees. Oxford University Press, New York, 1991.

'Harlem' is reprinted from 'The Panther and The Lash' by Langston HUGHES by permission of Alfred A. Knopf, Inc.. Copyright 1951 by Langston Hughes.

'If only I could live' by Higuchi ICHIYO is reprinted from 'In the Shade of Spring Leaves' by Robert Lyons Danly, 1992. W.W. Norton Co. Inc, 1992. 500 5th Ave, New York NY 10110.

Verses 5–18 of 'The Season of Frosts' are reprinted from 'KALIDASA: the Loom of Time' tr. Chandra Rajan. Penguin Books, 1989.

'Father' by Margit KAFFKA, tr. Laura Schiff is reprinted from 'The Penguin Book of Women Poets'. Copyright Artisjus, Budapest.

'The Distinct Impression', 'Open your Hearts', 'Words', 'Every Decent Family', 'Whenever That Happened', and 'Money in Love' are reprinted by permission of Bloodaxe Books from 'The Book of Judas' by Brendan KENNELLY (Bloodaxe Books, 1991).

'The Pig' and 'Willow' are reprinted by permission of Bloodaxe Books from 'A Time for Voices' by Brendan KENNELLY (Bloodaxe Books 1990).

'To a Young Man Driving His Own Car' is reprinted from 'Faint Shadows of Love', Poems by KWANG-KYU KIM translated by Brother Anthony of Taize. Forest Books, 20 Forest View, Chingford, London E4 7AY.

'There is a thing confusedly formed' is reprinted from 'Tao Te Ching' by LAO TZU, tr. D.C. Lau, Penguin Books 1963.

'The Broom' is reprinted from 'Poems from Giacomo LEOPARDI,' tr. and intr. John Heath-Stubbs. John Lehmann, London 1946.

'Fighting South of the Ramparts' is reprinted from 'The Poetry and Career of LI PO' by Arthur Waley. Allen and Unwin, 1950.

'I sing when my throat is wet, my soul is dry...', 'Still I have not died...' and 'Into the distance go the mounds of people's heads' are reprinted from 'Osip MANDEL'SHTAM: Selected Poems' tr. David McDuff. Writers and Readers Publishing Cooperative Society Ltd, 1983.

5 lines from 'The Word' by N. GUMILEV are quoted from p. 117 of 'Osip Mandelstam: The Collected Critical Prose and Letters' ed. Jane Grey Harris, Collins Harvill 1991.

'The Man Who Encountered a Bear' is reprinted from 'Self-Righting Lamp: Selected Poems by MARUYAMA KAORU', tr. Robert Epp. Copyright Robert Epp and Katydid Books.

'One Foot in Eden' and 'The Horses' are reprinted from 'Edwin MUIR: Collected Poems'. Faber and Faber, 1960.

'Eyes open wide, the poet weaves...' and 'No, I don't miss the dissipated nights...' are reprinted from 'PUSHKIN: The Bronze Horseman and Other Poems' translated by D.M. Thomas. Published by Martin Secker and Warburg, 1982.

'Oh God, Whenever...' is reprinted from 'Doorkeeper of the Heart: Versions of RABI'A' tr. Charles Upton. Threshold Books, RD4, Box 600, Putney, VT 05346.

'Untitled (Today I feel bearish...)' is reprinted from 'A Secretary to the Spirits' by Ishmael REED. NOK Publishers International, 1978.

'Saint Fursey on high' is reprinted from 'The Orgy' by Muriel RUKEYSER. Andre Deutsch, 1966, c. 1965 Muriel Rukeyser.

'Gaze on the cheeks of love...'. is reprinted from 'Mystical Poems of RUMI, Second Selection' tr. A.J. Arberry. Bibliotheca Persica, 450 Riverside Drive No. 4, New York NY 10027, USA.

My version of 'One handful of dust shouts I was hair' by RUMI is adapted from a translation in 'I am Wind, You are Fire: the Life and Work of Rumi' by Annemarie Schimmel. Shambhala, 1992.

'Trees' by Marina TSVETAYEVA is reprinted from 'A Life Through Poetry: Marina Tsvetayeva's Lyric Diary' by Jane A. Taubman. Slavica Publishers, 1989.

The Prologue to the Ramayana is from 'The Ramayana of VALMIKI' transcreated by P. Lal. Tarang Paperbacks, 1989.

'The Man Who Loved Islands' is reprinted from 'Collected Poems 1948–1984' by Derek WALCOTT. Faber and Faber, 3 Queen Square, London WC1N 3AU. Copyright Derek Walcott.

'Nervous Prostation'is reprinted from 'The Writings of Anna WICKHAM', Virago Press.

'..And Mr. Ferritt', 'Australia 1970', 'Builders', 'Encounter', 'Eve to her Daughters', 'In Praise of Marriages', 'Lament for Passenger Pigeons', 'Night Herons', 'The Flame-Tree Blooms', 'The Wattle-Tree', 'To Hafiz of Shiraz', 'Victims', and 'Two Dreamtimes' are reprinted from 'Collected Poems 1942–1970' by Judith WRIGHT. Angus and Robertson, 1971.

'Light Rain on the Road to Sword Gate,' by LU YU and 'Third Day of the Third Month, Rain: Written to Dispel My Depression' by Yang Wan-Li are reprinted from 'Heaven my blanket, Earth my pillow: Poems by YANG WAN-LI', introduced and translated by Jonathan Chaves. John Weatherhill, Publishers.

2. REPRINTED FROM ANTHOLOGIES: ALPHABETICALLY BY EDITOR.

'The Old Commander' by WANG WEI is reprinted from 'Selected Poems of the Tang and Song Dynasties' tr. Rewi Alley. Hai Feng Publishing Co., 1981.

'This evening when I spake with thee, beloved' by Juana ASBAJE is reprinted from 'Anthology of Mexican Poetry' tr. Samuel Beckett. Indiana University Press 1959.

My version of TCHERNIKHOVSKY's 'Behold, O Earth' is an adaptation of Hilda Auerbach's translation in 'An Anthology of Modern Hebrew Poetry' edited by Abraham Birman. Abelard-Schuman, 1968.

'To Etan', by Fadwa TUQAN is reprinted from 'Women of the Fertile Crescent' edited by Kamal Boullata. Three Continents Press, 1978.

'Testament' by Alda LARA is reprinted from 'A Horse of White Clouds: Poems from Lusophone Africa' tr. Don Burness. Ohio University Press, 1989.

'The Ruined City' by PAO CHAO is reprinted from 'Poems of Solitude' by Jerome Ch'en and Michael Bullock. Abelard–Schuman Ltd, 1960.

'A Reminiscence' by Egan O'RAHILLY is reprinted from 'A Gaelic Anthology' by S.P.D. Clough, privately printed 1987.

'Lament' and 'Prayer' by Endre ADY, tr. F. Marnau and M. Hamburger, are reprinted, by kind permission of Michael Hamburger, from 'New Road 1944' ed. Alex Comfort and John Bayliss.

PRAXILLA's fragment 'Adonis Dying' tr. John Dillon and 'Father' by Margit KAFFKA, tr. Laura Schiff, are reprinted from 'The Penguin Book of Women Poets' ed. Carol Cosman, Joan Keefe and Kathleen Weaver 1973.

'The ever-touring Englishmen' is reprinted from 'Folk Songs of the Maikal Hills' by V. Elwin and S. Hivale, Oxford University Press, Madras, 1944.

'Ancestral burden' by Alfonsina STORNI, tr. Richard O'Connell is reprinted from 'Anthology of Contemporary Latin-American Poetry', ed. Dudley Fitts, 1947.

'Song of Songs' 5, 3–8 is reprinted from 'The Song of Songs and the Ancient Egyptian Love Songs' by Michael V. Fox. University of Wisconsin Press, 1985. My version of 'Two flowers on one stem' is from M.V. Fox's in the same book.

'Poem of Sorrow' by TSAI YEN is reprinted by permission of Oxford University Press from 'An Anthology of Chinese Verse' tr. J.D. Frodsham and Ch'eng Hsi (1967). Copyright Oxford University Press.

'The Unhappy Race' by Oodgeroo NOONUCCAL, 'Ode to Salted Mutton Birds' by Jim EVERETT, 'Homage to JC' by Maureen WATSON, 'Time is Running Out' by Oodgeroo NOONUCCAL and 'God Gave Us Trees to Cut Down' by Les RUSSELL are reprinted from 'Inside Black Australia' ed. Kevin Gilbert. Penguin Books Australia Ltd, 1988.

'Your house gleams with calm light' by SEDULIUS SCOTUS is reprinted from 'Poetry of the Carolingian Renaissance' by Peter Godman. Gerald Duckworth and Co., 1985.

'Two Requests' and 'Gone' by PROPERTIUS are reprinted from 'Some of Propertius' Love Poems' by Jack Lindsay. Fanfrolico Press, 1927.

'He is walking in the road' is reprinted from 'Songs of the Forest. The Folk Poetry of the Gonds' by S. Hivale and V. Elwin, Allen and Unwin, London, 1935.

'Goodnight, Wide World' by Jacob GLATSTEIN and 'Sparrows' by Mani LEIB are reprinted from 'A Treasury of Yiddish Poetry' ed. Irving Howe and Eliezer Greenberg. Schocken Books, 1976.

'Solitary pleasures' by Tachibana AKEMI is reprinted from 'An Anthology of Japanese Literature' ed. Donald Keene, Penguin Classics 1968.

'My Story', 'The Blackbird's Song', 'The Cliff of Alteran', 'The Old Woman of Beare' and 'Hope' are reprinted from 'Love of Ireland: Poems From The Irish' by Brendan Kennelly. Mercier Press, 1981.

'Shipwreck' by ARCHILOCUS is reprinted from 'Greek Lyrics' by Richard Lattimore, University of Chicago Press, 1955.

'O warmth of summer', 'Delight in Singing' and 'Song of the Lemming' are reprinted from 'Eskimo Poems from Canada and Greenland' tr. Tom Lowenstein. Allison and Busby, 1973.

'A Voiced Lament' by Gulten AKIN, 'Panic' by Behcet NECATIGIL, 'Shanty Town', by Orhan Veli KANIK and 'A Fable' by Nazim HIKMET are reprinted from 'The Penguin Book of Turkish Verse', ed. N. Menemencioglu, 1978.

'The Chariots go Forth to War' and 'The Rain at Night' by TU FU, 'They stampede in search of money and grain' by CHU YUAN, 'Clearing the Fields' (Anon), and 'To Tu Fu' by LI PO are reprinted from 'The White Pony' edited by Robert Payne, 1947.

The excerpt from 'The Adoration of Inanna in Ur' by ENHUEDANNA is reprinted from 'Ancient Near Eastern Texts' edited by James Pritchard. Princetown University Press, 1969.

'The Ruin (Fate has smashed these wonderful walls)', 'Riddle – Swan' and 'Riddle – Bookworm' are reprinted by permission of the Universitry of Nebraska Press from 'Poems from the Old English' tr. Burton Raffel. Copyright University of Nebraska Press, renewed 1992.

'There, in the very middle' by AUVAIYAR, 'The old woman's shoulders' by KAKKAIPATINIYAR NACCELLAIYAR, 'What She Said (to her friend)' by KAPILAR, 'A Poet's Counsel' by KOVUR KILAR and 'Where the Lilies Were in Flower' by KUMATTUR KANNANAR are reprinted from 'Poems of Love and War' by A.K. Ramanujan. Copyright Columbia University Press, New York, 1985. Reprinted with permisssion of the publisher.

'Other men are thorn' by MAHADEVI is reprinted from 'Speaking of Siva' translated by A.K. Ramanujan. Penguin Books, 1973.

'On a Visit to Ch'ung Chen Temple...' by YU HSUAN CHI is reprinted from 'The Orchid Boat: Women Poets of China' translated and edited by Kenneth Rexroth and Ling Chung. The Seabury Press, Inc. 1972.

'When will mankind realise it is one' by SRINIVASA is reprinted from 'An Anthology of Indian Literatures' ed. K. Santhanam, published 1969 by S. Ramakrishnam.

'The Pan, the Pot, the Burning Fire I Have in Front of Me' by Ishigaki RIN and 'To Inscribe on a Picture of a Skull I Painted' by RYOKAN are reprinted from 'From the Country of Eight Islands', edited and translated by Hiroaki Sato and Burton Watson. Anchor Press/Doubleday, 1981.

'Clear the autumn wind' and 'To His Wife' by LI PO, 'The Song of the Savage tiger' by ZHANG JI and 'After the Wars' by XIN YUANG are reprinted from 'Love and Protest; Chinese Poems from the Sixth Century B.C. to the Seventeenth Century A.D.' by John Scott. Andre Deutsch, 1972.

'Amagoduka at Glencoe Station' by Oswald Mbuyiseni MTSHALI and 'The Motoka' by Theo LUZUKA are reprinted from 'Poems of Black Africa' ed. Wole Soyinka, Heinemann International, 1975. ('The Motoka' was first published in the magazine Dhana.)

'In a tangle of cliffs I chose a place' by HAN SHAN is reprinted from 'Riprap and Cold Mountain Poems' by Gary Snyder. Four Seasons Foundation, San Francisco, 1969. Reprinted by permission of Gary Snyder.

'To whom shall I speak today' is reprinted from 'Documents from Old Testament Times' ed. D. Winton Thomas. Copyright Thomas Nelson and Sons Limited, London, 1958.

'The Rain Man Praises Himself' and 'Song of Caribou etc.' are reprinted from 'The Unwritten Song', ed. Willard Trask. Jonathan Cape, 1966.

'Aphrodite' by SOPHOCLES is reprinted from 'Translations from Greek Poetry' by R.C. Trevelyan. Allen and Unwin, 1950.

'Now I must mend my manners' by MARBOD of Rennes, 'The Old Man of Verona' by CLAUDIAN, 'This bird was happy...' by BOETHIUS and 'The Roman was the victor of the world' by PETRONIUS are reprinted from 'More Latin Lyrics' by Helen Waddell. Victor Gollancz, London, 1980. Copyright Dame Felicitas Corrigan.

'Zip, zip the valley wind!' and 'I climb that wooded hill' are reprinted from 'The Book of Songs' tr. Arthur Waley. Allen and Unwin, 1937.

'Planting Flowers on the Eastern Embankment' by PO CHU-I, 'In the month of June the grass grows high' 'Drinking Wine 1' and 'Drinking Wine 2' by TAO CH'IEN are reprinted from 'Chinese Poems' by Arthur Waley, Allen and Unwin 1961.

Index of Titles or First Lines

Index of Poets